NEW DISCOVERIES
IN CHINA

DANIELLE AND VADIME ELISSEEFF

NEW DISCOVERIES IN CHINA

Encountering History Through Archeology

Translated by
Larry Lockwood
Typography by
Arts & Letters, Inc.

CHARTWELL BOOKS, INC.

Homage to the discoverer of ancient China
To Henri Maspéro (1883–1945
On his one hundredth anniversary

Published by
CHARTWELL BOOKS, INC.
A Division of **BOOK SALES, INC.**
110 Enterprise Avenue
Secaucus, New Jersey 07094

© 1983 by Office du Livre, Fribourg (Switzerland)

Reprinted with permission by William S. Konecky Associates, Inc.

ISBN 0-89009-840-9

Printed and bound in Shen Zhen, China.

TABLE OF CONTENTS

INTRODUCTION

It is said that China is changing as it responds to the temptations and attractions of the outside world. What if this very process were to impel China to suddenly regain something of its former faith and confidence in itself? Although the physical and intellectual legacies of the past have been repudiated and even eradicated during the last three decades, it is now possible to see the past emerging from the earth, cleansed of the disdain of daily life by the awe-inspiring endeavors that reveal its full vigor and radiance. It is outmoded to regard the discoveries as mere evidence of man's exploitation of man. Today the Chinese are excitedly discovering the creativity of their ancestors and the prodigious landmarks bequeathed by a vast stream of artists, artisans and craftsmen — those who for two thousand years have been cited in the pages of official chronicles. But the official documents refer to them in terms of profits and production, and within the context of an economic philosophy that vacillated between the demands of the state and the rights of the individual.

There is still a great temptation to make use of historical evidence for philosophical, social and political purposes. Nevertheless, it should be emphasized that archeologists seek to aid society by finally restoring to the Chinese people its memory and sense of historical continuity.

Before the Song dynasty, texts were the only avenue for approaching antiquity, or more generally, history itself. These texts were usually created for official, didactic or political purposes. Artifacts attracted attention insofar as they contributed to clarification of events contained in the annals or in important historical documents. Apparently, artifacts were associated with death or the afterlife, and hence, inspired fear.

Striking changes occurred during the first half of the eleventh century: With the fortuitous discovery of ancient bronzes at Anyang, scholars who subscribed to the routines of Buddhist philosophy rather than traditional Chinese thinking suddenly were awakened by a more critical spirit — a new form of interest in ancient China. The aura of mystery surrounding ancient tombs whetted the curiosity of learned men. Inspired by a scholarly penchant for cataloging and classifying, they immediately began to develop inventories of the principal antiquities known at that time. These consisted of illustrated guides called the *Kaogutu* (1092) and the *Bogutulu* (around 1120), each of which consisted of four sections, or at least four ways of approaching artifacts: cataloging, description, identification and the study of intended functions. Descriptive texts were accompanied by drawings and especially by rubbings through a technique which was widely adopted during the Five Dynasties period (tenth century); in modern times this technique has been considered one of the most interesting aspects of Chinese art. The fascination with the past mingled with contemporary tastes and an imperial edict issued during the reign of Huang-yu (1049–54) served to create an extensive series of reproductions of the Anyang bronzes. Admiration for the curios under an ancient guise produced two consequences, one of which was directly linked to archeology. On the one hand the repertoires of artists were enriched by the perpetuation of ancient creations, and on the other, significant distortions concerning the past were introduced through the reproductions.

In China, as in the Far East generally, indeed throughout the "world of characters" (as opposed to the "world of letters",) the concepts of replicas or forgeries has not been clearly understood. Since Xie He (sixth century), one of the fundamental principles of painting has been a belief that the content of art is far more important than the medium, and that there is greater merit in conveying a master's spirit than in expressing the message of an artistic heir.

Although fascination with antiquities diminished to some extent under the Yuan emperors, it flourished under the Ming dynasty whose ascension was interpreted as a regeneration of China. During the reign of Xuan De (1426–1436), another imperial edict ordered the creation of a vast number of bronze reproductions listed in the Song catalogues. Hence, the desire to own works reflecting ancient styles spread throughout China while the imitators' skills improved to such a degree that it even became possible to reproduce flaws found in the original creations. Gao Lian (sixteenth century) was a scholar who attempted to expose the imitators' deceptions but the criteria adopted by his contemporaries continued to be extremely simple: a hastily applied patina was often sufficient to declare a bronze object authentic.

Indeed, it was not until the eighteenth century that a truly archeological perspective emerged, and then within the context of philology with the completion of a lengthy treatise concerning inscriptions on ancient bronzes by Liang Tongshu. His work, however, relied heavily on Zhao Xihu's *Dongtianggingluji* (thirteenth century) which was the work of scholars under the Qing dynasty who had limited knowledge and were easily misled. Even Yuan Yuan, who published an extensive catalogue in 1804 that heralded a renewed interest in bronze items with inscriptions, appeared to display a sublime lack of interest in the matter of forgeries and reproductions. He gave equal attention to all of the ostensibly ancient bronzes that were accessible to him. It was only during the 1840s that Chen Jie-qi introduced the problem of the authenticity and origins of ancient relics. But even at this point reproductions did not disappear. When the demand arose in the West, they acquired renewed popularity; but this is another matter.

While on the subject, it would be unpardonable not to cite European contributions in the field of Chinese archeology.

Initially, at the end of the nineteenth century and during the early twentieth, visits in the form of expeditions had been undertaken by intrepid travelers who were both scholars and adventurers. A recent and extremely interesting study evokes such figures as Grünwedel and Albert von le Coq of Germany; Sir Aurel Stein and Dudley A. Milles from England; Berezovsky, Oldenburg, and Kozlov from Russia; Langdon Warner, Berthold Laufer and Torrance from the United States; Otani, Tachibana and Sekino from Japan; and from France, Jacques Bacot, Paul Pelliot, d'Ollone, Edouard Chavannes and Victor Segalen.

After 1920 such European geologists and prehistorians as the Swedish scholar J.G. Andersson and Father Teilhard de Chardin began to explore and study prehistoric sites. In 1923 their research led to the discovery of an early Paleolithic collection of implements at the edge of the Ordos Desert and in December 1928 to the discovery of the "Peking Man's" skull at Zhoukoudian.

During this period Chinese scholars initiated archeological excavation and research projects under the supervision of the *Academia Sinica* (Academy of Sciences). During 1928 the efforts of Luo Zhenyu, Wu Qicheng and Guo Moruo, under the supervision of Doctor Li Ji, the director of the archeological division of the Academy of Sciences, led to the well-known excavations in Henan Province at Anyang for the Shang Period, at Cheng Ziyai in Shandong Province for the Neolithic Age, and in Shaanxi Province for the Han Period.

Immediately before this landmark year, Henri Maspéro, who was then the most eminent specialist in Chinese historical research, published a summary of accomplishments from the turn of the century to 1927. Far more effectively than a lengthy commentary, a few lines from Maspéro's foreword emphasize the irreplaceable contributions of archeology of the past, present and future to a deeper understanding of the societies that arose in ancient China: "Despite recurrent affirmations to the contrary, the history of ancient China does not extend extremely far into the past, and texts originating in antiquity only possess limited merits. Instead of a continuous history, we have obtained glimpses of certain eras, separated by periods that are relatively unfamiliar. Thus, we have begun to learn about conditions in China at the end of the Yin dynasty (approximately the twelfth or eleventh century B.C.) because of a recent archeological find which has endowed this period with a bit of life. Nevertheless, later centuries which have traditionally been regarded as the zenith of the Zhou dynasty represent a blank space; the shadows only have become less dense toward the end of the ninth century. Beginning with the end of the eighth century, for two hundred and fifty years, or from 722 until 480, we possess relatively extensive historical knowledge because of a chronicle pertaining to this period. Then, for the subsequent period which lasted until the end of the third century, where documents are scarce and unreliable, the mist reappears, although it is less impenetrable than for more remote eras."

This passage admirably expresses two elements in a precise form: firstly, the scholar's perceptiveness in demarcating obscure periods that, unfortunately, have not been fully illuminated; and secondly, the inherent nature of contributions that Chinese archeology may furnish today in terms of replacing deficient texts, unless it becomes possible to unearth not only artifacts but also rare manuscripts which would predate the Imperial tradition.

Although since 1949 Chinese archeology has not abandoned political objectives, it has been guided by a scientific outlook that does not exclude humanistic methods or aims. Its increasingly vigorous development has depended upon the coordinated efforts of various institutions. All research and excavation projects in particular are administered by the National Office for Cultural Resources (*Guojia wenwu shije guanliju*). This institution appoints and pays archeologists. It is also responsible for the enormous task of administering China's museums, either directly or through regional or municipal subdivisions known as the Cultural Office (*Wenhuaju*). Museums actually occupy a dual role as depositories and research centers. They have absorbed the prior Local Commissions for Preservation of Cultural Resources (*Wenwu quanli wei yuan hui*).

This extensive regional network is crowned by two scientific institutes: The Institute of Vertebrate Paleontology and Paleo-anthropology and the Archeological Institute (*Kaogu yanjiusuo*). Each of these institutes is under the supervision of the Academy of Sciences (*Academia Sinicia, Zhongguo kexue yuan*).

The Archeological Institute which has been administered for many years by Professor Xia Nai, is now an extremely vast entity. The central division in Beijing employs more than 2,000 persons: archeologists, librarians, paleographers, draftsmen, restoration specialists, librarians and archivists. There are three permanent regional branches, respectively located in Xi'an, Anyang and Luoyang. In addition, the Institute coordinates all of the information furnished by archeological centers within three different prefectures and sends specialists to significant sites upon request. The Institute likewise supervises or assumes responsibility for preparation of reports and scientific articles that are published in two periodicals directly sponsored by the Institute, or in other publications issued under the authority of the publishing entity known as *Wenwu chubanshe*. In conclusion, we shall mention the individual merits and obvious value of these extensive and informative publications, not-withstanding their sometimes unimpressive external appearance.

Archeologists are divided into two categories: those who pursue their careers full-time with local museums or with commissions, and those who are hired on a part-time basis, assigned to sites while a particular one is being excavated after which they are reassigned to their usual activities. The government selects local archeological specialists from this latter category. Its members furnish the volunteer brigades that are always prepared to participate in emergency excavations or in large-scale projects.

Eight universities are set up to train professional archeologists: Beijing, Qirin, Shandong, Xibei, Nanjing, Sichuan, Xiamen (Amoy) and Zhongshan. Until recently, candidates, after completion of their secondary education and at least two years in the work force, had to obtain permission from their fellow workers, peasants or soldiers as well as their group leaders, to be admitted to the university. These regulations now appear to be less rigorous, but access to a university education continues to depend upon approval of government agencies which still determine the number of openings in relation to needs. It is clear that the Archeological Institute exercises the right to supervise young archeologists by first accepting them as trainees and then providing further guidance on the basis of their interests and skills.

Since 1979 China's archeologists have sponsored annual conventions. The published proceedings of the first convention held in Xi'an in April 1979 to commemorate thirty years of activities, give indications of the principal areas that are shaping current interest. Many of these areas represent a continuation of the traditional orientation of Chinese historical research.

One can cite such endeavors as the deciphering and interpreting of oracular texts and inscriptions on bronzes from the Shang and Zhou dynasties, the dating of bronzes and of their ceramic prototypes and the careful investigation of the Great Wall along China's western border erected to prevent incursions by nomadic invaders. One can also observe the beginnings of comparison of new archeological information from China proper with prior discoveries in outlying regions of the Empire: investigation of Paleolithic, Neolithic and Chalcolithic strata in areas surrounding the Great Plain such as Inner Mongolia, Heilongjiang, Zhejiang, and Yunnan; increasingly more accurate and diverse descriptions of the many cultures inhabiting China during the Neolithic era; and analysis of relationships that linked or separated different cultures. Lastly, considerable emphasis has been given to investigation of the so-called Southern autochthonous civilizations such as the one that arose in the Tai Hu region at the mouth of the Blue River (Yangtze) as the cradle of the Kingdom of Yue, the civilization erected by the impressive Kingdom of Chu whose expansion appears to have profoundly influenced Northern China, or the accomplishments of smaller cultural units in Sichuan and Yunnan that participated in the

CHRONOLOGY

Xia Dynasty			Circa 2100-1600 B.C.
Shang Dynasty			Circa 1600-1100 B.C.
Zhou Dynasty	Western Zhou Dynasty		Circa 1100- 771 B.C.
	Eastern Zhou Dynasty		770- 256 B.C.
	Spring and Autumn Period		770- 476 B.C.
	Warring Kingdoms		475- 221 B.C.
Qin Dynasty			221- 207 B.C.
Han Dynasty	Western Han Dynasty		206 B.C.- 24 A.D.
	Eastern Han Dynasty		25 A.D.-220 A.D.
Three Kingdoms	Wei		220- 265
	Shu Han		221- 263
	Wu		222- 280
Western Jin Dynasty			265- 316
Eastern Jin Dynasty			317- 420
Northern and Southern Dynasties	Southern Dynasties	Song	420- 479
		Qi	479- 502
		Liang	502- 557
		Chen	557- 589
	Northern Dynasties	Northern Wei	386- 534
		Eastern Wei	534- 500
		Northern Qi	550- 577
		Western Wei	535- 556
		Nothern Zhou	557- 581
Sui Dynasty			581- 618
Tang Dynasty			618- 907
Five Dynasties	Later Liang		907- 923
	Later Tang		923- 936
	Later Jin		936- 946
	Later Han		947- 950
	Later Zhou		951- 960
Song Dynasty	Northern Song		960-1127
	Southern Song		1127-1279
Liao Dynasty			916-1125
Jin Dynasty			1115-1234
Yuan Dynasty			1271-1368
Ming Dynasty			1368-1644
Qing Dynasty			1644-1911
Republic of China			1912-1949
People's Republic of China			1949-

From *China, Sights and Insights,* Vol. 1, No. 3 (Beijing, China Travel and Touring Press, August, 1981)

life of China but were not influenced solely by the traditional norms of the Great Plain.

One can see that a substantial proportion, and perhaps the majority of the articles and reports on excavations, insofar as specialized publications may be concerned, approach the problems that have been cited heretofore: there is an unabated interest in pre-Imperial China. This trend does not mean that the appeal of excavating sites of Imperial provenance is diminishing. Nevertheless, it cannot be denied that a major portion of the finds that are decisively contributing to knowledge of China's past are pre-Imperial, representing eras prior to the development of an extraordinarily centralized government whose archives appear to have actually preserved vital information.

Therefore, in relation to China it is appropriate to add another distinction apart from the traditional one between historic and prehistoric archeology and Imperial archeology. Both involve efforts to reconcile textual information with information from the earth itself but they belong to such different spheres that they sometimes appear to be in conflict; the pre-Confucian society, in contrast to one in which Confucianism triumphed, is charac-terized by the consolidation of the ideal of state authority whatever its transitory fortunes had been, notwithstanding their frequency. This is the same idea currently expressed in Marxist terms in most publications nowadays on archeology; initially, the birth, development and decline of slavery, and then the rise of feudalism. Wherein the archeology of Imperial China furnishes supplementary information, adjustments and corrections within a relatively familiar context, the archeology of periods before the Empire introduces new perspectives, confirms some texts, invalidates others, brings new information to light and suddenly illuminates regions or periods that have been plunged into darkness for two thousand years.

Through these discoveries entire generations have been brought to life. The most diverse ideologies immediately attempt to classify them in accordance with conflicting viewpoints, but all of these intellectual edifices are destined to become obsolete from one discovery to the next. One of the surprises of archeology is that, aside from giving us the joy of knowledge, it provides lessons in humility.

I. PRE-BRONZE AGE CHINA: A NEW FACE

Paleolithic Discoveries

The history of primitive man may represent one of the most significant triumphs of contemporary archeology.

In China, as discoveries have taken place in vast regions that had still been left empty or blank at the beginning of our century, it has been possible from one year to another to observe the humanization of an entire continent.

These discoveries began in a somewhat belated form during the 1920s with the discovery of the remains of a hominid who lived 500,000 to 600,000 years ago: this creature, known as *"Sinanthropusu"* or "Peking Man" (*Sinanthropus pekinensis*), was a predator who did not hesitate to eat members of his own species when the need arose. A curious set of events ensued. After having been buried within the bowels of the earth *Sinanthropus* reappeared in the twentieth century to create turmoil among scholars, contributing to the rise of field archeology in China and possibly providing philosophical inspiration for Father Teilhard de Chardin. Nevertheless, *Sinanthropus* quickly faded into darkness almost immediately after being discovered: the crates containing his priceless remains were transferred from one province to another in flight from Japan's advancing armies and were ultimately lost at the end of the Second World War. Thus, the remains of this ancient phantom-like hominid have vanished, lost — or stolen.

The relative importance of this question has diminished since the discovery of a slightly older brother or cousin of the *Sinanthropus* in Shaanxi Province in 1963, namely the "Lantian Man" or *Sinanthropus lantianensis*. This hominid lived 600,000 or 700,000 years ago. Furthermore, another *Sinanthropus* was recently discovered at Nanzhao in Henan Province, in 1979. In comparing these fossil remains with an assortment of stone implements discovered at Houjiapo which is also in Henan some

archeologists have concluded that the earliest civilization in China must have originated in this central portion of the Great Plain and advanced up the valley of the Wei River as far as the Shaanxi loess plateaux; this is an extremely important element when one recognizes that thirty years ago hardly any Paleolithic discoveries had occurred in this region.

It has now become necessary to associate this northern region divided into two sections — Shaanxi and Henan — with a southern region offering comparable characteristics although the latter, represented by the "Yuanmo Man" of Yunnan (discovered in 1965) and by tools from the Guanyin Cave (Guanyindong) in Guizhou found in 1964, undoubtedly represents an earlier epoch. Chinese prehistorians currently estimate that the "Yuanmo Man" lived 1,700,000 years ago. He may have been the earliest specimen of *homo erectus* in China (cf. *Vertebrata Palasiatica,* 4, Beijing, 1976, p.267), and it is probable that he produced simple stone tools (cf. *Kaogu,* 3, 1976, pp. 153–160). In turn, the three thousand stone fragments found beneath eight meters of soil at Guanyindong in a complex stratigraphy constitute the most extensive Lower Paleolithic discovery thus far in areas south of the Yangtze River.

For Middle Paleolithic times it is necessary to return to central China where Changyang Man, a Neanderthal type who lived 200,000 or 300,000 years ago inhabited Hubei Province. Another Neanderthal, Maba Man, who inhabited the Guangdong region approximately 100,000 years ago, was discovered in 1958 while the upper cave at Zhoukoudian also contributed a human link of the same type, discovered in 1966. Ziyang Man from Sichuan Province and Hetao Man from Inner Mongolia also appear to represent the same phase of the Upper Paleolithic period while Dingcun Man from Shaanxi represents advances in human settlement of that region, even though his tools which were of a Clactonian type, appear to be somewhat primitive for that point in time.

From this fragmentary evidence which deserves continued investigation for many years, it can be ascertained that China as a whole was capable of nourishing and sustaining the human species from its origins without relying upon a complex theory of migrations. In this way we encounter one of the most venerated theses among Chinese archeologists and to an even greater extent among their leaders: the concept of Sinocentrism or the endogenous origins of Chinese culture. Although this viewpoint may appear to be convincing with respect to evidence from the Paleolithic Age or indeed for certain aspects of the Neolithic Age, its strengths diminish for a certain number of features of Bronze Age civilization; in the latter case, Chinese archeologists no longer deny external links but continue to interpret China as the point of departure. This perspective does not always exercise such a strong attraction upon foreign archeologists.

The theories of migration and of Chinese originality at the beginning of the Upper Paleolithic Age have been confronted by the discovery of a *homo sapiens* who lived 30,000 or 40,000 years ago at Liujiang in Guizhou Province in the Himalayan portion of China. The most striking characteristic in this instance is the presence of distinctive Mongolian racial features. Thus, it is confirmed that racial characteristics did not originate at the same time as the human species; instead, they emerged when mankind had practically attained its current level of development under conditions that have not yet been identified. Hence, it now appears that China may have been "Mongolized" from the South when a highly advanced level of human inhabitation had already emerged. This is a viewpoint which may be invalidated or, on the other hand, confirmed by future discoveries in Northern China. The answer that excavations shall provide — if there is ever truly an answer — shall be capable of significantly modifying the concept that the presumably "Han" and "non-Han" peoples of China have adopted with respect to themselves and other ethnicities.

ADVANCES AND COMPLEXITY DURING THE NEOLITHIC AGE

"Toward the point where the civilizations of Western Asia were reaching their zenith at the other end of the Asiatic continent in the vast low-lying plains which form the shores of the Bohai Gulf and the Yellow River, the farmers who inhabited the banks of the Yellow River slowly began to advance toward civilized life and, unaware of the magnitude of their future creations, began to develop the foundations of the Chinese Empire."[1]

The Earliest Agrarian Societies

Whereas the identification of a coherent group of Paleolithic cultures within the confines of the Chinese mainland constitutes one of the most significant feats of contemporary archeology, the existence of Neolithic society in China has already been confirmed since the earliest projects sponsored by the *Academia Sinica* at the end of the 1920s. No doubt current research will provide important results because it will help develop comprehensive regional portraits[2] of the earliest agrarian civilizations which will reveal the pervasiveness of a technological level that appears to have been attained at about the same time throughout the principal areas of China.

Situated between the Paleolithic and Neolithic periods, Microlithic culture — characterized by small tools carved from stone — covered the Asian steppes in a broad layer from the Caspian Sea to Northern China, extending to Tibet, Xinjiang, Inner Mongolia, but also at Xiachuan in Shanxi, and Hutouliang in Hebei. Microlithic craftsmanship, which created small and delicately sharpened cutting tools and arrowheads, survived in many locations for a considerably longer period than the technological and chronological framework that archeologists have established in relation to its earliest origins. Carbon-14 dating techniques, which rely upon adjacent organic substances, tend to confirm this evidence and Microlithic artifacts may have

1
Urn decorated with four large circles. Neolithic painted pottery. Discovered in 1956 at Yongjing (Gansu). Height: 49 cm.
This large-bellied jar with two small handles is a marvelous specimen of painted pottery from Western China from the Neolithic civilization known as the "Yangshao" period. This type of pottery produced from clay containing lead was retouched by hand although pieces of exceptional quality were sometimes finished on potters' wheels at the end of the "Yangshao" period. Fine specimens were distinguished by painted decoration, often consisting of geometric motifs of the type seen here. This

form of decoration was characteristic of the so-called "Banshan" style, whose name is derived from the site where wares of this type were discovered as early as 1923. Adornment often consisted of medallions filled with various motifs such as concentric circles or large spirals although it is still not possible to interpret the meaning of these symbols. To a significant extent these motifs appear to be derived from extremely stylized recreation of zoomorphic or originally anthropomorphic forms. Decoration was always confined to the upper portion of the vessel. This was a practical necessity because the bottom part of the urn was designed to be firmly set within the ground.

originated more than 20,000 years ago. Nevertheless, along the Great Wall for example, a variety of chronological stages have furnished relatively significant quantities of Microlithic flints from cultures that produced primitive pottery decorated with a comb to sites in Longshan where the effects of metal work were foreshadowed by refined ceramic pieces with delicate and shiny surfaces.

Beyond the Mesolithic Age Chinese history once again becomes obscure. Nevertheless, recent discoveries have revealed the beginnings of agrarian societies within the Great Plain: Peiligang in central Henan Province and Xishan in Hebei both contain the vestiges of agriculturally-oriented societies, complemented by a harvesting economy which especially thrived at Xishan. The inhabitants bred domestic animals such as pigs and were concerned with providing honorable burials for the dead. They produced crude pottery which was baked at relatively high temperatures; the oblique kiln found at Peiligang which is comparable to the Yangshao kilns provides a basis for assuming that here the potters' techniques were slightly more advanced than at Xishan, even though the Xishan wares displayed greater variety in decoration and shapes. If one accepts the results of Carbon-14 dating, these two sites typologically and chronologically provide a portrait of society approximately 6,000 or 5,000 years B.C. They prefigure subsequent development of the Yangshao culture, corresponding to the flowering of the first fully recognizable Neolithic culture in China — whereas the second is the so-called Longshan culture.

Discovery of these extremely primitive agrarian societies has considerably enriched Chinese prehistory, although it has not yet been possible to identify links between Mesolithic periods and these indications of a firmly established Neolithic way of life.

The Yangshao Culture

As Peiligang and Xishan are left behind darkness descends once again until the rise of the Yangshao culture. This culture developed a highly advanced farming economy where towns occupied hundreds of square yards and even larger areas in some instances. Another of its distinguishing features was the production of polished and painted ceramic ware. Carbon-14 analysis has situated the Yangshao culture between 4515 and 2460 B.C. but delineation of its various characteristics remains difficult and continues to give rise to disagreements. Contemporary Chinese historians regard this era as the height of the Age of Matriarchy.

On the basis of current knowledge four regional categories are usually established with respect to the Yangshao culture: the loess plateaux, the plains, Shandong Province, and an area encompassing the upper valley of the Yellow River. The first region, which incorporates the entirety of the loess plateaux, is represented by such sites as Banpo, Miaodigou, Beishouling and Xiwangcun.

The large Neolithic town of Banpo, discovered in 1954, became a "museum-school" after 1958 and continues to serve as a model site. Multitudes of visitors come there to learn about the finds and subdivisions of prehistory. Indeed, this location eloquently reveals the lifestyle during the height of the Neolithic period. Its sedentary inhabitants were not only farmers but also hunters and fishermen.

They resided at Banpo more than 6,000 years ago and the traces of their activities are now located three or four meters underground, covering an area of more than ten hectares. The eastern portion of the village was allotted to pottery production, whereas the burial ground extended northward. The discoveries have included more than fifty dwellings, more than a hundred trenches for storing food, more than ten thousand utensils and tools, more than two hundred graves of various types and countless bones of domestic animals. In the mirror of archeology the soil of Shaanxi has generously permitted an entire way of life to be reconstituted before everyone's eyes.

Insofar as it is possible to furnish estimates, the village that constituted the center of this settled area covered three hectares. It was surrounded by a trench that may have helped to protect the community from wild beasts inhabiting the adjacent forests. This trench was still in a usable condition when it was discovered. Within the area demarcated in this way, Chinese historians have observed the presence of a society with clearly distinguished strata, where the quality of individual dwellings reflected the owners' respective status within the community.

These dwellings, whose foundations have been identified according to differences in soil density, could be round or square and large or small. Some were built upon the surface of the ground but others were partially underground. In some instances the largest dwellings occupied several dozen square meters whereas the smallest only occupied a few square meters. The average surface area varied between sixteen and twenty square meters. All of these dwellings were open on the southern side and were built from simple materials: tree-trunks, dried mud, branches and masses of leaves. In some dwellings a hole was provided within the roof in order to allow smoke from the hearth to escape, but this feature was not always included. Indeed, certain dwellings did not contain hearths.

It is obvious that few if any portions of the superstructures of these dwellings have been preserved: there are only ashes, wood and remnants of a form of masonry containing a high proportion of plant matter. The tamped dirt foundations that were used in all Chinese dwellings during later periods had not yet been introduced and on the basis of current knowledge the earliest indications of floors of this type are only attributable to the end of the Neolithic Age.

The site has also yielded a substantial number of tools — 735 farming implements, for example — and utensils for daily use. These items were produced from stone or bone and were characterized by exceptional diversity. Analysis of animal bones has also allowed certain interesting observations. The high number of bones from pigs demonstrates that this animal had already become an important source of nourishment and that it undoubtedly helped improve the inhabitants' capacity to perform their labors. It also appears that large quantities of fish were consumed. Not far from their dwellings the villagers grew their crops, notably berries and fruit as well as chestnuts.

Crafts seem to have been as extensively developed as agriculture insofar as the number of tools may furnish an indication: the 1133 tools which were discovered were used for preparing hides and fur, as well as bones, woven products and pottery. The distinct area allotted to potters, located in the eastern portion of the village, is especially interesting. There were six kilns: five with an oblique draft and one where the draft was placed at the center. Each kiln was situated within a suitable excavated area, and consisted of two sections. There was a hearth, above which was a supporting slab containing two holes — and later, slits — where pottery was placed during baking. The holes within the supporting slab allowed heat and smoke to be released. Whenever baking took place, the following steps were carried out. After the unbaked wares had been positioned upon the crude grid placed above the fire, a protective cover made of mud

2
Flat-bottomed amphora. Neolithic painted pottery. Discovered in 1958 near Wushan (Gansu). Height: 38 cm.
This amphora possesses two small handles which are actually loops for hanging, carrying or emptying the vessel. The amphora, noteworthy for the quality of its composition, is adorned with an extremely rare and impressive reptilian zoomorphic motif. The legs suggest that this is undoubtedly an image of a dragon, whose presence is associated with clouds, rain, and water, or ultimately with fecundity.
Cf. *Kaogu xuebao,* 1960, 2, p. 14 and pl. I, no. 9.

3

Basin with striped decorative motif. Neolithic painted pottery. Discovered in 1966 at Dadunzi, Sihu, Pixian (Jiangsu). Height: 10 cm. Diameter: 18 cm. This item with elegant shapes and bold decoration consisting of spirals and diagonals represents the so-called "Qingliangang" culture. This culture, belonging to the Yangshao group, produced painted pottery from clay containing lead. The relative fineness of the surfaces and the soft luster of this specimen, as well as the imaginative and harmonious development of decorative patterns, are aspects which foreshadow the next technological stage: the Longshan culture, whose vestiges have subsequently been discovered throughout China, but especially in nearby Shandong Province. Cf. *Wenwu,* 1972, 3, p. 77.

and materials from plants was positioned around them. This cover contained a hole in order for smoke to escape. In this way there was no direct contact between the fire and the pottery and baking was permitted to continue for several hours. The potters' labors required a considerable amount of time because these small kilns could only accommodate a limited number of ceramic items. Hence, it was necessary to repeat the process many times. Nevertheless, modern potters acknowledge the merits of these ancient kilns which are not extremely different from present-day kilns for baking simple pottery in terms of the fundamental

principle. Thus, we can understand why the quality of pottery produced at Banpo was so outstanding.

Pots were usually hand-turned in cylindrical shapes although potters' wheels were already being used for certain extremely small cups.

After baking the best pottery was painted red, black or ashen gray. Indeed, the inhabitants of Banpo appear to have possessed strong artistic inclinations. Not only were there decorated ceramic items, but also wooden carvings representing people, birds and animals, as well as ornaments produced from such materials as bone, ivory and jade. Indeed, 900 different items represent the villagers' decorative skills, and this category even includes two ceramic wind instruments *(ocarinas)*.

Lastly, one of the most astonishing discoveries at Banpo consisted of symbols engraved upon ceramic pieces as a portent omen of the development of writing. Twelve types of symbols have been identified and it is probable that each possessed a meaning which remains undecipherable thus far. Nevertheless, some scholars believe that these symbols were merely intended to identify individual potters.

Two hundred and fifty tombs were found within the village. Whereas graves for 76 children were discovered inside dwellings, most of the 174 adult graves were located in burial areas north of the village. Separation of adults from children, as well as the diversified characteristics of the adults' graves, constitutes one of the most significant features of the Banpo site. In some instances, the bodies were extended full length and at times were arranged in fetal positions. Some were buried alone and others were buried in groups of two, three or four, with their heads facing westward. Certain graves (71) contained funerary accoutrements consisting of five or six commonplace objects. Accoutrements of this type were especially lavish in the women's graves, thereby providing additional evidence to support the current belief that primitive Chinese society was predominantly matriarchal.

Seventy-three of the 76 children were buried in large terracotta urns in accordance with a custom that later reappeared in Japan during the Bronze Age (third century B.C. — third century A.D.). The archeologists also discovered a lavish grave for a young girl who was approximately six years old. She had been buried lengthwise like an adult within a coffin made of slabs which is the earliest coffin to have been discovered in China.

Another interesting characteristic of the tombs is that none of the adults appears to have lived past the age of thirty. This circumstance indicates the brief life expectancy of people born during this era. Contemporary Chinese historians have derived an ideological conclusion from this situation: the Confucian scholars of earlier times committed a substantial error by placing the "Golden Age" in the distant past when children had died like flies and when an adult's life seldom lasted beyond the thirtieth year. In China archeology is not merely a means of investigating the past; it contributes to perspectives about our own times.

The second region representing the height of the Neolithic Age includes a site at Dahe,[3] northeast of Zhengzhou in Henan Province. This site was discovered in 1972 southeast of the previously cited area at the foot of the loess plateau; it is located in the flatland area constituting the center of the Yellow River Basin. Dahe is especially important because without any discontinuities it provided objects representing not only the Yangshao culture — over a period of two thousand years — but also items associated with the Longshan culture. It has therefore been possible to establish an uninterrupted chronological sequence and Chinese archeologists have identified six stages in the rise of civilization.

Because the exceptional complexity of the oldest stratum at Dahe renders analysis difficult, further investigation will still be necessary. Indeed, red and gray pottery has been discovered within this layer but there have also been two fragments of white pottery — whereupon difficulties arise. Are these fragments forerunners of Longshan pottery or do they represent a stratigraphic aberration derived from some accidental event in the distant past? These shards are characterized by a sinuous engraved or painted decorative motif, in white, pale yellow and black. Exceptional variety has been observed not only in their shapes but also in ornamentation, and the entire output of the potters at Dahe appears to have been distinguished by vigorous originality. It is tempting to conclude that even during this epoch techniques had become more advanced in Henan than in peripheral regions. Once again theories and ideological premises tend to merge: this particular site is located at the very center of the authentically Chinese realm. The customary tools of Neolithic farmers were found alongside the pottery: stone axes, adzes, and scrapers as well as arrowheads or needles produced from bones. It appears that, immediately afterwards — and directly above in stratigraphic terms — tools were rapidly improved and diversified to such an extent that classification according to general categories becomes exceedingly difficult. The mysterious fragments of white pottery — which are not to be confused with the conventional painted pottery of this era — gradually became more numerous, and the quality of decorated pottery improved. Many specimens contained symmetrical motifs or cleverly arranged alternating patterns (xiangziwen) conveying a rhythm akin to that of writing.

With another leap in chronology the third layer offered an exceptional abundance of items. This layer contained not only dwellings but also urns for the dead. At this juncture the inhabitants of Dahe were living in sophisticated houses with several interconnected rooms — usually three or four whose dimensions were approximately 3.7 by 1.5 meters. At least it is possible to derive a design of this type by reconstructing the foundations that contained holes marking the positions of columns placed adjacent to the walls. According to whether they served as main pillars or merely as additional means of support, the diameters of columns varied from eight to ten centimeters and from sixteen to eighteen centimeters. From one room to another the floor level varied by five to ten centimeters. The hearth was located either in a corner or in the center of the house. Thus, the principal features of the traditional Chinese dwelling had already appeared. Primitive foundations consisting of tamped dirt and

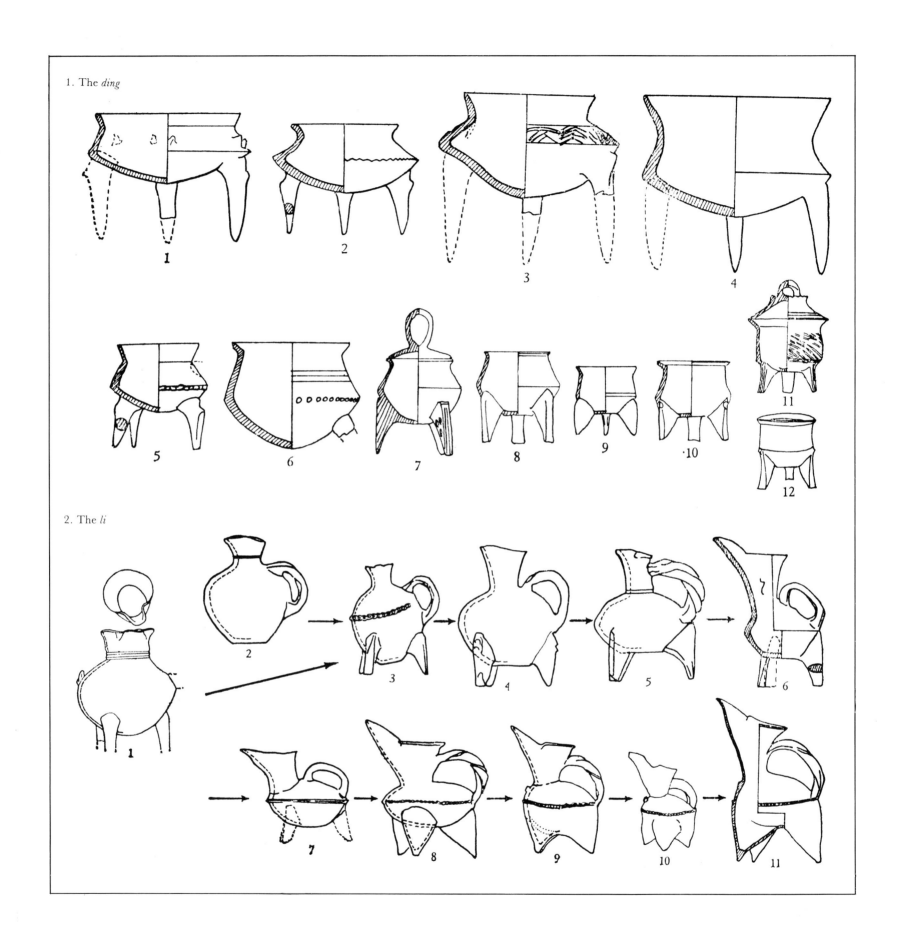

1. The *ding*

2. The *li*

Fig. 1.   Development of Dawenkou ceramics. Source: *Kaogu xuebao,* 1982, 3, p. 279.

a framework with wooden posts provided a versatile layout that would undergo subsequent adaptations in relation to the requirements of religious ceremonies and geomancy.

During the next period at Dahe the design of tombs appears to have been the primary preoccupation. Indeed, the respective stratum contained sixty tombs with urns and another thirty-seven that were surrounded by carefully tamped dirt; still another innovation was found here, namely underground trenches of the type that would be extensively used during the Shang dynasty at the beginning of the Bronze Age.

These trenches were primarily occupied by male bodies. Indeed, there were twenty-four male cadavers and only seven females but burial accoutrements for women still appear to have been more lavish than for men. This circumstance has also been cited as supporting evidence for theories concerning the rise of matriarchy.

The same layer also contained certain items used by those who were alive. There was an extensive assortment of necessary articles and utensils for daily survival, such as red and gray pottery with engraved decorations and complex shapes. These vessels were painted red instead of white or were adorned with patterns in black in smaller dimensions than had been customary during earlier eras. There were also new creations destined to undergo further development such as long-handled pots with perforated spouts for straining liquids and pots with multiple holes which were intended for cooking with steam.

After these extremely active phases the Dahe community appears to have become dormant between 2500 and 2000 B.C. The elegant Longshan culture is only represented by an obvious impoverishment reflected within the two uppermost strati-graphic layers. What happened? What sort of relationships did the inhabitants maintain with their neighbors? Perhaps interpretation of analogies with adjacent or typologically comparable sites will ultimately provide answers, thereby shedding light upon China's probable role as a crucible of civilization from the very beginning.

At least with respect to the third stratum containing remnants of dwellings, it has been possible to recognize affinities. This layer possessed certain characteristics that also existed at the Dawenkou site in Shandong Province where extensive excavation was completed between 1959 and 1979. The latter site represents the third regional category for the Yangshao culture. During a twenty-year period more than a hundred sites discovered throughout the Shandong Peninsula have irrefutably demonstrated the presence, not merely of isolated settlements but of an entire society that imperceptibly underwent a transition from the purely Neolithic Age to the dawn of the Bronze Age, from the Yangshao to the Longshan culture.

The Dawenkou Culture

The Dawenkou culture which originated as early as 4000 B.C. and survived for 2000 years covered an immense area; to the south it spread as far as the northern portion of the Anhui River, extending throughout Shandong Province and as far west as the northern bank of the Yellow River. For historians this aspect represents a significant phenomenon: the extremely ancient ties among vast geographic areas that centuries of feudal subdivisions and imperial administrations have conditioned us to perceive as separate entities.

Apart from Sanlihe[4] whose pottery is distinguished by elegant animal-like shapes, one of the most impressive sites within this region is certainly Chengzi,[5] where both architectural and funerary vestiges were discovered. Most of the graves within the oldest level were individual graves: each body was placed in a coffin accompanied by burial accoutrements, even in the simplest graves. The inhabitants undoubtedly constituted one of the earliest groups in China to adhere so unmistakably to the belief that life after death would resemble life on earth. This was a different concept from the outlook represented by double burial where two inhumations, separated by a brief interval, were performed in order to ensure more effective preservation of corpses. During the Neolithic Age this concept emerged not only in China but also throughout the world, and it persisted in Chinese civilization independently of the influence of foreign religions. At Chengzi a few collective graves were situated beside individual tombs. Perhaps these were graves intended for persons of low rank such as slaves, or they were intended for entire families that had suddenly been decimated by nature or by their fellow men. The bodies were heaped atop one another without being arranged by age or sex.

The most recent level contained the remains of a circular building with a diameter of 4.5 meters and with a roof supported by twenty-six pillars. Despite its complexity this configuration was reintroduced during the Shang and Zhou dynasties, but it essentially disappeared before regaining its prestige under the Yuan emperors who were Mongol rulers accustomed to building in ways other than those favored in Imperial China.

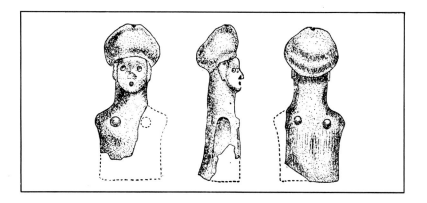

Fig. 2. Neolithic figurine from Lintongxian (Shaanxi). Source: *Kaogu yu wenwu*, 1982, I, p. 6.

The first differentiation among social classes becomes clearly observable at this point: as the Neolithic Age was ending, tombs became extremely numerous but they also began to be divided into three categories according to size with separate burial areas. The largest tombs contained an abundance of ceramic objects whereas the most humble graves were unadorned and, in some instances, did not even contain coffins. Chinese sociologists have attributed the rise of social classes to this era, regarding it as the transition from a society composed of clans to a society where state authority and hierarchies had emerged: individuals were now defined according to their social roles instead of solely according to bonds derived from consanguinity.

Establishing the origin of these people whose remains are being discovered today remains a difficult question to answer, because it calls into question the Chinese way of perceiving their ancestors, and emotion sometimes collides with logic. Yan Yan, the author of the first study of the Dawenkou culture, regarded the members of this society as being of Polynesian origin in contrast to the group that had developed the so-called Yangshao culture in central China. Han Kangxin and Pan Qifeng[6] ultimately furnished a different explanation when they approached the difficult question of the origins of the Chinese. Rejecting the Polynesian hypothesis, they emphasized certain physiological similarities between the Dawenkou group and the Yangshao group, finally concluding that the two communities were directly related to the vast family of Mongolian ethnic groups in Eastern Asia. Thus, we have once again encountered the perpetual conflict that, for both scientific and political reasons, still inspires advocates of the endogenous or exogenous nature of Chinese civilization.

The Upper Yellow River Valley

The same problem arises in relation to the cultures of the upper valley of the Yellow River. They constitute a fourth category where a certain number of distinct characteristics emerged, especially in terms of art forms and ornamentation. For example, there was the elegance of motifs that relied extensively upon curves and countercurves. Consequently, the cultures of this region have been collectively given the name "Yangshao culture of Gansu Province" or the "Majiayao culture" (identified by J.G. Andersson in 1924 and clearly defined since 1958). There are three fundamental types, matched by the same number of sequences: Majiayao, Banshan and Machang (discovered in 1923 – 1924). Nevertheless, it is acknowledged that each of these categories is slightly more recent than the Miaodigou culture of the central plain. Carbon-14 techniques have established 3000 B.C. as an approximate date for Majiayao, 2500 B.C. for Banshan, and 2400 B.C. to 2000 B.C. for Machang.

Furthermore, it is now possible to adopt a conclusion that no one would have dared to advance fifteen years ago: namely that the "Yangshao" culture in spite of chronological differences and localized variations existed throughout China, solidified by a series of characteristics linking cultural groups that were separated by considerable distances.

Graphic symbols had already been introduced within this milieu where writing had not yet arisen and detailed studies of pottery from Banpo (3000 B.C.) have been cited heretofore. There was also a system of numerical notation — from 1 to 8 — as well as points placed in a triangular arrangement, similar to the practices of the ancient inhabitants of Chaldea.

It has likewise been demonstrated that art had already become important in this society: geometric patterns for urns and the few animal or human figures characterizing the final phase at Banpo were widely recognized. An even more surprising element has been introduced by recent excavations (1977–1978): the head of an elderly man, molded from terra cotta, has been discovered at Egoubeigang, a large Neolithic village in

4
Basin. Neolithic painted pottery. Discovered in 1963 in Tomb Number 44 at Dadunzi in Sihu (Jiangsu). Diameter: 30 cm.
This basin, decorated with clusters of eight-pointed stars, represents the final more angular phase of the so-called "Qingliangang" culture, a late Neolithic culture of the lower Yangtze region.
Cf. *Kaogu xuebao,* 1964, 2, p. 32 and pl. I, no. 2.

5

Cup with a stem (dou). Black pottery with thin "egg-shell" inner side. Discovered in 1960 at Yaoguanzhuang, Weifang (Shandong). Height: 16.3 cm. This lustrous black cup perfectly represents the so-called "Longshan" civilization. Its pottery, which was formed on potters' wheels, is extremely fine and shiny. Instead of relying on painted decoration, potters allowed the contours and the hues of their materials — white, ochre, reddish brown, gray, or black — to be emphasized to the fullest extent. The existence of white, gray, or red wares has been confirmed by excavations completed since 1949 but black pottery had been discovered considerably earlier: the first specimens had been unearthed as early as 1930 at Chengziyai in Shandong. As the cup shown here demonstrates, recent excavations have confirmed the degree of technical virtuosity which is illustrated not only by the quality of the clay but by boldness of contours, suggesting mysterious affinities between the potter's craft and metal work.
Cf. *Kaogu xuebao,* 1963, 7, p. 349 and pl. 2, no. 4.

Henan Province, and by comparison with an adjacent stratum whose age was determined by Carbon-14 techniques, it would appear that this item was created in 5290 B.C. Moreover, a comparable discovery has recently occurred in the Lintong district near Xi'an in Shaanxi Province. Thus, we are encountering one of the most significant revelations from excavations undertaken during recent years: the presence of human figures within a repertory of forms that Shang and Zhou bronzes had induced us to regard as predominantly consisting of geometric or zoomorphic forms.

The Longshan Cultures

The final and least remote phase of the Neolithic Age in China has been given the name *Longshan* which is derived from the name of a site at Chengziyai in Shandong Province. During the late 1920s and at the beginning of the 1930s excavations at this location uncovered a culture that was distinguished by shiny ceramic pieces with delicate surfaces and complex rounded shapes. Although it was initially believed that this culture was confined to Shandong Province, its presence within the plains region, in Henan, was soon confirmed. Some scholars even spoke in terms of a "coastal Longshan culture" and a "Longshan culture at the mouth of the Yangtze River."

Current discoveries have corroborated this view: Longshan artifacts have now been discovered in many regions of China. Therefore, the prevalent opinion during the past twenty years has been that a civilization resembling Longshan superseded the more ancient civilization represented by the Yangshao culture. Sociologists have interpreted this transformation as the transition from matriarchy to patriarchy.

Nevertheless, theories and models constantly waver between the temptations toward an all-round global view and the temptations toward arbitrary compartmentalization. Today, there is a tendency toward a form of proliferation or somewhat exaggerated regionalization, whereby each site or each stratigraphic layer comes to be perceived as a separate entity or as a separate culture. As a result evidence has been scattered among an array of subdivisions that ought to be classified since these groups undeniably display shared or similar features, including at least one feature that must be expressed in negative terms: namely that they do not belong to the mid-Neolithic periods represented by the Yangshao culture, nor to the obviously Chalcolithic civilization which had arisen during the initial

Fig. 3. Characteristic creations of the Qujialing, Dawenkou, and Liangzhu cultures. Source: *Kaogu,* 1982, I, p. 44.

phase of the Shang dynasty. Archeologists have also reached universal agreement concerning another aspect of the Longshan civilization although a satisfactory explanation has not yet emerged: the realm of Lu — which was subsequently the homeland of Confucius — was a transitional region in certain respects. Traces of the Longshan civilization discovered in this region are not precisely identical, depending upon whether they have been found east or west of the small principality that entered history during the Spring and Autumn Period (770 B.C. −476 B.C.).

The many facets of Longshan culture that have emerged today are open to interpretation.

In the region where the provinces of Henan, Shanxi, and Shaanxi are contiguous, the so-called Miaodigou II culture, which superseded the "Yangshao" culture of Miaodigou, was characterized by exclusive use of the type of gray pottery that was produced everywhere during this era (2700 B.C.). Two hundred years later (2500 B.C.), however, black pottery produced on potters' wheels had already appeared in Henan. It appears that by this time the use of potters' wheels had been introduced everywhere, after having represented a secondary procedure for a lengthy period where it had been principally employed for finishing high-quality items that were initially hand-crafted.

Similar cultures arose in the valley of the Yangtze River and their ties with the cultures of Northern China appear to be obvious, although the southern farmers, instead of growing millet or rice in unirrigated fields as farmers in the north and in the Gansu region had done, were introducing rice paddies in the lowland areas of southern China. Furthermore, it is possible to identify such cultures as the Daxi in Sichuan and the Qujialing in Hubei above the Yangshao strata that are observable throughout China. In these regions it appears that perhaps to a greater extent than elsewhere development continued toward diversification and multiple regionalization of human communities.

The Daxi culture extended as far as the "Three Gorges" region (Sichuan, southwestern Hubei, northern Henan), and Carbon-14 dating techniques have established 2900 B.C. as its approximate period of existence. The influence of the Qujialing culture was especially pronounced in northern Hubei and southwestern Henan around 2500 B.C. Lastly, the Longshan culture of Hubei — in the Han valley and the central portion of the Yangtze River — was significantly different from the Longshan culture of the Great Plain. Whereas gray pottery was widely used in 2400 B.C., it was solely hand-turned and imprints derived from wicker work were often applied. Indeed, it has been confirmed that for a considerable period of time in southern China there was no rush to adopt the potters' wheel except for finishing, and that baking temperatures were relatively low: 750° C. to 810° C. at Daxi; 600° C. to 700° C. at Honghuatao in Hubei; 880° C. at Mengxi in Henan; and even at Qujialing no more than 900° C. The levels of 1000° C. or 1050° C. that had become popular among the northern Longshan potters were not yet a possibility. Perceptibly higher temperatures were not introduced in southern kilns until the final phase of the Neolithic Age: at that point, a level of 1100° C. was attained and from then on baking temperatures increased over the centuries.

25

This situation predominated in the heart of central China. Further down the Yangtze River or toward the south a more complex set of patterns gradually emerged.

Three cultures arose in the Lower Yangtze regions: the Hemudu, Majiabang and Liangzhu cultures. The Hemudu culture flourished in the Gulf of Hangzhou, whereas the Majiabang and Liangzhu cultures successively arose in the Tai Hu region. Hemudu craftsmen produced sophisticated wooden agricultural implements as well as a porous and relatively crude black pottery that was adorned with lively engraved motifs. The Majiabang culture produced simple or more elegant red pottery as well as some gray, and in rare instances black pottery. Liangzhu specimens, which represent a later period and indicate use of potters' wheels, appear to be of a significantly superior quality. Nevertheless, the abundance of rice grains observed at the three sites confirms at least one shared characteristic: cultivation of rice.

Further south few clear conclusions have emerged yet: Carbon-14 techniques have not yet furnished precise results because a coherent method has not yet been developed for determining the age of shells and animal bones situated within the same strata.

In many instances Chinese archeologists are now confronted by a considerable quantity of uninterpreted evidence, and the concept of extreme diversity prevails over the tendency to establish unity. In conclusion, it is nevertheless appropriate to observe that whereas materials, methods and technology for ceramic work varied greatly from one location to another, thereby reflecting the vigorousness of local creativity, a pervasive series of forms suggests a certain degree of unity, or an undeniable bond with later Chinese civilization: the *ding,* the *gui,* the *he,* the *dou,* and the *hu* that we recognize in lavish bronze versions were forms which Chinese potters were already producing from one end of the mainland to another before writing emerged.

Today, the art of the bronze workers appears to have originated from two distinct traditions: the tradition of the northern Chinese forest dwellers who undoubtedly created wooden items with carved surfaces in the same manner as their cousins in Siberia; and the tradition of the potters who worked with rounded shapes and whose talent is confirmed by excavations in every region of China.

II. THE REAPPEARANCE OF A FORGOTTEN DYNASTY: THE XIA

"It was not an easy matter for the Chinese countryside to have been prepared in this manner: amid the extreme obstacles which the landscape offered to settlers ... All of these efforts were so ancient that any recollection was shrouded in the mist of legends ...

During the period when the short treatises which are now contained in a compilation entitled the *Zhou jing* were written, during the eighth century before our era and during subsequent centuries, all of these legends were woven into a semblance of a continuous narrative ..."[7]

One of the most fascinating characteristics of contemporary Chinese archeology is its tendency to provide confirmation for ancient texts and to enhance legends by establishing their authenticity.

All ancient Chinese texts, including the extremely venerable *Li Ji,* affirm that traditional society, characterized by distinctions among social classes and by possession of wealth, emerged during the era of the first royal dynasty, the Xia dynasty, whose geographic cradle was defined by Si Ma Qian (*circa* 145–90 B.C.) as the region where the Yellow River bends, from the Luo to the Yi, precisely around the Xia district which is the birthplace *par excellence* of the Xia dynasty. Represented by the benevolent figure of the demiurge Yu the Great, who regulated streams and rivers, this dynasty until recent years appeared to have been lost in the haze of traditional myths pertaining to the origins of the Empire. Nevertheless, the question arose: until the excavations at Anyang in 1928, it was conventional to regard this dynasty's successors, the Shang emperors who are described in historical texts, as having been purely fictional. It is possible that comparable discoveries could confirm the existence of the Xia dynasty, independently of the exaggerations or distortions that are inherent to subsequently created chronicles whose aim was to establish the origin of the State.

For thirty years Chinese archeologists have labored incessantly to solve this riddle. Although extensive excavations in the Xia district were interrupted in 1963 and resumed in 1973, artifacts have been unearthed from the principal stages in the rise of Chinese civilization, from the Neolithic to the Iron Age. If the Xia — a dynasty attributed to the beginning of the Bronze Age — truly existed, it should be possible to find signs of its presence. In 1976 the ruins of a city erected approximately 2000 B.C. were discovered precisely within the Xia district (Xia Xian). Could these be the ruins of China's most ancient imperial capital? For such an affirmation evidence that would allow comparisons is indispensable. Indeed, it now appears that such evidence has existed since the discovery (in 1954, although investigations began much later) of the Erlitou complex[8] in Henan Province, which is stratigraphically situated between Longshan layers and the so-called Erligang layer, corresponding to the earliest Shang emperors. This particular site which was inhabited for an extremely long period offers many significant features — such as a palace that represents the height of the Bronze Age — and have been attributed to 1500–1300 B.C. by Carbon-14 techniques. That period already represents the beginning of the Shang dynasty. Directly beneath this layer the soil yielded another cultural layer that possibly represents the origins of the written word.

The materials found in this older layer are usually extremely ordinary: simple gray pottery, rather thick, was baked at low temperatures. This pottery is decorated with sinuous lines, and resembles pottery found in all regions adjacent to China, both in the Asian steppes and in the islands of the Pacific or even in the central basin of the Yangtze River. Nevertheless, the extremely varied shapes, despite a more precisely identifiable affinity with Inner Mongolia, suggest a new chronological, technological and sociological stage that is occasionally represented by items discovered throughout the central basin of the Yellow River. Two sites that are comparable to Erlitou have been discovered in Shanxi Province at Dongxiafeng and at Maputou. There is little difference between these sites, although the potters of Dongxiafeng appear to have specialized in producing tripods with hollow legs (*li*), while their counterparts in Maputou primarily created vessels with four solid legs (*fang ding*).

These differences may represent a mere evolutionary phase within the Neolithic context, but there is a specific aspect that tends to place Dongxiafeng among the cruel societies of the Bronze Age. One of the tombs there contained the partially embalmed body of a youth, accompanied by urns containing various offerings of customary burial accoutrements in keeping with a widespread practice whose development can be traced since the Yangshao culture. Beside him, however, there lay the body of a young woman who was nearly thirty years of age, unaccompanied by any offerings. She had undoubtedly been chosen to accompany the deceased into the afterlife, and indeed, sacrifices of this type originated throughout the world during the Bronze Age.

Furthermore, the actual demarcation of the beginnings of the Bronze Age in China is now undergoing modification. Since the Song dynasty, scholars and archeologists have specifically associated the Bronze Age with the prodigious Shang and Zhou dynasties because of the quality of their sumptuous metal vessels. In 1977, however, a small bronze knife which measured 12.6 centimeters was discovered 1.2 meters below the current surface level at Majiayao in Gansu Province. This phenomenon would not be of any particular significance unless it had been corroborated by comparable finds: at Machang, Huangniang-niangtai or Dahezhuang (Gansu), Sanlihe (Shandong), or Dachengshan (Hebei). It would be difficult to imagine how juxtaposition of archeological layers could have occurred in the same way at five different sites for the same small objects. Hence, on the basis of current evidence it is possible that the Xia civilization had developed bronze-working techniques in a rudimentary form, thereby foreshadowing the accomplishments of the Shang Period. Thus, there might be a grain of truth in the famous legend of Yu the Great's having cast the nine *ding* pots which symbolize his civilizing influence whereas his son Qi later began to mine and work metal ores.

Without rejecting these poetic portrayals but without granting them excessive authority, archeologists are attempting to correlate or superimpose the various categories that are now available: the Longshan culture of Henan, the older Erlitou culture and the Dongxiafeng culture. Professor Xia Nai, who is the Director of the Archeological Institute, has cited four possible choices. It could be that the "Longshan culture of Henan" and the four stratigraphic layers at Erlitou constitute a continuous evolutionary sequence that entirely corresponds to the Xia dynasty and not to a primitive phase of the Shang which only originated during the height of the Bronze Age, or that the Xia dynasty only occupies intermediate layers representing the end of the Longshan culture and the beginning of the Erlitou one? Or it is possible that only the most ancient strata at Erlitou should be regarded as the Xia Period. Finally, there is still another hypothesis: that the Longshan culture of Henan remained purely Neolithic whereas the entire Erlitou site corresponds to the origins of the monarchy under the Xia.

Indeed, present-day archeologists with some degree of certainty will uncover evidence of the existence of the Xia dynasty. Such an accomplishment is regarded as a scientific necessity, or as the discovery of the missing link. Nevertheless, only its shadow has thus far been discerned.

III. THE ERA OF KINGS IN CHINA

THE SHANG DYNASTY AND EARLY BRONZE AGE

China's entry into history coincides with the appearance of written communication during the Shang dynasty but it can be situated even earlier if one considers the symbols traced upon Neolithic ceramic wares. In terms of a system of notation consisting of more than simple mnemotechnical or numerical references, however, the era of the Shang represents an indisputable beginning.

The Shang constituted a clan or an ethnic minority comparable to those that, even until modern times, have incessantly gained control of the major portion of the Chinese land mass. Initially they established their domain in the Lower Basin of the Yellow River. From there they extended their authority as far as Henan and became significantly more powerful. Having strengthened themselves by uniting several other tribal groups which became their allies or had been subjugated, the Shang, according to traditional accounts, ultimately waged war against Jie, the last Xia ruler. In this way they seized power — a form of power called *wangdao* — the extent and development of which has been described in recent publications by Leon Vandermeersch whose scholarly endeavors are comparable to those of Marcel Granet fifty years earlier.

From the sixteenth century until the fourteenth and thirteenth centuries before Christ, the Shang dynasty experienced a difficult formative period, marked by extensive unrest. The site of the capital, which was to be the seat of royal power and the home of the Shang rulers, was changed at least five times until King Pan Geng (before 1370 B.C.) chose Anyang in Henan Province at a location that the Chinese of later eras would call

Yinxu, or "the Yin ruins," adopting the name given to the Shang as their dynasty entered its final period. The Shang rulers maintained their capital at this location for 273 years until their authority ended in the twelfth century B.C.

Anyang

Although the city of Anyang had been discovered during the Song Period (960-1268) and was subsequently ignored, it was identified once again as the Shang capital by the end of the nineteenth century, and scientific excavation began in 1928 under the *Academia Sinica.*

At that time a vast and lavish series of tombs and monuments was discovered adjacent to the village of Xiaotun on the southern bank of the Yuan River. Nevertheless, the archeologists were compelled to abandon the site during the Japanese invasion in 1937, and it was not possible for research to begin again until thirteen years later, after the new government had been established.

Accordingly, research at this site began again in 1950. It was possible to identify a populated belt around Xiaotun on the southern bank of the Yuan River. North of this zone there were remnants of buildings — undoubtedly with thatched roofs but clearly of significant dimensions. To the east at Hougang were simple dwellings. Hence, it appears that the southern bank of the river had been primarily allocated to the realm of the living.

The domain of the dead was situated on the opposite bank to the north, or at Wuguancun (discovered in 1950) and at Houjiazhuang, where the aristocracy had established its final resting place beside the ten large royal tombs that have been discovered thus far.

6
Li tripod. Bronze. Shang Dynasty, Zhengzhou Period (*c.* 1600 B.C.–1300 B.C.). Discovered at Zhengzhou (Henan), the original Shang capital in 1955. Height: 16.5 cm.
This vessel is a *liding,* a tripod with a trilobate belly in the shape of udders which permitted firing to be completed more easily. It began to appear during the Neolithic Age but its form was subsequently adapted by bronzesmiths. The principal motif, situated between two rows of small circles, is a series of stylized *taotie* masks. The triangular heads do not possess eyes and only the S-shaped spirals evoke these creatures' snouts, or their horns and eyebrows. This form of advanced stylization represents a continuation of late Neolithic zoomorphic motifs.

7
Gu vessel. Bronze. Shang Dynasty, Zhengzhou Period (*c.* 1600 B.C.–1300 B.C.). Discovered in 1965 at Minggonglu (Tomb No. 2), northwest of Zhengzhou (Henan). Height: 18 cm.

This vessel is a *gu,* a drinking cup which appears to have been used only until the end of the Shang Period. The two cruciform openings, often regarded as imprints from the attachments for inner and outer molds, could be used as vents when the vessel was placed upon hot coals in order to heat alcohol. The waist contains a "carcajou" (*taotie*) decorative motif.
Cf. *Kaogu,* 1965, 10, p. 502 and pl. 3, no. 2.

8
Jia vessel. Shang Dynasty, Anyang Period (*c.* 1300 B.C.–1030 B.C.). Discovered in 1959 at Anyang (Henan). Height: 30.8 cm.
A *jia* was a vessel for heating wine, and its form closely resembled *jue* containers although there was no pouring spout. This specimen contains a dedication to *Mu Ya,* "Mother Ya." There are three categories of decoration: "carcajous" (*taotie*) with S-shaped horns; at the top, a row of *taotie* with elongated bodies; and lastly, a series of triangles resembling the silhouettes of grasshoppers' bodies.

Nevertheless, the southern bank also contained burial sites; here, and at Dasikongcun on the northern bank, the cemeteries were humble, leaving no doubt as to the lowly status of their occupants.

Consequently, it is possible to define the social geography of Anyang in the following terms; a populated area existed at Xiaotun and at Hougang between the royal cemetery and the cemetery for the poor, but consistent use of this area is undoubtedly the reason why tombs were also located at those sites, amid the ruins of dwellings.

Excavation is still being carried out in every portion of the Anyang complex although several thousand tombs have already been unearthed. This figure suffices to express the historical and human significance of a location where it seems that each new investigation ultimately yields its own rewards.

Thus, large-scale excavation between May, 1969 and May, 1977[9] in the western portion of ancient Yinxu has recently brought to light within a zone of three hectares 1,003 Shang tombs as well as five trenches containing the remains of horses and more than two hundred other tombs representing an extensive span of time, from the era of the Warring States to the Song and Yuan dynasties. Indeed, ordinary tombs predominate in this area and — among more than a thousand — there are only five tombs that contain entry corridors. One of the objectives of current excavations is to investigate conventional characteristics or types of materials that, in spite of their having been recognized for a considerable period, have not always been properly understood in terms of their respective roles in the development of society. The extensive array of documentation originating from coordinated excavation projects will allow more accurate comparative analysis of such exceptional monuments as the royal tombs.

Indeed, a broad panorama of life at Yinxu[10] during several centuries is now being revealed. It has been ascertained that the necropolis expanded without precisely defined plans or principles even though most of the tombs were placed in a semblance of a north-to-south alignment. The dead were usually positioned lengthwise, although some lay in bent positions; in accordance with traditional Chinese cosmogony, some bodies faced southward and others faced northward. In the latter instance, however, the bodies had been placed slightly at an angle in relation to due north.

Some of the dead were only protected by crude coffins. For others the coffin consisted of a relatively large sarcophagus capable of accommodating burial accoutrements. Coffins were made of wood and were coated with layers of red lacquer or, occasionally, a yellowish-green lacquer. In rare instances there were more ornate sarcophagi containing bright red, bright yellow, black, or white adornments. The decorative motifs included not only geometric forms such as triangles, circles, or zig-zags, but floral motifs. In some instances the entire coffin was covered with colored hangings suitable for placement of various offerings. Hence, it is possible to recognize the origins of burial customs that, apart from a few relatively limited changes, persisted in China until the apogee of imperial authority.

The dead were often accompanied by substantial numbers of animals: horses, pigs, oxen and fish, although dogs were far more numerous since 439 were discovered among the 339 tombs at this location. In Shang society the dog had indeed acquired a significant role the origins of which can be traced to the Neolithic Age. Sacrificing of dogs is mentioned in oracular inscriptions, and every excavation within the confines of an ancient town uncovers a collection of canine skeletons. Large tombs always contained small trenches (*yaokeng*) where human beings were buried in some instances and where the remains of sacrificial dogs are inevitably discovered. There can be no doubt

9

Gu drum. Bronze. Shang Period (XV–XIV century B.C.). Discovered at Chongyangxian (Hubei) in 1977. Height: 75.5 cm. Length: 49 cm. Hubei Provincial Museum.
This bronze drum is the second Shang Dynasty drum of its type to have been discovered thus far. The Sumitomo Collection in Kyoto (Japan) contains another specimen which was acquired prior to World War II. These two drums, originating from the same region, are extremely similar, but the decorative style suggests that the more recently discovered specimen is slightly older. Analysis of attachments for molds also reveals interesting differences. It appears that the drum from the Sumitomo Collection was created with a more complex set of molds than this specimen. With the exception of the saddle-shaped top portion, this drum was cast by means of a one-time procedure requiring four molds. Although the "carcajou" (*taotie*) decor, highlighted by protruding "eyes," is extremely stylized and exceptionally simplified, it is still perfectly identifiable. On the other hand, uncertainty persists with respect to the nature of the uppermost portion which, in the drum from the Sumitomo Collection, resembles two mythical birds facing opposite directions. Perhaps this portion of the drum was a holder intended for the drumsticks but it is more likely that this portion of the drum permitted it to be hung from a beam in order to allow greater resonance. There is a possible reference in the "Classic on Rituals," which cites "Xia drums on stands, Yin drums fastened to posts, and hanging Zhou drums." These bronze drums, with excellent resonance, possess the form of instruments produced from several different materials and retain all of the respective functional pieces such as rivets for attaching an animal's skin to a wooden frame. In the instance of the Sumitomo drum, this aspect is figuratively expressed by the scales of a reptile's skin.
Cf. *Wenwu*, 1978, p. 94 and pl. 8.

10

Zoomorphic guang wine vessel. Bronze. Shang Period (XIV–XII century B.C.).
Discovered at Shilou, Luliang (Shanxi) in 1959. Height: 19 cm. Length:
41.5 cm.

This bronze in the form of a dragon with sharp fangs is a *guang,* a vessel used
to store wine. The back served as a lid, and the mouth constituted a spout.
The artisan adorned the body with animals representing good fortune, such
as reptiles, dragons, serpents and tortoises. These engraved motifs
anticipate the decorative patterns of the Early Zhou Period. The two rings
fastened to the sides suggest the possibility of attaching flexible handles or
any other items which would have allowed carrying or hanging of this vessel.
Cf. *Wenwu,* 1960, 7, pp. 50–51.

11

Squatting human figure. Jade. Shang Dynasty, Anyang Period (*c.* 1300
B.C.–1030 B.C.). Discovered in 1976 in Tomb No. 5 at Anyang (Fu Hao's
tomb). Height: 6.9 cm. Beijing, Archeological Institute, Yinxu, Tomb No.
5, no. 371.

This figure is squatting in the manner which is still widely practiced in
Japan, although this custom disappeared in China during the Song Period
when the use of chairs became widespread. Although they are extremely
rare similar jade carvings are not unknown. There are two specimens at
the Musée Cernuschi, although the workmanship is more sophisticated and
therefore undoubtedly represents a later period. The material is the same:
ochrous jade with flecks of green and brown, where certain traces of red
which are probably derived from cinnabar are observable. The somewhat
rustic simplicity of this creation is truly impressive, and the meaning of two
of its essential attributes has not yet been deciphered: a flat headdress with
a coiled edge and a large appendage on the figure's left hip. Could the latter
item be the scabbard of a ceremonial weapon, or, as R.W. Bagley (*The Great
Bronze Age of China,* p. 189) has suggested, could it be an extension of a
serpent-like motif which begins on the left thigh? The carved decorative pattern consists of the double lines which are characteristic of the Shang style.
Cf. *Kaogu,* 1977, 3, pl. 7, no. 1 and *Kaogu xuebao,* 1977, 2, pp. 80–81 and
pl. 26, no. 3.

12

Bird of prey pendant. Jade. Shang Dynasty, Anyang Period (*c.* 1300 B.C.–1030 B.C.). Discovered in 1976 in Tomb No. 5 at Anyang (Fu Hao's tomb). Height: 6.2 cm. Beijing, Archeological Institute, Yinxu, Tomb No. 5, no. 390.

This jade pendant in the form of a bird of prey with extended wings contains carving on both sides; there are double incisions on the obverse and single incisions on the rear side.

Cf. *Kaogu xuebao,* 1977, 2, pp. 85–86 and pl. 33, no. 5.

that in the realm of shadows, just as in earthly life, the dog would presumably serve as a loyal protector or guide.

Burial acccoutrements included conventional objects or stone ceremonial pieces such as flat, oval, crescent-like or irregularly shaped daggers. These daggers sometimes contained engraved decorative motifs resembling those appearing on bronzework from the Shang Period. Indeed, large quantities of bronze pieces have been discovered and they often contain inscriptions that reappear in groups at specific locations within the burial area. It is tempting to conclude that these inscriptions are the emblems of clans or tribes whose tombs were arranged in a close proximity, according to family membership. Efforts to define the possible duration or indeed the genealogy of these social units will be a challenging endeavor.

In addition to a thousand ordinary or humble graves, recent excavations at Yinxu have also revealed five large tombs with entry corridors. Each tomb is from seven to nine meters long and approximately three meters wide.

According to the structural outlines that have been defined since 1950 in relation to the large royal tombs at Wuguancun,

stairs or steps located on the southern side permitted access to these tombs. In keeping with royal or aristocratic customs, human victims were buried alongside deceased dignitaries. Seventeen of the tombs contained thirty-eight sacrificial victims, representing a relatively low but inherently horrifying percentage. Thus, only two percent of the bodies were accompanied by persons who had been put to death, among whom adolescents constituted the majority.

The most beautiful of these lavish tombs is indisputably the tomb currently identified as Number Five.[11] Chinese archeologists have emphasized that it constitutes the most impressive archeological discovery of recent years.

Although the upper portion had been severely damaged, the tomb still measures 5.5 meters from north to south and 5 meters from east to west. The bottom portions of the entry pathway can still be identified on the eastern side. This tomb was relatively small but it is an extremely important archeological landmark because of its sumptuous decorations.

There are six postholes for pillars situated above the tomb, which still contain stone bases. Three of these bases which were covered with ashes suggest the original presence of a superstructure that was ultimately burned. Other holes for pillars are situated on the eastern, western, and northern sides of the monument. Thus, these pillars must have demarcated both the tomb and a small temple enclosure where ceremonies were performed to venerate the occupant of the tomb.

13

Aviform figurines. Jade. Shang Dynasty, Anyang Period (*c.* 1300 B.C.–1030 B.C.). Discovered in 1976 in Tomb Number 5 at Anyang (Fu Hao's tomb). Height: 5.3 cm., 7.7 cm., 5.5 cm. Beijing, Archeological Institute, Yinxu, Tomb No. 5, items 403, 507, and 508.

The center figurine portrays an owl whereas the figurines beside it consist of mythical creatures with bird-like bodies, although they possess rams' horns. A hole was drilled in the owl's crest, undoubtedly in order for this figurine to be worn as an amulet. Decorative motifs were created with double lines which are characteristic of Shang engraving techniques for human figures as well. The upright pieces are reminiscent of the contours of zoomorphic *zun* or *you* vessels made of bronze, which often portrayed owls or other birds of prey.

Cf. *Kaogu xuebao,* 1977, 2, pp. 84, 85, and 87, and pl. 31.

14

Goose, crane, and frog. Jade. Shang Dynasty, Anyang Period (*c.* 1300 B.C.–1030 B.C.). Discovered in Tomb No. 5 at Anyang (Fu Hao's tomb) in 1976. Height: 7.8 cm., 9.8 cm., 7.1 cm. Beijing, Archeological Institute, Yinxu, Tomb No. 5, items 386, 416, and 356.

Each of these plates, which contains finely carved double lines typifying the Shang style, possesses a hole permitting the plate to be sewn onto or suspended from a garment. These aquatic creatures always suggested good fortune because they represented water and fertility.

Cf. *Kaogu xuebao,* 1977, 2, pp. 86–88 and pl. 34.

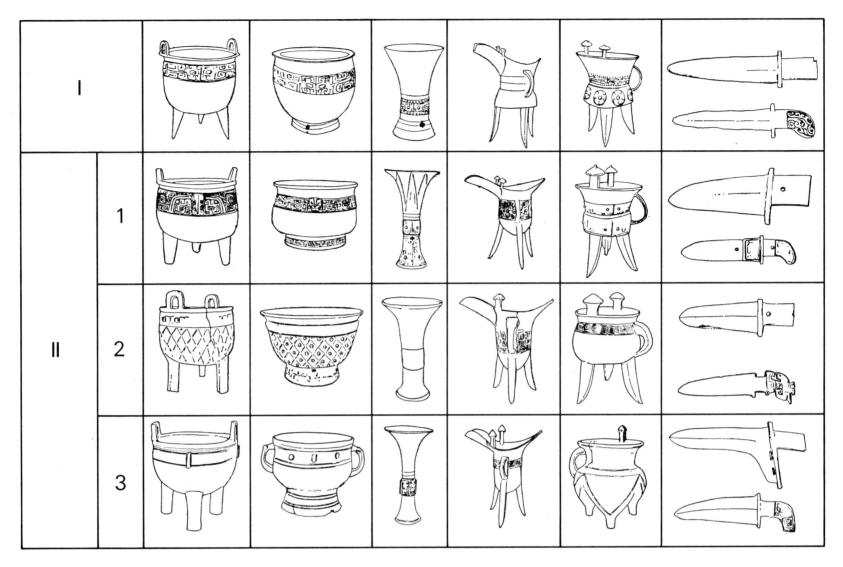

Fig. 4. Shang bronzes: principal stages of development. Source: *Shang Zhou kaogu*, 1979, p. 35.

The burial vault (5.4 meters × 4 meters, with a depth of 5.7 meters) rested upon a platform composed of tamped red clay with a thickness of 20 to 30 centimeters. A layer of foundation stones was added for reinforcement. The western and eastern walls of the burial vault contained two niches (1.7 meters × 0.3 meters × 0.35 meters) that were 6.2 meters deep and the bodies of several sacrificial victims were placed within these niches.

It has been possible to locate sixteen human victims, accompanied by six dogs, but excessive deterioration of their remains has rendered it impossible to identify eight of them even in the most general form. On the other hand, archeologists have identified the other victims as four men, two women, and two children. The causes of their death remain a mystery with only two exceptions: one victim's throat had been slit and another had been stabbed in the chest before being interred.

15
Drinking vessel. Ivory inlaid with turquoise. Shang Dynasty, Anyang Period (*c.* 1300 B.C.–1030 B.C.). Discovered in Tomb No. 5 at Anyang (Fu Hao's tomb) in 1976. Height: 30.3 cm. Neck diameter: 11.2 cm. Thickness of inner surface along neck brim: 0.1 cm. Beijing, Archeological Institute, Yinxu, Tomb No. 5, no. 100.
This vessel and another similar vessel constitute a pair. The turquoise inlaid work adorns the body with motifs which accentuate a complex series of finely carved lines. These motifs offer recognizable affinities with the bestiary for bronzes; on the body, a stylized grasshopper represented by a triangle, with its head resembling a *taotie* whose eyes are set off by eyebrows, while the horns extend in a manner evoking the insect's front legs. This form of decoration is set between two accompanying series: *taotie* masks at the top, where the short horns may be attributable to a lack of space, and *taotie* masks with long horns at the bottom. The handle portrays a bird of prey with a hooked beak; its claws are bent inward and the tail is erect. Cf. *Kaogu xuebao*, 1977, 2, p. 90 and pl. 37, no. 2.

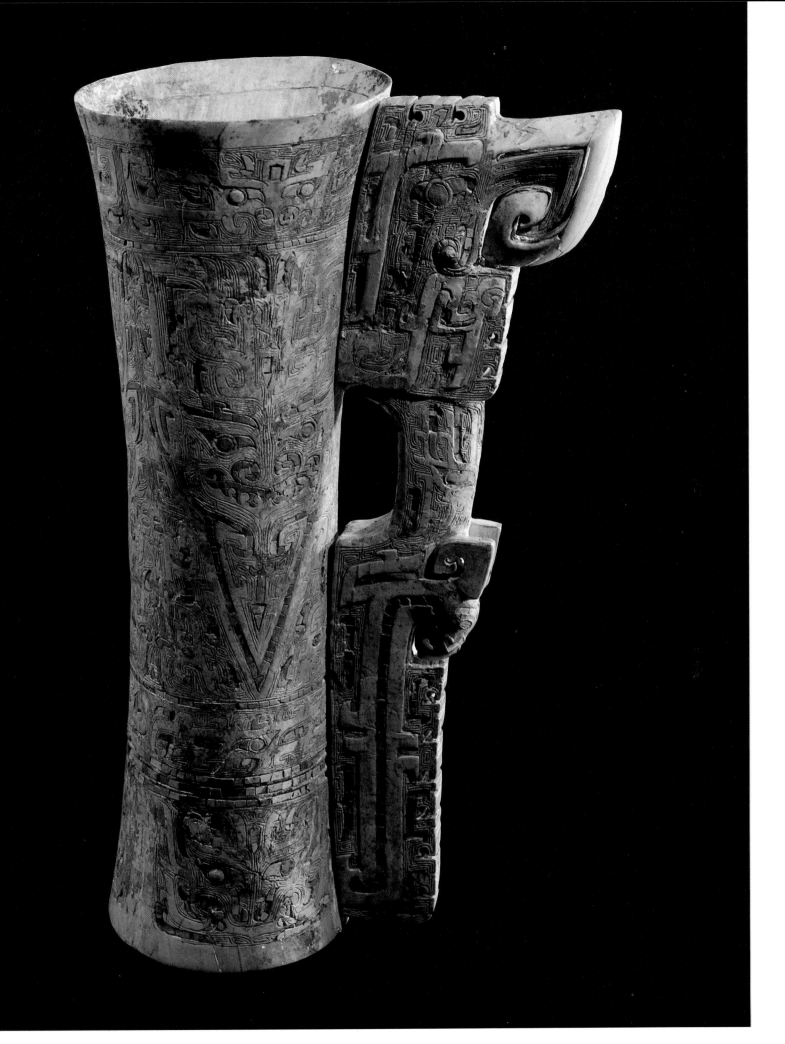

Earthen bases were placed around the entire burial vault in order to accommodate offerings. In the middle of the vault the trench appears to have been reinforced by coffer-planks that have decomposed, with the exception of a few portions of the ceiling that contain traces of red paint. Nevertheless, from a few pieces of black lacquer and some remnants of woven materials which appear to have been hemp and possibly silk no indications of the tomb's occupant nor of the sarcophagus or coffin have been found.

Because the fifteen hundred items comprising the burial furnishings were made of imperishable materials, their luxurious qualities have been fully preserved. There were 440 bronze pieces, nearly 500 pieces carved from jade and from bone, as well as stone and ivory carvings, ceramic pieces, and nearly 7,000 cowry shells (which were used as currency).

The jades have been divided into four categories: ceremonial items, propitiatory objects placed adjacent to the corpse, utensils or commonplace items and ornamental pieces. There was also an impressive collection of small sculptures: seven human figures kneeling, squatting on their heels, or bent so as to conform to the curvature of the original jade with their arms and legs folded together; a single piece of jade whose respective sides contain a naked couple possessing recognizable sexual organs and large ears with headdresses reminiscent of a deer's antlers; and, finally, an exceptionally diversified bestiary including tigers, bears, elephants, horses, cattle, monkeys, rabbits, ducks, owls, grasshoppers, fish and frogs. None of the small figures placed inside the tomb measures more than 12.5 centimeters but the pricelessness of the jade compensates for the small dimensions.

The 440 perfectly preserved bronze pieces represent the largest and most beautiful collection of this kind to have ever been discovered. Apart from weapons, mirrors, large and small bells, axle caps for chariots, and various tools — including a spade — there are more than twenty categories of ceremonial vessels. It is even more significant to observe that seventy of these vessels contain inscriptions that permitted identification of the occupant of this tomb, the contents of which were so lavish in spite of its relatively small size. The inscriptions referred to a personage whose presence was wholly unexpected: Fu Hao, the spouse of King Wuding (1324–1266 B.C.). Fu Hao is not mentioned in any classical texts: those accounts originated considerably later in a period where women had already lost their former authority. Nevertheless, oracular inscriptions — these extremely ancient but numerous chronicles of China's past that had been sold as "dragons' bones" by nineteenth century apothecaries — cited her no less than 170 times. As a queen and sorceress who interceded between divinities and human beings, she accompanied her husband during wars and in some cases she determined the advisability of doing battle. On some occasions she recruited soldiers whom she personally led on expeditions against tribes living on the periphery of regions ruled by the Shang dynasty. It is obvious that Fu Hao was also a mother because the oracle bones describe King Wuding's doubts and questions with respect to this topic. She died earlier than her royal husband and it appears that he venerated her memory. Wuding erected this underground palace for her remains and continued to communicate with her through sacrifices that were faithfully recorded by the scribes.

Zhengzhou: Erligang

Aside from Anyang, whose treasures sometimes appear to be inexhaustible, archeological discoveries during recent decades have shed light upon two or three centuries of the history of the Shang dynasty, namely, the period preceding relocation of the Shang court to its prestigious seat at Anyang.

In 1952 a Shang level — Erligang — was discovered at Zhengzhou in Henan Province. This location corresponded to the ancient "city of Ao" which had been the Shang capital during the reign of the Shang dynasty's tenth monarch, King Zhongding, whom archeologists currently believe to have ruled between 1562 B.C. and 1550 B.C.

This town — indeed, it must be defined as a town comparable to those of the Neolithic Age — was situated within a tamped earth enclosure protected by a perimeter of 6,960 meters. Insofar

16
Vessel. Bronze. Shang Dynasty, Anyang Period (*c.* 1300 B.C. – 1030 B.C.). Discovered in Tomb No. 5 (Fu Hao's tomb) at Anyang in 1976. Height: 34.2 cm. Beijing, Archeological Institute, Yinxu, Tomb No. 5. No. 796. This vessel, discovered at the same time as two similar specimens, is a *pou,* which contained beverages. Pieces belonging to this category were only produced for a relatively short period of time, approximately from the thirteenth century B.C. until the tenth century B.C., corresponding to the Anyang Period. The two characters of the inscription "Fu Hao" appear on the inside in the bottom portion. The decoration for the waist, which is divided into six sections by prominent ridges, includes three *taotie.* It is enhanced by an ornamental sequence at the top, where dragons with uplifted snouts face a prominent mask, and by a bottom strip containing browsing dragons. The principal motif reappears in an inverted form (top to bottom) on the lid. Creation of motifs accompanied by linear adornment on a background filled with spiral shapes is typical of bronzes from this period.
Cf. *Kaogu xuebao,* 1977, 2, p. 68 and pl. 11, no. 1.

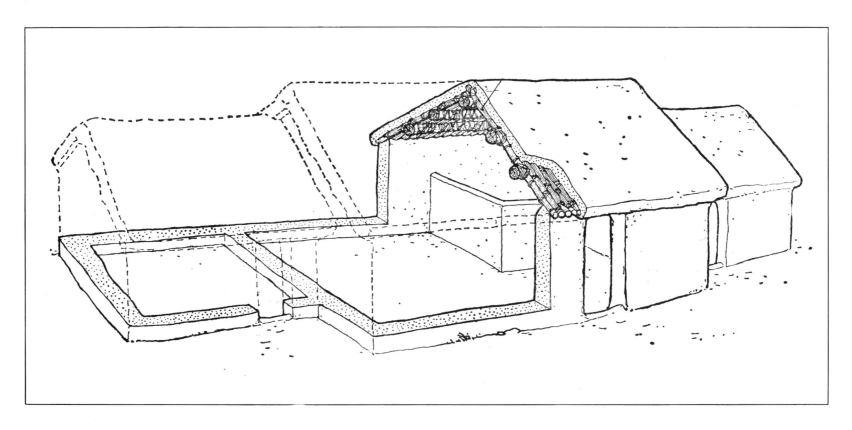

Fig. 5. Reconstruction of a dwelling at Mengzhuang. Reproduced from *Kaogu xuebao*, 1982, p. 53.

as it is possible to determine, the northern and southern sides measured 1,700 meters and 1,690 meters respectively, whereas the western and eastern sides measured 1,870 meters and 1,700 meters respectively. There were eleven openings undoubtedly corresponding to gates.

The town was surrounded by a prosperous community of artisans: bronzesmiths on the northern and southern sides; potters on the western side; and to the north craftsmen who created bone carvings from both human and animal bones. The potters had developed techniques for producing protoporcelain, or *yuanshixi,* the origin of which now appears to be attributable to the twentieth century B.C. Their creations included large-mouthed vessels coated with a bright greenish or greenish-yellow layer. Like the high-quality green porcelain of later eras, these extremely hard pieces are identifiable by a distinctive sound.

As a result of an extensive series of excavations during 1976 and 1977, an "Erligang" layer was likewise discovered at the site known as Mengzhuang, also in Henan Province.

At this location a village covering approximately 400 square meters contained nine dwellings, twenty-five trenches for storing food, a foundry, a pottery kiln and two tombs. One of the dwellings (Number FI-3) is particularly interesting: three main buildings or, in more precise terms, three cottage-like structures had been erected in a row upon a tamped earth foundation.

17

Zoomorphic "simu xin" guang vessel. Bronze. Shang Dynasty, Anyang Period (*c.* 1300 B.C. — 1030 B.C.). Discovered at Anyang in Tomb No. 5 (Fu Hao's tomb) in 1976. Height: 36 cm. Length: 46.5 cm. Beijing, Archeological Institute, Yinxu, Tomb No. 5. Number 803.

This composite animal is one of the six *guang* vessels found in Fu Hao's tomb. Its shape is comparable to that of a gravy dish with a cover evoking the head and the back of a dragon whose horns are curled in this particular instance, so that its appearance partially suggests the head of a bull or a goat. Although the *guang* was a typical category during the Shang, it disappeared at the beginning of the Zhou Period in approximately the tenth century B.C. This specimen is extremely rare for several reasons. As a pure reflection of a set of images whose meanings have been lost, the composition of the head reflects a perceptible naturalist tendency. The diversity of specific details does not render interpretation any less difficult. The wings on the sides and the claws on the rear legs give the hindquarters the appearance of an owl, whereas the *kuei* motifs on the front legs evoke the protective presence of the dragon. At the beginning of the tail, there is a face which could be a human face. Similar *guang* pieces which anticipated the four-legged *yi* vessels of the Zhou Period were extremely rare during the Shang Period (there are two other specimens; one is owned by the Freer Gallery in Washington, D.C., and the other belongs to the Fujita Collection in Osaka), because this type of vessel usually possessed an oval base. Lastly, this specimen of bronze craftsmanship contains an invocation to Fu Hao, who is probably being designated by a posthumous title (*si mu*) by a descendant invoking her as a "mother" (*mu*): the Shang precepts concerning kinship suggest that the donor may have been her son or her nephew.
Cf. *Kaogu xuebao*, 1977, 2, pl. 8 and p. 69.

44

Although the roofs do not appear to have been situated at the same heights, this elongated complex nevertheless constitutes the oldest fully completed version of the type of Chinese dwelling that would emerge over the centuries.

In particular the Erligang period is represented by the oldest bronze vessels to have been discovered thus far: extremely small *jue*, or ewers with three slightly curved legs possessing a triangular shape. Ewers of this type ultimately became a commonplace item during the Shang Period.

Later, the necks of *jue* were adorned with one or two studded posts which were decorated in various ways: archeologists still do not agree on the function of these protrusions although it is usually assumed that they were handles intended to facilitate removal of the ewer from a brazier.

On account of the diminutive *jue* from Erligang and of the chemical analysis of more recent *jue*, such as those that were found in Tomb Number 5 at Yinxu, it is necessary to reconsider this interpretation. The legs or the bottom portions of these vessels do not display any traces of fire nor any signs of exposure to heat. Therefore we can conclude that these *jue* were ceremonial vessels never intended for daily use, or that heated wine was poured into a container that remained cold. If these vessels were never heated it would be easier to understand the function of the double-bottomed *jue*, such as the specimen at the Shanghai Museum whose outer bottom contains holes corresponding to a small brazier.

Accordingly, the posts may be vestiges of the top portions of small rods used to support a vessel originally having the shape of a cornucopia. It is also possible, however, that the posts are attributable to technical aspects of production. The edge of the neck of the small *jue* from Erligang is bent backward, and the extremely thin bronze consists of flattened leafwork in this particular location. In the corner where the lower portion of the spout is situated, the opposite side of this portion is thicker, extending slightly beyond the rims of the spout. Hence, there are two protuberances that may actually have evolved into the two posts associated with later periods. Nevertheless, the existence of *jue* with only one post appears to offer a more plausible explanation: in order to reinforce the lower portion of the spout that was joined to the main portion of the ewer, the craftsmen incorporated a supporting element such as a band, the two uppermost portions of which formed a knob above the spout. This knot may have been the source of the center post, whereas double posts may have been derived from tightening of the band on either side.

Whatever the answer may be the inturned edge of this small *jue* continues to engender a host of questions. Some scholars, such as John Laplante at Stanford (University), have even advanced the hypothesis that the vessel was produced from bronze leafwork that had been molded prior to cooling. Such a procedure appears to be complicated, however, and many persons consider it improbable. Nevertheless, rejection of this hypothesis does not suffice to explain the presence of this hem-like brim. It is possible, indeed, that even in the most minute details the bronze vessel was adapted to the contours of the clay vessel which it was intended to emulate in a more prized material. Is it not possible to a significant extent to explain the exceptional beauty of Chinese bronzes in relation to the advanced techniques of early Chinese potters? The affinities between the potter's craft and the craft of bronze workers during the Bronze Age continue to represent an area where an aura of mystery persists.

18
Four-legged fang ding with thin "leafwork" legs. Bronze. Shang Dynasty, Anyang Period (*c.* 1300 B.C. — 1030 B.C.). Discovered in Tomb No. 5 (Fu Hao's tomb) at Anyang in 1976. Height: 42.4 cm. Length: 33.3 cm. Width: 25.1 cm. Beijing, Archeological Institute, Yinxu, Tomb No. 5. No. 813. This piece, which was discovered at the same time as another similar specimen, belongs to the vast category of cauldrons used for cooking food: they were directly exposed to the fire. Four-legged vessels are a variation upon the more common three-legged category. The body possessed a hemispherical shape (*ding*) in some instances or consisted of three hollow portions ending in sharp tips (*li* or *liding*, cf. pl. 6). The legs of square *ding* vessels (*fang ding*) were usually cylindrical. This specimen, which is one of the most beautiful bronzes to have been discovered in Fu Hao's tomb, represents a variant which was previously unknown, namely the *fang ding* with leafwork legs that looked like standing dragons. Legs of this type were ordinarily used for certain tripods whereas their presence in a tetrapod is exceptional. The four sides of this piece are adorned with *taotie*, whose bodies evolve into vertically arranged dragons on each side. The inner surface contains an inscription: *Fu Hao*.
Cf. *Kaogu xuebao*, 1977, 2, p. 63 and pl. 19, no. 2.

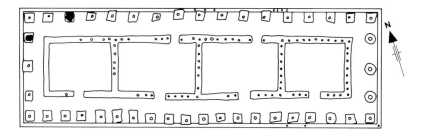

Fig. 6. Layout of palace (F I) at Panlongcheng. Reproduced from *Shang Zhou kaogu*, 1979, p. 67.

Lastly, one of the most significant results of recent excavations is that it has been possible to modify to some degree our formerly undisputed ideas concerning the territorial breadth of the Shang culture which was far more extensive than had been initially assumed. Maspéro had anticipated this modification when he wrote: "...The actual realm of the Yin encompassed both banks of the Yellow River, from the plains region to the foot of the Shanxi plateau, and from the foot of the Taishan to the periphery of the Huaiho Basin, possibly extending as far as the sea. Apart from this area which they ruled directly, their authority must have extended over all the Chinese portions of the north and the east ... Their presence has been observed toward the southeast ... in the northern portions of Gansu and

19
Vessel for boiling food. Bronze. Shang Dynasty, Anyang Period (*c.* 1300 B.C. – 1030 B.C.). Discovered at Anyang in Tomb No. 5 (Fu Hao's tomb) in 1976. Height: 15 cm. Beijing, Archeological Institute.
This *zeng* vessel containing a "boiling mushroom" (a short pipe, with a cap containing holes mounted at the top) that suggests an antique washing kettle, resembles pots which are still used today from Mongolia to Japan for boiling meat. The character "*Hao*" appears on the inside. There are two comparable specimens: a bronze counterpart with a round base (*yu* was discovered at Anyang (Tomb M. 1005 at Xibeigang, Houjiazhuang), whereas a ceramic counterpart with handles was discovered in the northern portion of Wuguancun (Tomb M. 230; cf. *Kaogu,* 1977, I, p. 28 and pl. 10, no. 9), which is also within Anyang. It appears that this type of utensil was relatively common from the Shang Period on because conventional ceramic versions had already begun to appear.
Cf. *Wenwu,* 1981, 9, p. 84.

20
Warmer with three warming pots (xian). Bronze. Shang Dynasty, Anyang Period (*c.* 1300 B.C. – 1030 B.C.). Discovered in Tomb No. 5 (Fu Hao's tomb) at Anyang in 1976. Total height: 68 cm. Beijing, Archeological Institute, Yinxu, Tomb No. 5. Nos. 770 and 790.

At the present time this warmer is the only one of its kind. The only comparable items are two altar stands originating from Baoji (Shaanxi), where they were respectively discovered in 1901 (altar from the former collection of the viceroy Duan Fang, with twelve vessels; now at the Metropolitan Museum of Art in New York) and during 1925–1926 (altar currently at the Cultural Resources Office in Tianjin). Both altars have rectilinear stands without the six legs which in this case permitted the warmer to be set among hot coals and have allowed identification of its intended use. The inner surface of one of the pots contains the inscription *"Fu Hao."*
Cf. *Wenwu,* 1981, 9, p. 83.

Anhui where the barbarian inhabitants, at least at certain times, must have acknowledged their authority..."[12]

Current archeology confirms this perspective: in July, 1981, two tons of Shang bronzes, including fifty-six pieces of exceptional quality, were discovered at Changping (in the vicinity of Beijing). It has not yet been possible to obtain photographs of this collection, but the press has enthusiastically called attention to an unfinished trumpet-shaped vessel. Who were these northern bronzesmiths? For such regions as Beijing, Gansu and Hubei, the existence of cultures resembling the Shang civilization does not imply that the inhabitants of these regions were vassals of the Shang monarchs or that they had been fully subjugated.

48

21
Three-legged ding vessel with aviform legs. Bronze. Shang Dynasty, Anyang Period (1300 B.C. — 1030 B.C.). Discovered in Tomb No. 5 (Fu Hao's tomb) at Anyang in 1976. Height: 50 cm. Beijing, Archeological Institute. At the time of its discovery, this tripod was in extremely poor condition and substantial restoration was required. Instead of having been formed from strips of metal in the usual manner, the legs of this vessel consist of round knobs, representing a relatively uncommon technique for creating zoomorphic legs during this period.

22
Fang yi vessel (zoomorphic decoration on the surface). Bronze. Shang Dynasty, Anyang Period (*c*. 1300 B.C. — 1030 B.C.). Discovered in Tomb No. 5 (Fu Hao's tomb) at Anyang in 1976. Height: 60 cm. Length: 88.2 cm. Width: 17.5 cm. Beijing, Archeological Institute, Yinxu, Tomb No. 5. No. 792. This *fang yi*, a rectangular vessel having the shape of a dwelling, was intended for beverages. The dimensions are relatively uncommon and the two handles placed upon the roof would even suggest the designation "double *fang yi*." The composite decoration portraying birds of prey supported by their tails is typical of this period. There are also *taotie* and dragons which are walking, standing, grazing, or reclining upon their serpent-like tails. In addition, there are birds in flight situated opposite a mask with ram's horns and a mask with a trunk on the wider side of this piece, or alongside a *taotie* mask appearing on the lid. Apart from these forms of decoration, archeologists have been interested in the dentate motif on the edge of the roof as well as the seven protuberances situated upon the neck of this vessel. These protuberances, resembling shields on one side, have a triangular shape on the other. They suggest joists protruding beyond the principal supporting beams which must extend between opposite sides of a building. Cf. *Kaogu xuebao*, 1977, 2, p. 67 and pl. 21, no. 1.

Panlongcheng and Peripheral Regions

The walled city of Panlongcheng[13] in Hubei Province is the brightest jewel of the Shang civilization outside of Henan. Excavations began in 1974 to locate the heart of a region where Shang-style items have been discovered for the last twenty years although it has not been possible to associate these finds with a specific point of origin.

Panlongcheng was protected by tamped earth ramparts (*hangtu*). The remains of a palace complex, as well as exceptionally lavish tombs, were found inside the walls. Although the reason is still not understood, it appears that the inhabitants deserted this town very early at the beginning of the Anyang Period.

The town covered slightly more than ten hectares. Its eastern border was demarcated by a lake and to the south the Fuhe River, which is a tributary of the Yangtze, served as a boundary. During the summer and autumn floods the site would have been surrounded by water on three sides and would therefore have been more easily defended.

The small remnant of the ramparts demonstrates that the *hangtu* technique, at least during the period when construction of Panlongcheng began, continued to be primitive: the builders had not yet begun to use the wooden molds fastened by cords which would have permitted dirt for the walls to be compacted according to procedures resembling those that are now used for cement.

In the northeastern portion of the enclosed area, a tamped foundation provided a raised platform for the palace buildings. The vestiges of superstructures formed by wooden pillars resting upon stone beds established within pre-hardened soil have been identified here and can be compared with elements which are still characteristic of Chinese dwellings.

Tombs were scattered nearly everywhere and were often situated amid the ruins of dwellings, as if the burial grounds and the area intended for the city itself had been intermingled several times from one century to another. Nevertheless, the most impressive tombs were located *extra muros,* at a site known as Lijiazui, located east of the town. Two of these tombs represent the most beautiful tombs from the Erligang Period to have been discovered thus far. The same period, of course, coincided with establishment of the Shang dynasty's capital at Zhengzhou.

Examination of the bronzework from the tombs has not revealed any signs of provincialism, insofar as comparison of the Panlongcheng pieces with bronzes from Zhengzhou may be concerned. Should it be concluded that the power of the Shang had expanded to this region, or did Panlongcheng merely represent a colony established within a hostile region? The fact that written symbols resembling those of the north have been discovered on stone or ceramic molds at Wucheng in Jiangxi, three hundred kilometers south of Panlongcheng, suggests that the Shang civilization, constituting a new era in technology — represented by bronzework, and within the intellectual domain by writing — must have burst forth everywhere or that it must have spread like a vast undercurrent, extending far beyond the boundaries of Henan.

This phenomenon also suggests another facet of the rise of civilization: many communities on the periphery of the Great Plain were not as backward as earlier scholars may have believed. Indeed, there were many instances where Bronze Age civilization even coincided — is there a possible cause and effect relationship? — with a decline in the power of the Shang monarchs. The decline is represented by the abandonment of Panlongcheng precisely during the period when the rulers in the actual heart of the Shang domains were moving their capital northward from Zhengzhou to Anyang. The vitality of southern China would also seem to be corroborated by many oracular inscriptions from the reign of Wuding (1324–1266 B.C.). These sources allude to the monarch's campaigns in the valley of the Han which was undoubtedly difficult to control and perhaps unconquerable.

Recently, Virginia Kane,[14] like certain other authors, has pointed out that, during the final phase of the Shang dynasty, artisans in southern China were producing strikingly original creations which were placed in tombs alongside works that were wholly of northern origin: it is tempting to regard this situation as reflecting extensive and long-standing interchanges of a quasi-commercial nature between these two portions of the Chinese mainland.

23

Four-legged fang ding vessel. Bronze. Final period of the Shang Dynasty (*c.* XI B.C.). Discovered at Ningxiang in Hunan Province in 1959. Height: 38.7 cm.
This tetrapod vessel is a *fang ding:* a quadrangular vessel for cooking or heating food. Whereas the design, including the ridges at the corners, is entirely conventional, the decor with four faces is unique for this category. The features of the masks are comparable to those of other portrayals of human beings which have recently been found in Shang tombs, such as Tomb No. 5 at Anyang.
Cf. *Wenwu*, 1960, 10, pp. 57-59.

The Bestiary on Bronzes

Long before it was rediscovered in the form of a coherent cultural entity, as has occurred in modern times, the Shang civilization already inspired admiration and for many centuries scholars admired the extraordinary bestiary that adorned the surfaces of ancient bronze pieces. Influenced by ancient literary sources, the scholars experienced a passionate encounter with literal representations of the fantastic creatures cited in texts which constituted an essential element of their literary background: the serpent with two bodies, cited in the *Shan Hai Jing* (*circa* 220 B.C.) as a fearsome creature whose presence foretold the arrival of devastating droughts; of the *kui,* which the *Shuowen,* the great dictionary of the Han Period, described as resembling a bull but possessing no horns and only one foot while its body was as luminous as the sun or the moon and its thundering voice created strong winds and rainstorms whenever it entered the water or emerged. It was said that only Huangdi succeeded in capturing this creature and that he used its skin to fashion a drum that he played with the monster's bones: the notes of this strange musical instrument could be heard for a distance of more than 500 *li.* In turn, each author appears to have formulated his own image of the dragon. Today, however, it would seem impossible to trace the sources of this ancient tradition merely by examining comparatively recent texts from the earliest period of the empire. Although these texts describe the fabulous creatures inhabiting scholars' imaginations during that era, they do not furnish any reliable information for understanding the minds of the considerably more ancient generations who created the elaborate bestiary of antiquity.

After the empire had arisen it appears that the entire tradition underwent a rapid transformation: less importance was given to certain fabulous images appearing on bronzes and elegant or astonishing literary descriptions became predominant. For example, the description of the carcajou (*taotie*) mask that appears in the *Lushi Chunqiu* gained special prominence, and this frequently portrayed creature haunted the imagination: a carcajou represented by a head that lacked a lower jaw, devouring men without swallowing them. In ancient catalogues certain poorly understood motifs that were difficult to interpret tended to be associated with the *taotie.* In other words the original tradition ceased to be understood and, to some extent, confusion dominated interpretation of decorative motifs for a considerable period of time. Thus, archeological discoveries have made an extremely valuable contribution in this domain, and have especially enriched the interpretations and forms of classification that Western and Chinese scholars had developed on the basis of bronze items in collections or on the basis of pre-war excavations.

In fact, a new general method for classifying decorative motifs is being developed today. It has been possible to confirm the extremely ancient origin of certain themes, although not in every instance, by recalling Neolithic jades and pottery produced by

24
Oracular inscription. Tortoise shell. Beginning of the Zhou Period (*c.* 1100, B.C.). Discovered at Qishan, Fengshu (Shaanxi), at Point H.11. No.1. This inscribed shell was discovered at Qishan in the western wing of the palace at Point H.11. (cf. *Wenwu,* 1979, 10, p. 38). In quantitative terms, the oracular inscriptions found at Qishan represent the largest discovery to have occurred thus far: 16,700 inscriptions on tortoise shells, with another 300 inscriptions on cattle bones. The inscribed items have not yet been fully catalogued. The characters are observable in their most ancient form. Some suggest the lines of present-day characters, whereas others are extremely different and certain others have not been identified elsewhere. Thus, it is difficult to provide accurate translations of the texts where these characters appear. For the entire series of inscriptions from Qishan, paleographers have been able to identify more than 600 characters within inscriptions whose lengths vary considerably, from only one character to more than 300 characters. This inscription evokes the ceremonies and sacrifices which the Zhou rulers conducted in honor of the ancestors of the Shang in order to demonstrate that, prior to the overthrow of the Shang by the Zhou monarch Wu (reign: 1122–1116 B.C.), the Zhou had at least acknowledged the moral authority of the ruling dynasty.
Cf. *Wenwu,* 1979, 10, pp. 39, 43; pl. 4, no. 1.

25
Guang vessel. Bronze. Zhou Period (*c.* 1100 B.C.–771 B.C.). Discovered in 1963 at the Qijiacun site, Fufeng (Shaanxi). Height: 31.6 cm.
This vessel belongs to the *guang* category which was actually beginning to disappear during the early Zhou Period. A *guang* was a vessel used for storing alcohol and it was somewhat similar to a gravy dish with a stylized zoomorphic design. In this case the quadrangular body of the vessel is accentuated and it therefore represents an advance in relation to typically Shang specimens. The sides of the cover are decorated with dragons while the neck contains a coiled dragon with prominent horns, situated opposite a crouching bird of the same type as the birds appearing on the bottom portion of the base. The body contains a full *taotie* mask with an extended upper lip. An inscription consisting of eighteen characters appears on this vessel: "Priceless ceremonial vessel offered to Ri Ji. May his sons and grandsons make eternal and worthy use of it for ten thousand years."
Cf. *Kaogu*, 1963, 8, p. 14 and pl. 2, no. 2.

the Yangshao culture; in this way there would be an explanation for the striking complexity of some of the motifs appearing on bronze pieces. Transposition of these motifs onto metal occurred as a result of simplification of more sophisticated designs or sets of designs whose stages of development are indicated by ceramic creations: for example, the frog motif was gradually reduced solely to the gridwork pattern used for creating and adorning these forms at Banpo. Today, as they strive to emancipate themselves from concepts that have prevailed for two thousand years, Chinese archeologists who have adopted the methods of Western specialists tend to emphasize solely the graphic aspect

26-27
Chamfron. Bronze. Zhou Period (*c.* 1100 B.C.–771 B.C.). Discovered at Zhangjiapo, Xi'an (Shaanxi) in 1955. Height: 13 cm. Xi'an, Shaanxi, Provincial Museum.
This top portion of a chamfron in the form of a mask contains holes for attachment to a harness. It demonstrates the careful efforts to ensure that the trappings of steeds or carriage animals belonging to dignitaries would properly represent the owners' rank.

of decorative motifs while overlooking categories that had been employed until recently. Thus, Chinese archeologists now prefer to counterpose a more typologically rigorous distinction between animal motifs *per se* and motifs which combine portrayal of humans with images of animals. The traditional distinction was between motifs evoking animals which exist in nature and motifs derived from mythical and legendary bestiaries.

Two masterpieces in the category of combined portrayal of animals and humans consist of bronze vessels portraying

28
Zun vessel with handles. Pottery with brown glaze. Zhou Period (*c.* 1100 B.C.–771 B.C.). Discovered at Yiji, Tunqi (Anhui) in 1965. Height: 11.9 cm. Beijing, Gugong bowuguan.
This vessel is a *zun* with a short neck and a limited brim. It was used for storing beverages. Decorated with two handles which resemble willow branches, it contains a pair of horned masks and in the top portion a series of cross-bars. This is an example of the wares referred to as *yuanshici*, or "protoporcelain," by Chinese archeologists. Actually, this is ordinary pottery which has been glazed. Instead of mere fragments of ashes which had been vitrified by the fire, there is an evenly distributed glaze which must have been applied with a brush.
Cf. *Wenwu*, 1965, 6, p. 52

tigresses and human beings. One of the vessels belongs to the Sumitomo Collection in Japan and the other is owned by the Musée Cernuschi in Paris. Despite their beauty and the quality of their patina, these two vessels have been the source of impassioned disputes for a long time. Indeed, some portrayals of human figures in jade or bronze creations from the Shang Period are displayed throughout the world, notably at the Freer Gallery in Washington or especially at the Musée Cernuschi, although these creations are small in size. Recent finds at Anhui, at Ningxiang in Henan (discovered in 1959), at Houjiapo, at Xibeigang, or even more recently in the sepulchre of Fu Hao, have finally provided irrefutable evidence or hypotheses with respect to authenticity. Human figures or faces have been observed consistently on items with relatively large dimensions.

29-30

Gui vessel. Bronze. Western Zhou Period (*c.* 1100 B.C.–771 B.C.). Discovered at Tunqi (Anhui) in 1965. Height: 19.7 cm.

This *gui* vase was found in a tomb with a somewhat unusual layout. Instead of being buried within a trench dug into the floor, the decedent and the mortuary accoutrements had been placed upon a bed of small stones. A tumulus with a height of two meters and a diameter of twenty meters was erected above the burial location. The body of the vase contains two series of motifs. The upper set consists of stylized *taotie* masks on each side and the creature's body is merely represented by squares. The lower set consists of a series of motifs where two squares are combined. The short neck has a linear motif with spirals, while the base shows extremely stylized coiled dragons. The two zoomorphic handles are adorned with rams' heads. The inner surfaces contain a combination of strips where the motifs consist of elongated brackets and extended commas in a head-to-tail arrangement, along with spirals filled with stripes or cross-bars. This type of adornment, where sets of angular lines and surfaces covered with dashes or dots predominate, is typical of southeastern China. It is also interesting in terms of possible analogies with pottery originating from this region.

31

Ding vessel. Bronze. Western Zhou Period (*c.* 1100 B.C.–771 B.C.). Discovered at Zhuangbocun, Fufeng (Shaanxi) in 1975. Height: 22 cm. Neck diameter: 22.3 cm. Depth: 12.3 cm.

This pot (*ding*) for cooking food is noteworthy on account of the elegant harmony among shapes with flattened profiles, typifying the style of this period. It is also unusual on account of the presence of semi-circular stubs attached to each leg. Perhaps a plate which disappeared at the time of discovery was placed in this area or perhaps there was a stand capable of accommodating hot coals. The refined but restrained decoration portrays elongated dragons with their heads turned rearward; they are arranged in three pairs. An inscription consisting of five characters appears on this vessel: "This priceless *ding* was made for Dong."

Cf. *Kaogu yu wenwu*, 1981, 4, p. 30.

32

Fang li vessel. Bronze. Western Zhou Period (*c.* 1100 B.C.–771 B.C.). Discovered at Fufeng (Shaanxi) during 1976–1977. Height: 17.7 cm. Length: 11.9 cm. Width: 9.2 cm. Depth of *li*: 6.3 cm.

This unusual creation is a square *li* (*fang li*). Instead of being referred to as a *ding*, as its shape suggests, this type of vessel was given the name *li*, which was usually reserved for tripods with hollow legs because one of the legs contains a character which includes the *li* suffix in addition to the word "metal." This cooking vessel was combined with a brazier outfitted with doors which could be closed by means of a carved knob. It appears that a slave was responsible for stoking the fire. At least five comparable vessels are known to exist, including one which was also discovered at Fufeng. One is owned by the Fogg Museum (Cambridge, MA) and another belongs to the Palace Museum (Gugong bowuguan) in Beijing (the latter specimen, which lacks handles, legs, and corner adornments, possesses an especially austere appearance). Cf. *Kaogu yu wenwu*, 1981, 4, p. 31.

Usually, an animal, or a *taotie,* is shown with its human prey. Regardless of the species, the animal always evokes the ferocity of a man-eating tiger even if this quality is solely conveyed by details. In contrast, the human being is never portrayed as fearful and is almost ready to smile. Hence, it is essential to observe that Chinese art at the height of the Bronze Age, in a manner comparable to the end of the Neolithic Age, began to attribute greater emphasis to human figures, and displayed less devotion to abstract elements than prior sources have indicated.

This aspect did not exclude development of a vast repertory of geometric decorative motifs, although it is not known whether these motifs should be interpreted as purely ornamental or as a form of symbolic language. Some art historians have emphasized the continuing complexity of this problem and the role which graphic counterparts may have played in transmitting or perhaps transforming ancient themes. Clearly, this possibility should not be excluded, especially with respect to secondary or auxiliary motifs. Nevertheless, allusions to shamanism and to the omnipotence of the natural environment that surrounded mankind may seem more obvious and more powerful than an evolving series of forms, even though such a grammar of forms may have played a role as it always does whenever symbols are transmitted.

The Zhou Dynasty: The Birth of Classical Architecture

The reign of the Shang lasted several centuries until a new clan, the Zhou, overthrew them. This clan originated in the region of the high loess plateaux. Indeed, King Wen erected his capital at Fengjing, currently situated in the center of Shaanxi Province in a region whose civilizing role had already emerged during the Neolithic Age. Nevertheless, significant changes had occurred in Central Asia. Nomadic peoples had developed on the fringes of the domains inhabited by farmers whom the nomads periodically threatened and occasionally looted. Furthermore, the Chinese realm had already become too vast to be ruled from peripheral regions: King Wu (1122–1116 B.C.) soon erected the city of Luoyang in the Great Plain region. From then on and for many centuries, Luoyang served as the eastern capital of China, in conjuction with Shaanxi which continued to represent the western capital. The ruling dynasty completely withdrew to Luoyang in 771 B.C. when barbarian raids had rendered its position untenable in the western regions. Nevertheless, as one recent study has indicated, the development of Chinese society did not undergo immediate changes: "... it is not sufficient to acknowledge that the earliest Zhou monarchs were initially the heirs of those whom they had overcome or that they merely oversaw a transitional period between two types of social and cultural systems which are to be regarded as fundamentally different, with one representing a continuation of primitive communism and with the other already foreshadowing an organized government, or with one representing a slave-owning society and the other a feudal one. Between the Yin and the Zhou, there is not only a transition but also profound unity among social phenomena... As for the suspension of continuous development, it was caused solely by gradual reinforcement of a countercurrent arising from turbulence created by the Zhou monarchs' retreat from the eighth century barbarians, ultimately leading to a hegemonic regime and to the authority of laws, to be followed in the end by the empire."[15]

To a significant extent the countless vestiges of the Zhou dynasty demonstrate the stability of a culture that was already

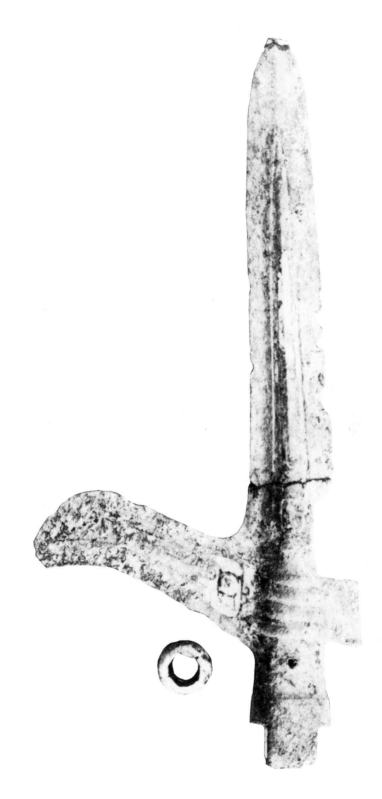

33
Halberd. Bronze. Western Zhou Period (*c.* 1100 B.C.–771 B.C.). Discovered at Xian Jiaoxian (Shandong) in 1976. Length: 29 cm. Changwei (Shandong), Office of Cultural Resources.
This *ge*, or halberd with a spur, which contained traces of blood on both blades, was found in a chariot pit. Along with a spear, it lay beside the chariot driver whose skeleton (or the remaining portion of his skeleton, namely his upper torso) remained inside the chariot drawn by a team of four horses. The silhouette with a short stub is of the ancient type. Later, the stub was arranged in a more horizontal form and it was given a rounder shape.
Cf. *Wenwu*, 1977, 4, p. 67 and pl. 8, no. 4.

a thousand years old. Excavations constantly furnish evidence of the civilizing affinities that link the Shang and Zhou dynasties to each other, and hence, to the subsequent development of Chinese civilization.

For this period archeology still yields occasional surprises. For example, in 1977, unknown texts and the ruins of an extensive palace complex were discovered at Qishan in Shaanxi Province.[16] Indeed, this site provided 17,000 oracle bones (*jiagu*), 16,700 tortoise shells, and 300 cattle bones containing relatively long texts — at least thirty characters in most instances — with an already developed language of at least 600 words. These oracle bones, which were carefully arranged in various storage locations inside the palace buildings or in their immediate vicinity, served as archives. Perhaps they shall contribute to

partial filling of a gap which Léon Vandermeersch has recently cited: "For the late Zhou Period there are no oracular inscriptions because the Yin custom of recording divinatory precepts as an accompaniment to osteomantic diagrams was replaced by another form of notation which relied upon strips of silk or bamboo which, unfortunately, were perishable."[17] Or perhaps these oracle bones are more ancient. In any event their having been stored in the vicinity of a Zhou palace also leads to speculation.

The most spectacular or the most immediately understandable discovery from recent excavations is of architectural forms that were already quite complex. If, as Pierre Gourou has said, a dwelling is "a condensed portrayal of a civilization," it can be affirmed that the relationship between the Zhou and their environment is gradually being revealed to us today.

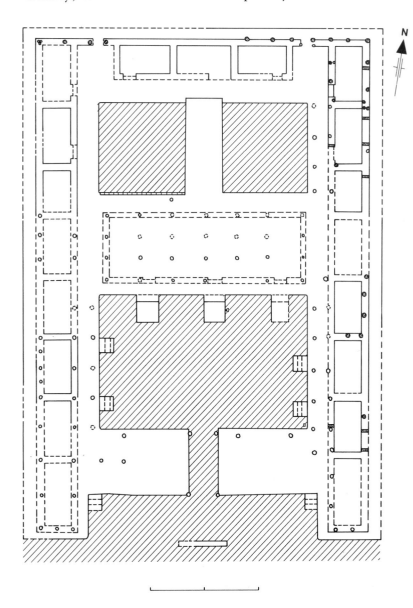

Fig. 7. Layout of palace (no. 1) at Qishan. Reproduced from *Shang Zhou kaogu*, 1979, p. 182.

34
Zoomorphic zun vessel: water buffalo supporting a tiger. Bronze. Western Zhou Period (*c.* tenth century B.C.). Discovered in 1967 at Hejiacun in the Qishan region (Shaanxi). Height: 24 cm. Length: 38 cm. Xi'an, Shaanxi Provincial Museum.
This vessel for beverages containing alcohol was closed by means of a cover adorned with a cat-like creature (probably a tiger) at the top. The cover was secured to the body by means of a ring which also provided a handle. The mouth of the water buffalo constitutes a pouring spout. It is difficult to distinguish the linear decoration but the eye appearing on the side of this vessel suggests a motif which may have originally consisted of an inwardly coiled plumed bird, although this particular version is an entirely geometric representation.
Cf. *Wenwu*, 1972, 6.

35
Zoomorphic zun vessel: elephant. Bronze. Western Zhou Period (*c.* tenth century B.C.). Discovered at Rujiazhuang, not far from Baoji (Shaanxi) in 1974. Height: 24 cm. Length: 28 cm. Baoji, Municipal Museum.
This massive bronze elephant is a *zun*, which was a vessel for storing alcoholic beverages. In very general terms, the *zun* category includes the distinct sub-category of zoomorphic vessels with legs, which has been familiar among collectors for a considerable period of time and is represented by such pieces as an owl at the British Museum, a rhinoceros belonging to the Brundage Collection, an elephant at the Musée Guimet, or the elephant at the Freer Gallery of Art. Another *zun* resembling an elephant was recently discovered at Lilingxian, southeast of Changsha (Hunan Province) (1975). Whereas these vessels had been introduced during the Shang, the form was reproduced during the Zhou Period although with a certain lack of skill. In comparison with the magnificent elephant from Lilingxian (attributed to the Anyang Period, *c.* 1300 B.C. — 1030 B.C.), the Baoji elephant appears to be extremely crude. The animal, which bears some similarities to a pig, is only identifiable by its trunk or the outlines of its tusks. The sides contain two large medallions, which are adorned with spirals consisting of groups of coiled birds with elongated bodies. As H. Brinker and R. Goepper (*Kunstschatze aus China*, p. 77) have done, it is possible to wonder whether the Zhou bronzesmiths had ever seen elephants and whether they permitted their imaginations to depart freely from themes bequeathed by the preceding period. Perhaps this situation is due to climate changes which may have occurred in China during this period.
Cf. *Wenwu*, 1976, 4.

36

Dou goblet with open-work foot. Bronze. Western Zhou Period (*c.* 1100 B.C–771 B.C.). Discovered at Qiangjiacun, Fufeng (Shaanxi) in 1974. Height: 15.2 cm. Diameter: 27 cm. Depth of vessel: 5 cm.

This *dou* goblet with an open-work foot containing multiple strips of eyelet motifs (derived from the traditional theme of the dragon) belonged to a set of seven bronzes comprising a buried treasure. All of these bronzes shared certain characteristics: relatively large dimensions, lengthy inscriptions, and sometimes the presence of banded motifs which are typical of the late Zhou Period. These pieces had been produced at different times for different families and by at least four artisans. Hence, questions continue to arise concerning their having been buried together. The region where this treasure was found, namely the northern portion of the so-called "Zhouyuan," or "Zhou Plain," has yielded many similar abundant collections of Western Zhou bronzes. Discoveries had already taken place prior to World War II, and the most significant subsequent finds included those of 1952, 1953, 1960, 1966 and 1970. Usually, these relatively large hiding places (more than 1 cubic meter) appear to have been intended to conceal the treasures of several families and this factor explains the diversity of the bronzes which have been discovered during the present era. It is probable that these hiding-places were created as a result of widespread social and political upheavals, such as those of the year 771 B.C. which marked the end of the reign of King You and the withdrawal of the Zhou Dynasty to the region located east of the Great Plain. For example, another *dou* was discovered in 1975 at Dongjiacun, Quishan (Shaanxi), as part of a buried treasure which included 37 bronzes (cf. *Wenwu,* 1976, 5, pl. 3, no. 1). Cf. *Wenwu,* 1975, 8, p. 59.

37

Fang yi vessel. Bronze. Zhou Period (end of tenth century B.C.–beginning of ninth century B.C.). Discovered at Licun, Meixian (Shaanxi), in 1956. Height: 18.2 cm. Shaanxi Provincial Museum.

A *fang yi* is a "square sacrificial vessel," whose shape provides a resemblance to a small dwelling or a shrine. This type of vessel for storing water or wine was introduced under the Shang Dynasty in the Anyang Period, or during the thirteenth century B.C., and it disappeared under the Zhou Dynasty or shortly after the tenth century B.C. This vessel contains elephant-trunk handles which are typical of the late Zhou Period. The same observation is applicable to the ornamental work arranged in thin strips, where dragons face rearward in the direction of a whirlwind motif evoking the sun. The lid and the base contain simplified motifs consisting of plumed birds with double tails extending onto their backs. The inner portion of this vessel is divided into two compartments. The lid is adorned by a dihedral handle. Unsophisticated casting techniques appear to have been used in this instance. The same lengthy inscription appears beneath the lid and in two locations inside the vessel (it was also reproduced on another *zun* of the same provenance) and it contains 106 characters: "The King visited the Zhou temple during the first quarter of the eighth month. The Duke of Mu guided Li to the central courtyard where he stood facing northward. The King ordered his servants to offer scarlet cloth, black jade, and a bridle-bit to Li, saying to him: "With these, you shall oversee the royal functionaries and the Three Ministers — the Seneschal, the Constable, and the Master of the Artisans." Then the King said to Li: "You shall henceforth lead the Six Regiments (of the West) and the Eight Regiments (of the East)." Li knelt and stated that, in acknowledgment of the trust which the King had placed in him, he would have priceless vessels cast for his noble ancestor Yi Gong. Li said, "May the deeds of the Son of Heaven defend our Empire forever! I prostrate myself before him and I swear that I shall be worthy of those who have served before me." (cf. R.W. Bagley, *The Great Bronze Age of China,* pp. 246–247.)
Cf. *Wenwu,* 1957, 4, p. 5.

38

He pouring pot. Zhou Period (*c.* ninth century B.C.–eighth century B.C.). Discovered at Qijiacun, Fufeng (Shaanxi) in 1963. Height: 38 cm.
An unusual bestiary which includes a cat-like creature whose head has been turned rearward to provide a handle, a dragon's mouth as the pouring spout, and a bird of prey with a curved beak as the lid has been placed around the flat body of this composite pouring pot. The ornamentation appearing on the body — broad spiral motifs arranged like scales — is typical of the end of the Zhou Period. This piece was found in a trench close to the one discovered in 1960. It was undoubtedly hidden under the same circumstances — although not at the same time — as the *hu* vessel dedicated to "Ji the Father" (see Illustration 39). Another comparable pouring jug was discovered in 1976 in the Lintong District in Shaanxi Province.
(Cf. *Wenwu,* 1977, 8, pp. 2–3 and pl. 3, no. 3).
Cf. *Kaogu,* 1963, 8, p. 415 and pl. 2, no. 6.

The site of Qishan (Fengshu) in Shaanxi actually permits interpretation of the principal aspects of ancient Chinese architecture. These characteristics, involving a precisely defined geometric configuration, were already observable at Erlitou or at Panlongcheng for the earliest phases of the Shang Period.

Each pavilion — as a unit within a larger whole — was built on a square plan, and all of the pavilions are arranged in a row within a square or rectangular area demarcated by a trench or by a tamped earth enclosure. The foundation of each building was firmly tamped, and multiple layers were applied according to a thickness of 40 to 50 centimeters in order for the pillars to be embedded in the foundation and provide a stable base. Today, archeologists are discovering remnants of these pillars,

39

Hu vessel. Bronze. End of Western Zhou Period (ninth century B.C.). Discovered at Qijiacun, Fufeng (Shaanxi) in 1960. Height: 59.4 cm. Xi'an, Shaanxi Provincial Museum.
Hu were used for storing fermented beverages. This specimen was discovered with other bronzes comprising a treasure which must have been buried hastily during the eighth century B. C., at the time of the barbarian raids which persistently threatened the Zhou rulers and induced them to move the capital city to the central plain. This piece is remarkable for its elegant form and for the ornamental strip, where a dragon's head appears at the center. There is a dedication to "Ji the Father" (*Ji fu*), to whom this *hu* had been offered. The Brundage Collection includes a similar bronze. Another less elegant specimen with similar decoration was discovered in 1973 in Hubei Province, not far from Xiongjiao (cf. *Kaogu,* 1975, 4, pl. 1, no. 4), in a tomb situated within the former Kingdom of Zeng.
Cf. *The Bronzes from Qijia Village, Fufeng,* (Beijing), 1963, p. 7, fig. 4.

which still convey the design of ancient palaces as if their imprint had been engraved upon the earth.

The pavilions were centered around a principal structure known as the *tang* which was specifically intended for ceremonial purposes. It extended from east to west, as indicated by the alignment of pillars placed at intervals of two meters along the four sides. The pillars were sunk 50 to 70 centimeters into the ground, depending upon their height. A row of lighter pillars was sometimes placed one meter in front of the building in order to support the overhanging portion of the roof or weatherboards that protected the veranda. The roof of the main building could include one, two, or even four sharply sloping portions: insofar as it is possible to determine from the diameters and numbers of holes for pillars, the angle was usually 45°. The ceiling initially consisted of a layer of planks mounted directly upon the pillars and the rafters: thatches were placed directly upon these planks, or, beginning with the Zhou dynasty, tiles were also used for princes' palaces.

The walls connecting the pillars and defining the interior of a building were composed of blocks produced from baked dirt (*tupei*) and plants. This mixture was flattened between two rows of tree trunks and then dried. The finishing layer which was applied to the walls consisted of a coating produced from white ashes in accordance with a procedure that had already been employed during the Neolithic Age at Dahe. Nevertheless, it soon became customary to apply a similar coating to the side walls and to foundations; this practice, which required considerable quantities of materials, eventually led to the use of lime.

The vestiges of the palace at Qishan also contained many fragments of jade or shells which were scattered throughout the site. It is tempting to consider this fact as a confirmation of ancient texts: indeed, the *Shang Shu* and the *Zhou Shu* indicated that, during the reign of King Cheng (1115–1079 B.C.), the Zhou palaces were adorned with murals created by using shells of various colors and floral forms cut from jade. This must have been the "combination of ostentation and barbaric luxury" cited by Maspéro and amply represented by the sumptuously decorated bronze work of this period.

The general layout of the palace was centered around the previously described main building: in front of this building, at the southern entrance, there was a gateway large enough to allow horse-drawn chariots to enter, as well as a separate small building intended as a barrier against evil spirits. At the rear, extending to the northern wall where there was a smaller gateway were pavilions, or ordinary rooms and living quarters

that are comparable to Yangshao dwellings. These areas can be reconstructed by the substantial number of pillars, whose traces reveal an extensive series of small rooms or servants' quarters adjacent to the edifice constituting the main palace.

The various sections of this vast complex were connected by one or more corridor-verandas. The evidence offered by Qishan, where it seems that many pillars were placed haphazardly or in a winding pattern, would appear to suggest that the covered passageways (*lang*) and rain-shelters (*yuda*) which contribute to the beauty of contemporary Far Eastern dwellings originated more from necessity than from esthetic intentions. Three thousand years later, this possibility is evoked amid the tamped earth of the foundations at Qishan by a series of pillars that, with precision and for any given arrangement, enclosed multiple walkways that are not yet identifiable. Nevertheless, the positions of chambers and corridors demarcating gardens inside the palace suggest an equally observable tendency to maintain the set of "four combined courtyards" (*siheyuan*) which would predominate in the classic Chinese dwelling — an enclosed area containing a series of smaller enclosures, evoking a world where multiple sets of elements coexist and intermingle.

Lastly, Qishan also possessed a substantial system for supplying water made of terra cotta and stone ducts. Supplying drinking water was ensured by means of rainwater basins that were connected to tamped earth cisterns. The porous yellow earth of northern China possesses a quality that explains certain features of Chinese architecture: when it is properly tamped, the surface as a result of humidity forms a strong and impermeable crust. Thus, at Erlitou and at Panlongcheng the Chinese were already using yellow earth to create ducts or to drain and irrigate their land. The same phenomenon can be observed at Qishan, and these primitive clay conduits are sometimes interpreted as

40
Gui vessel belonging to Hu (Hu gui). Bronze. Western Zhou Period (c. mid-ninth century B.C.). Discovered at Famen, Fufeng (Shaanxi) in 1978. Height: 59 cm. Fufeng Museum and Library.
This vessel is a *gui,* a round container (which usually possessed a lid) intended for storing unheated food. Similar specimens exist at the Musée Cernuschi, the Shanghai Museum, the Saint-Louis Museum, and the Cleveland Museum. This *gui* is noteworthy on account of the fullness and elegance of its handles, whose extravagance is counterposed to the austerity of the waist. The size of the handles is not uncommon but the array of heads with distinguishable eyes is a rare form of totemic evocation. On the inner surface, a lengthy inscription of 124 characters recounts the origin of this vessel: it was created at the request of Li Wang (a Zhou monarch who ruled during the middle of the ninth century B.C.) for a ceremony in honor of his royal forebears. The inscription refers to Li Wang by his personal name *Hu;* hence, this piece has often been given the designation *Hu gui,* or "Hu's *gui* (vessel)."
Cf. *Wenwu,* 1979, 4, pp. 89–91 and pl. 9, no. 1.

the source of the curved tiles that, although they were initially used in the same way as gutters, were ultimately placed upon roofs in order to direct the rain away from the inhabited portions of buildings. Although precise archeological landmarks have not yet been established, it is already possible to identify the elements that may have represented the respective ends of such a chain: semi-cylindrical conduits created from dried earth since the beginning of the Shang Period, and ceramic tiles with the same shape during the Zhou era.

An even more astonishing aspect is that one of the buildings must have had a superstructure above the main roof. This phenomenon was extremely rare at the beginning of the Zhou Period, but is no longer unique since the discovery from the Western Zhou era of another extensive palace complex at Shaocheng in the Fufeng region of Shaanxi Province. In both instances a large pillar surrounded by smaller columns, which would appear to have supported a roof whose top was attached to the central pillar. was erected in the middle of an extremely large building. Hence, it is obvious that a belvedere had been erected, but what was its shape? Contemporary architects have readily envisioned a rounded superstructure, embodying a principle that only reappeared in Chinese architecture during the Song Period and especially during the time of the Yuan emperors. Nevertheless, there is less of a basis for certainty when one considers the pattern of pillar holes within the ground, and it also appears possible that a square design had been adopted, similar to the design which is ordinarily associated with the Han Period. Indeed, it is possible to retain doubts concerning the ability of carpenters during the Zhou Period to arrange the sections required for creating a round bell-turret. The only certainty that excavations have established thus far — and it is significant — is that the master carpenters of the Zhou Period were able to erect any type of square or rectangular building, without limits upon the dimensions and with at least one story.

41
Square fang hu urn with lid. Bronze. Spring and Autumn Period (770 B.C. –475 B.C.). Discovered in Tomb No. 13 at Zhangmacun, Houma (Shanxi) in 1961. Height: 86.6 cm.
This large urn for fermented beverages is extremely typical of bronzework from the Spring and Autumn Period. The ornamentation on the waist tends to blend with a lightly carved banded motif, whereas all of the externally situated features—ornamentation on the edges, the handles, the base and the lid—possess a sumptuous quality which was not present during the Zhou Period. In addition, there has been extensive use of open-work. Cf. *Kaogu,* 1963, 5, p. 238 and pl. 3, no. 5.

Thus, there is corroboration for the reconstruction that Maspéro had developed on the basis of ancient texts: "In terms of their daily life, the Zhou monarchs lived in the center of their capital city as mere noblemen. It is said that the capital of the Eastern Zhou constituted a small square with a perimeter of 17,200 feet (approximately 3,500 meters), north of the Lo River, which was the source of its name, "the Town on the Lo" or Luo-yi. The outer wall was a square embankment surrounded by a trench containing twelve gates (three on each side). The main gate, located in the center of the southern wall, was reserved for the King's use, while the nine famous tripods, or *kieu ding,* which were believed to have been cast by Yu the Great and were regarded as symbolizing the legitimacy of royal authority, were located adjacent to another gate, namely the southeastern gate …

"Essentially, the palace … was merely an extremely large aristocratic residence, with a reception hall in the middle, with the ancestral temple on the left, and with an altar to the Earth Deity on the right while pavilions for its inhabitants were situated at the rear. The entire structure was surrounded by a large wall

42

Open-work scoop. Bronze. Spring and Autumn Period (770 B.C.–476 B.C.). Discovered in an estuary in the Jingan region (Jiangxi) in 1979. Height: 8.8 cm. Length (with the handle): 46.5 cm. Width: 25.5 cm. Jiangxi Historical Museum.

A treasure of three bronzes from the end of the Spring and Autumn Period was discovered at this site: a deep *pan* basin, another basin which had contained embers, and this open-work scoop which appears to have been used for handling hot coals. The inscriptions upon both basins indicated that these items were associated with the Xu, one of the nine kingdoms of ancient China according to the traditional designations attributed to Yu the Great. The Kingdom of Xu extended from Taishan (Shandong) in the north, as far as the mouth of the Yangtze in the south, and as far west as Lake Poyang. Information about the Kingdom of Xu is extremely sparse and it is only cited in the *Zuozhuan,* for a period from 668 B.C. to 512 B.C. Some scholars believe that this kingdom was established at the beginning of the Zhou Period, under the authority of a prince who was a member of the royal family. It appears to have been absorbed or destroyed by the Kingdom of Chu at the end of the Spring and Autumn Period. This discovery, which has permitted identification of relationships between these engraved artifacts and other items discovered at locations on both sides of the Yangtze, has contributed to the reemergence of a small kingdom which had nearly faded into oblivion two thousand years ago. A similar scoop was discovered in 1978 in Tomb No. 6 at Pingshan (Hebei), within the former kingdom of Zhongshan (Warring States Period. Cf. *Wenwu,* 1979, 1, pl. 9, no. 2). Mortuary accoutrements within the Shang tomb of Fu Hao (Yinxu, No. 5), which was discovered in 1976, also included a scoop without holes. (Cf. *Kaogu xuebao,* 1977, 2, pl. 17, no. 1.)
Cf. *Wenwu,* 1980, 8, p. 14 and pl. 2, no. 3.

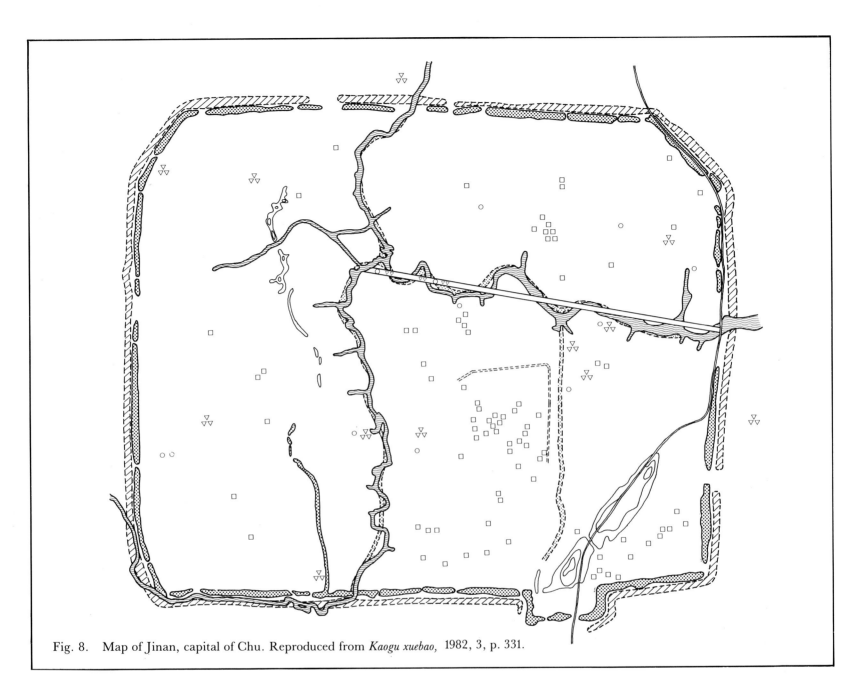

Fig. 8.   Map of Jinan, capital of Chu. Reproduced from *Kaogu xuebao,* 1982, 3, p. 331.

▽
▽▽   Neolithic relics

o   Ancient wells

□   Remains (foundations) of ancient buildings

▨   Remains of city wall

∿   Ancient watercourses

▨   Present-day watercourses

       Trenches

with an entrance on the southern side ... Three successive doors separated by a distance of a hundred paces led from the outer portions to the private chambers across courtyards containing various public buildings."[18]

The Flowering of the Regions:
The Spring and Autumn Period

At the end of the eighth century B.C. nomadic invaders whose power had increased along the periphery of regions inhabited by sedentary communities, killed the Zhou sovereign Yu (771 B.C.) and placed one of his sons, Prince Yijiu, on the throne as their vassal. One of the kingdom's dignitaries, the Duke of Guo, immediately chose another of Yu's sons and declared him to be the king; the dynasty, which was divided into two wings, with the Prince of Yuchen ruling in the Xi'an region and the Prince of Yijiu ruling at Luo Yi as King Ping, never recovered despite the departure of the barbarians. In fact, it is not

43

Carillon. Bronze. Spring and Autumn Period (early fifth century B.C.). Discovered in 1955 at Shouxian (Anhui) in the tomb of Marquis Zhao (518 B.C.–491 B.C.) of Cai. Height: 16.6 cm. to 28 cm.

This carillon had nine bells of the *bianzhong* type. These were hanging bells without clappers which had to be struck. This set of bells seems rather unimpressive since the discovery of the exceptional carillon of the Marquis of Zeng in 1978 at Suixian (Leigudun) in Hubei Province – 65 bells from the Warring States Period. The Shouxian carillon, along with another carillon discovered in 1957 at Changtaiguan, Xinyangxian (Henan), constitutes one of the oldest to have been discovered thus far. The bells were rung by striking the center or the undecorated bottom portions. On both sides of the trapezoidal overlay, there are two strips containing nine knobs whose design allowed manual retuning. The lower portion of each bell contains vermiculate adornment consisting of comma-like motifs.

Cf. *Kaogu xuebao,* 1956, 1, pl. 1, no. 5.

44

Gui vessel with lid. Bronze. Spring and Autumn Period (beginning of fifth century B.C.). Discovered in 1955 at Shouxian (Anhui) in the tomb of Marquis Zhao of Cai (518 B.C.–491 B.C.). Height: 36 cm. Diameter: 23.8 cm.

This round bronze vessel mounted upon a square base is a *gui:* a pot used to store unheated food. The ornamentation consists of a series of small motifs arranged in a vermiculate pattern. The lid is adorned with a corolla of five petals and the handles contain flat masks with broad horns. The inscription appearing upon this pot consists of six characters: "Vessel belonging to the Marquis of Cai." A comparable but considerably more ornate specimen which appears to have been produced in the Kingdom of Qi during the Warring States Period belongs to the Palace Museum's collection in Beijing.

Cf. *Kaogu xuebao,* 1956, 4.

implausible that the foreign invasion merely accelerated the fragmentation of authority that was inherent to the development of Chinese society and its multiple economic units. This possibility is at least suggested by recent excavations.

Hence, it is appropriate to reconsider traditional historical evidence that relies on ancient texts that have been clearly summarized by Maspéro. During this period large principalities tended to arise around the central basin of the Yellow River which continued to be the geographic center of the dynasty. In turn, these principalities were composed of certain small domains that reflected comparable interests. To the east, between the Yellow River and the sea in the northwestern portion of present-day Shandong, the principality of Qi developed around its capital Linzi: "This was a rich region, situated within the vast eastern plain ..." Moreover, "its wealth was derived from a form of monopoly on salt ...: the Prince profited from distillation of seawater in the Jiuchen salt-pits, and sold the salt after imposing a 50 percent tax ... It also appears that a monopoly was maintained on iron."

At the other end of the realm, the Counts of Qin gained power over the austere but highly civilized Wei domains in Shaanxi Province. These rulers displayed heroic cleverness by punishing the barbarians who had killed King Yu and by subsequently acknowledging the authority of King Ping who resided far away at Luo Yi instead of the ruler chosen by the Duke of Guo at Xi'an near the Qin domains.

Immediately adjacent to Qin's northern border, the principality of Jin gradually developed in the southwestern portion of Shanxi between the Fen River to the east and the Yellow River to the west. Nevertheless, "communication among the various valleys was difficult, and the loess plateaux with their sunken roads were a favorable environment for raiders and bandits."[19]

South of the Great Plain in the central basin of the Yangtze, there was a realm whose expansion has been defined in the following terms by Maspéro: "The barbarian tribes who inhabited the vast plain formed by the intersection of the Yangtze and Han River began to unite under Chinese influence, and a clan of minor chieftains within the region located immediately downstream from the Yangtze Falls at Yi-chang near present-day Kiang-ling established the powerful kingdom of Chu." One of the most significant results of current excavations is to have allowed certain modifications in the "Sinocentric" interpretation of events, and it is legitimately possible to wonder whether the Chu domains, represented by a site such as Panlongcheng in the remote era of the Shang dynasty, constituted an active element in China's development as soon as the era of writing had emerged.

Five years of excavations (1975–1980), in addition to furnishing a substantial quantity of information, have revealed two ancient walled towns: Jinan and Ying, the capitals of the Chu Kingdom which were located in the contemporary sub-pre-

fectures of Shashi and Jiangling in Hubei Province. A series of excavations in 1980 even led to discovery of the foundations of a Neolithic town within the most ancient portion of the walls of Jinan, on the southern side. After having initially razed this area, inhabitants during the Zhou Period used it as a foundation for the ramparts of a feudal city. Thus, their city arose upon an extremely ancient site, so ancient indeed that fragments of Neolithic pottery remained within the foundations. It is significant that these shards display affinities with pottery created by the inhabitants of Ba in present-day Sichuan.

Relationships between the small Kingdom of Ba and the Chu kingdom reintroduce the topic of east-west commerce in China. These contacts, or alliances, were called "horizontal" (heng) in feudal times, in order to distinguish them from north-south, or "vertical" contacts (cong). Indeed, ideas or artifacts must have flowed from one region to another and bronze weapons containing written inscriptions accompanied by "tiger" (huwen) motifs which are typical of the Ba region have been discovered at Changsha. These weapons may have been booty that had been buried with warriors who had seized it from their enemies, or perhaps they were rare items exchanged as gifts. Recent discoveries[20] continued to highlight the vigor and originality of the "men of Chu": during this transitional period following the

45
Fu dish with cover. Bronze. Warring States Period (early fifth century B.C.). Discovered in the tomb of Marquis Zhao of Cai (518 B.C.–491 B.C.) at Shouxian (Anhui) in 1955. Height: 23.5 cm. Length: 29.7 cm. Width: 22.7 cm.
This dish with vermiculate dragon motifs is a *fu,* a vessel which was used for heated food. The inner surface contains an inscription with six characters: "Serving dish belonging to the Marquis of Cai." It is appropriate to observe the symmetry of the bowl and the lid, which could also be used as a plate or as an uncovered dish. Comparable but more sophisticated specimens from the same period or of more recent origin have been discovered during contemporary excavations, for example at Feicheng in Shandong Province (Cf. *Wenwu*, 1972, 5, pp. 9–11 and pl. 6, no. 3) in 1963 and in Zeng Houyi's tomb at Suixian in Hubei in 1978 (Cf. *Wenwu*, 1979, 7, p. 22). Cf. *Kaogu xuebao*, 1956, 4.

46
Ding tripod. Bronze. Spring and Autumn Period (early fifth century B.C.). Discovered in the tomb of Marquis Zhao of Cai (518 B.C.–491 B.C.) at Shouxian (Anhui) in 1955. Height: 44.7 cm. Depth: 46.2 cm.
This bronze vessel is a *ding,* which was used for heating or cooking food. The inscription consisting of six characters reads as follows: "Serving vessel belonging to the Marquis of Cai." In keeping with the style of this period, there are long curved handles, an S-shaped waist, legs with tips and prominent zoomorphic edges. The concentric ornamentation, which suggests thick stippling and extensive vermiculation, represents increased geometric adaptation of motifs composed of small dragons in erect or reclining positions.
Cf. *Kaogu xuebao*, 1956, 4.

Zhou dynasty, they succeeded in transforming Henan into one of the most prosperous regions in China. It also appears that with the same aims they began to colonize the Great Plain from the Spring and Autumn Period until the beginning of the empire. Walled towns and tombs are being discovered constantly, along with previously unknown centers of productive activity such as the copper mines of Jiuguwan. Carbon-14 analysis has established a date of 780 B.C. for these mines, and they are the most ancient site of this type to have been thus far discovered.

The most elaborate development of certain techniques that originated elsewhere also occurred within this region: for example, production of bronze objects by the melted wax method has been discovered at Xiasi[21] in Henan Province where excavations during 1978 and 1979 revealed more than twenty tombs from the Spring and Autumn Period. The *cire-perdue* (lost-wax) method, whose origins had been attributed to an extremely remote time on the basis of the earliest specimens and then to a considerably more recent period, has only been fully confirmed for the era of the earliest principalities in the northern portion of the Kingdom of Chu.

Hence, current archeological discoveries appear to a significant extent to provide confirmation for accounts in historical texts. Until the beginning of the sixth century, central China continued to be a source of rivalry between two highly civilized peripheral kingdoms, Jin in the north and Chu in the south, which were magnetically drawn toward the Central Plains, a region where the monarchs' sacred power had originated and a region that continued to inspire or participate in innovation. The Kingdom of Chu was able to consolidate its *de facto* hegemony over all of the populated areas along the Yangtze from Sichuan to the sea. Its domains included the small principalities of Wu and Yue, whose fierce rivalries would ultimately tend to alter the balance of power between the north and the south. Ultimately, the Kingdom of Jin in northern China sank into a state of exhaustion from internal conflicts fostered by the political fragmentation dictated by its geography. The prosperous Kingdom of Qi in the east and the Kingdom of Qin in the northwest immediately profited from this situation in order to pursue their ambitions. Nevertheless, from Qi in the east to Qin in the northwest or Chu in the south, there was no kingdom that was yet powerful enough to subjugate its two rivals or weak enough to dissolve. The ensuing period of instability was clearly designated as the "Warring States" Period (*Zhanguo*) by Chinese historians. This era was marked by a noteworthy technological advance: the appearance of iron. Nevertheless, society evolv-

ed in an exceedingly gradual manner, as a recent discovery confirms.

A tomb (Number 1) discovered at Hougudui[22] in Henan Province contained the remains of a young woman about thirty years of age. According to inscriptions appearing upon the bronzes buried with her, she probably had been a member of the family of the Duke of Song. Song, which was a fief allotted to the descendants of the Shang rulers, was a tiny state within the central region of China in Henan and its powerful neighbors, Qi, Jin and Chu constantly sought alliances or domination. The deceased woman was probably the wife of the Duke of Jing (516–451 B.C.). Her regal burial accoutrements were enhanced by the presence of seventeen human victims even though sacrifices had become so infrequent during this period that no other examples have yet been discovered. This fact induces Chinese archeologists to affirm, in accordance with Marxist theory and terminology, that the transition from a slave-owning society to a feudal one had not yet been completed at the end of the Spring and Autumn Period. This was an unusual intermediate stage in which victims, with or without their consent, were selected for sacrifices but were showered with respect; each of the victims within this tomb had his or her own sarcophagus, and these sarcophagi were clustered around the resting place of the deceased woman whom they accompanied. Indeed, burial accoutrements had been provided for each victim. Does this situation represent an expression of kindness or does it embody an attitude of superstitious dread? Everyone in those times knew that the dead, like famished spirits, could be dangerous.

For the past thirty years an abundance of artifacts has emerged; for example, in Henan Province alone more than 2,000 tombs from the Kingdom of Chu have been unearthed. Analysis of their contents, which have been carefully catalogued and safeguarded, initially appears to offer significant clarifications. It is now recognized that the truth was far more complex. Certain tombs whose walls were adorned with paintings in the style of the Western Han contained pottery and bronzes of an earlier type. These items may have been old pieces or produced in imitation of an "ancient" style. These examples demonstrate that within the Chu domains and elsewhere, the study of furnishings does not allow reliable definition of dates for monuments. Thus, an important element of traditional methodology can produce misleading results. Regionalism and sometimes archaism are capable of disrupting any chronological scale which by definition must be absolute. Hence, it appears that for several

47

Spherical dou vessel. Bronze. Spring and Autumn Period (early fifth century A.D.). Discovered in the tomb of Marquis Zhao of Cai (518 B.C.–491 B.C.) at Shouxian (Anhui) in 1955. Height: 34 cm. Diameter: 17 cm.
This spherical vessel mounted upon a base is a *dou,* which was used for serving food. When the lid is removed, it can rest upon the four decorative zoomorphic legs in order to be used as a serving dish.
Cf. *Kaogu xuebao,* 1956, 4.

48

Large pan basin. Bronze. End of Spring and Autumn Period (early fifth century B.C.). Discovered in the tomb of Marquis Zhao of Cai (518 B.C.–491 B.C.) at Shouxian (Anhui) in 1955. Height: 16.2 cm. Diameter: 49.2 cm.
This large basin with four feline handles is a *pan,* a flat water basin which was used for washing a person's hands during ceremonies in accordance with the *"Yi Li"* ritual. The *pan* category had originated during the Neolithic Age and production of these basins continued until approximately two thousand years ago during the Han Period. The discovery of the Shouxian site was one of the most important "post-1949" discoveries because the tomb of Zhao, the Marquis of Cai (518 B.C.–491 B.C.), contained more than 500 artifacts, including engraved bronzes which have provided information concerning relationships between the kingdoms of Wu and Chu. The sixteen-column inscription of 93 characters appearing on the bottom of this *pan* refers to the marriage of the Marquis of Cai's eldest daughter to a dignitary from the Kingdom of Wu. Why would this basin have been placed in her father's tomb? Undoubtedly, this marriage greatly enhanced his prestige.
Cf. *Kaogu xuebao,* 1956, 4.

49

Spherical dui vessel. Bronze. Warring States Period (middle of fifth century B.C.). Discovered in Tomb Number 1 at Wangshan, northwest of Jinan (Hubei) in 1965. Height: 25.5 cm. Diameter: 19.5 cm.

This vessel, which consists of two identical three-legged semi-spheres containing two handles apiece, is a *dui,* used as containers for cooked food. When the lid and the body are taken apart, each can be used for the same purpose. The Shanghai Museum possesses a similar *dui* which is lavishly decorated with silver and copper inlaid work.

Cf. *Wenwu,* 1966, 5.

50

Zeng Houyi's carillon. Bronze and wood. Warring States Period (475 B.C.–221 B.C.). Discovered in the tomb of Zeng Houyi at Leigudun, Suixian (Hubei) in 1978.

The photograph shows this carillon of 64 hanging bells (*bianzhong*) which had been given to the Marquis of Zeng by the King of Chu, in the form in which it was discovered by archeologists in 1978. Hanging upon beams placed in an L-shaped arrangement, each bell occupied a position consistent with its size and resonance. At the time of the excavations, its musical qualities were still suitable enough to permit musicologists to perform a series of experiments, using an authentic "instrument" from Antiquity to play various tunes which have been preserved in texts. In the upper left portion of the photograph, it is possible to observe a wall reinforced by heavy planks, which is characteristic of so-called "Chu" tombs. These planks provided a degree of impermeability which accounted for the excellent condition of artifacts found within the tomb. In the lower right corner, it is also possible to see a drum whose base has been reproduced elsewhere (Illustration 52). The drum was still supported by its broken stand, and a syrinx had been placed on top of it.

Cf. *Wenwu,* 1979, 7, p. 16.

centuries and indeed for nearly a thousand years, the outlying regions maintained the Shang way of life: in the southern Kingdom of Chu, in the Kingdom of Qi near Shandong or in the northwestern Kingdom of Qin. It appears, however, that the Zhou civilization, at least during its initial phase, emerged as a restoration of the ways of the ancient Shang under the guidance of more effective sovereigns.

Thus, current research is casting doubts on theories concerning a vital center, from which civilization traveled to outlying areas in successive waves. Some historians and archeologists who still promote theories of this kind appear to be more strongly guided by polemical and political stances than by a scientific approach. To the great joy of scholars it would seem that this debate is far from having entered its final stage.

An Unstable Equilibrium: The Warring States

"The collapse of the Jin marked not only the disappearance of a noteworthy kingdom but of an entire mode of political organization embodied by a type of confederation where the rights of local princes received some degree of respect; after the fifth century the old system of hegemonies had truly vanished, and the major kingdoms no longer tried to reintroduce it for their own advantage. Instead they attempted to gain strength directly at the expense of weaker neighbors, until the definitive victory of one of these kingdoms would achieve for the first time the complete unification of the entire Chinese society."[23] Despite the complexity of the subject, Henri Maspéro's text in an elegant and lucid style continues to delineate the turbulent relationships among kingdoms that only appeared to maintain contacts for the purpose of waging war more successfully. This is the moral conveyed by ancient texts from the Chinese bibliographical heritage no later than the third century B.C. One example is the famous *Bamboo Chronicles (Zhushu Jinian)* which ancient scholars had already encountered in an undoubtedly corrupt form as early as 284 B.C. It comprises a grandiose and abstract image of history presented by events, in the form in which it had formerly been taught and as a foundation for perceiving history. It is no less true that recent excavations are furnishing indispensable physical counterparts to a body of knowledge that had previously consisted of nothing more than the arid enumeration of events and dates.

The Splendors of Central China

Although references within ancient archives had already provided a basis for suppositions, the extent to which artifacts confirm the important role of peripheral regions may constitute one of the most interesting contributions of recent discoveries.

Indeed, an astonishing image of thriving creative dynamism in central and southern China, which may have been on the verge of surpassing the Great Plain in technology, has arisen before archeologists' eyes. In such domains as metallurgy, lacquer-work, weaving, and production of mirrors and bronzes, it is now recognized that the Kingdom of Chu was inventive and creative instead of merely imitative. The same observation is true with respect to intellectual endeavors, formerly represented solely by the "Chu Elegies," which are one of the jewels of traditional poetry. Today, evidence is provided by manuscripts and paintings on silk or cotton, or by tests transcribed on sheets of bamboo. In this way it has been possible to confirm one of Maspéro's observations whereby "... at this point (the end of the fourth century B.C.) where a series of treaties defined the status of each kingdom, it appears that the Chinese world, after a century of incessant warfare, tended to be divided among the three large kingdoms of Ji, Chu and Jin whose respective zones of influence embraced smaller principalities ... Relationships among princes were governed by a type of protocol which tactfully respected the susceptibilities of the weakest rulers while maintaining appearances ... There were various levels of relationships: the least restrictive levels were represented by treaties sealed by marriages and exchanging of hostages ... but in some instances the dominant kingdom appointed one of its own officials as an adviser to a protected prince in order to ensure firmer control ..."[24]

Thus, it was a complex milieu whose vitality was derived from multiple exchanges. This characteristic is evoked by the well-

51
Caryatid. Lacquered bronze. Warring States Period (475 B.C.–221 B.C.). Discovered in the tomb of Zeng Houyi at Leigudun, Suixian (Hubei) in 1978. Total height: 80 cm. Height of human figure: 35 cm.
This human figure is one of the six warriors who, with their heads and both hands, supported Zeng Houyi's heavy carillon at the ends and at one corner. The three figures which rested on the ground, like this one, were placed upon a solid bronze base (more than 100 kg.) adorned with intertwined dragons. This figure depicts a soldier, as indicated by the short "Yue" sword worn at his waist. The figures in the upper row were not placed upon pedestals which actually support the entire set of 64 bells. Both types of figures are comparable to the terra cotta models discovered at Houma (Shanxi) in 1959.
Cf. *Wenwu*, 1979, 7, p. 5, 17.

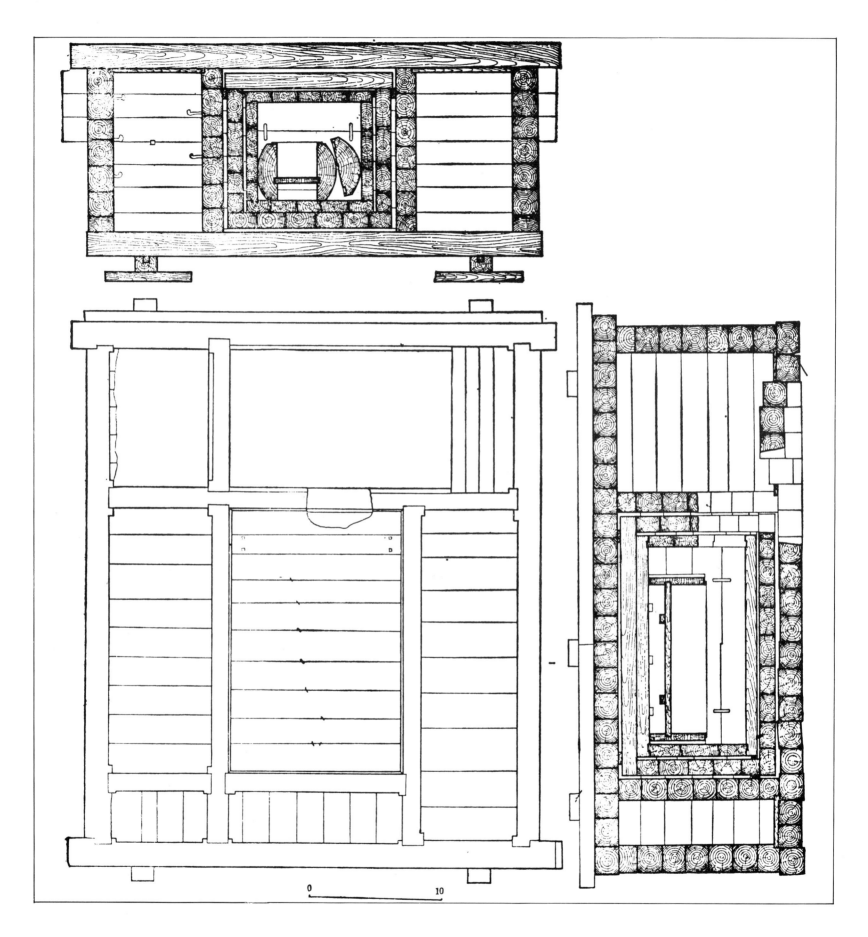

Fig. 9   Plan and sections of Tomb No. 1 at Tianxingguan (Jiangling) in the Chu Kingdom. Reproduced from *Kaogu xuebao*, 1, p.74.

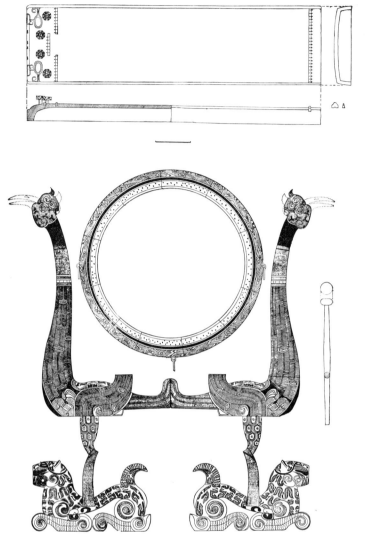

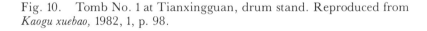

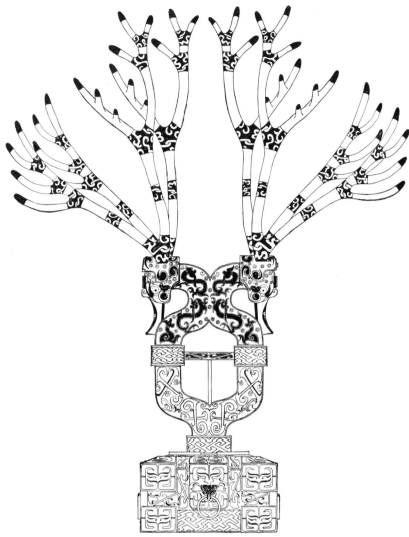

Fig. 10.   Tomb No. 1 at Tianxingguan, drum stand. Reproduced from *Kaogu xuebao,* 1982, 1, p. 98.

Fig. 11:   Tomb No. 1 at Tianxingguan, animal protecting the tomb. Reproduced from *Kaogu xuebao,* 1982, 1, p. 104.

known tomb of the Marquis of Cai, discovered at Souxian (Anhui) in 1955, and by the Wangshan tombs (Hubei), Tomb Number 1 at Tianxingguan in Jiangling (Hubei), and the tomb of the Prince of Zeng, "Zeng Houyi," at Suixian (Hubei).

Tomb Number 1 at Wangshan (Jiangling)[25] was discovered seven kilometers northwest of Jinan, the ancient capital of Chu, in 1965. This tomb contained an extensive collection of inscriptions on bamboo sheets in an alphabet containing nearly 1,000 characters. These disparate manuscripts represent an unending riddle that three scholars at the University of Beijing, Zhu Dexi, Qiu Xiqiu and Li Jiahao have been attempting to solve for a number of years. Li Jiahao has provided significant conclusions: the tomb could not have preceded King Zhuo of Chu (401–381 B.C.), and the name of its occupant was Zhaogu. He was a member of the royal family. Furthermore, at the end of the War-

ring States Period, such lavish tombs were only permissible for the most prominent aristocrats. The bamboo inscriptions also include a reference to the realm of Zhu, which until recently had only been cited in the *Mengzi,* written at the end of the Warring States Period. Thus, certain obscure references in classical texts are verified by fascinating human or historical evidence.

Apart from manuscripts, there were more than six hundred artifacts buried with the deceased nobleman: pottery and bronzes, of course, but also wooden plaques that had been carved and painted as well as a sword from Yue. Indeed, the high quality of blades from the realm of Yue, at the mouth of the Yangtze River, was recognized throughout China at a very early point. During the Spring and Autumn Period members of royal families were the only persons allowed to own these swords. The weapon discovered at Wangshan contains an inscription, "King

52

Drum leg. Bronze. Warring States Period (475 B.C.–221 B.C.). Discovered in the tomb of Zeng Houyi at Leigudun, Suixian (Hubei) in 1978. Height: 50 cm. Diameter: 80 cm.

Zeng Houyi's tomb contained four drums mounted upon legs. These drums had wooden bodies and leather covers. The drum shown here was found beside two smaller drums in a different style, in the center room, alongside the large carillon with 64 bells (see Illustration 50). A handle which supported a large sound chamber (Length: 100 cm. Diameter: 80 cm.) was inserted into the middle portion of the leg. The bronze stand shown here is entirely composed of dragons overlapping as if they had been piled onto a *pan* basin, in keeping with a design for which no counterparts have been discovered thus far.

Cf. *Wenwu*, 1979, 7, p. 6 and pl. 4, no. 3.

53

Stand in the form of a dragon. Bronze. Warring States Period (475 B.C.–221B.C.). Discovered in the tomb of Zeng Houyi at Leigudun, Suixian (Hubei) in 1978. Height: 109 cm.

This bronze dragon and another similar dragon whose head is turned in the opposite direction supported rods from which two rows containing 32 musical stones were suspended: twelve small stones and twenty large stones (six small stones and ten large stones within each row). Over-all dimensions of the stand: Length — 215 cm.

Cf. *Wenwu*, 1979, 7, pp. 6 and 17.

of Yue's sword," which indicates its origin and provides a basis for determining when it may have been produced. The sovereign for whom this sword was forged reigned from 496 B.C. until 465 B.C. When the sword arrived in the Kingdom of Chu remains an unanswered question. Obvious stylistic analogies between Tomb Number 1 at Wangshan and Zeng Houyi's tomb at Suixian, or to a lesser extent the Marquis of Cai's tomb at Shouxian suggest a relatively early point during the Warring States Period. Some scholars, however, believe that the sword did not fall into the hands of the Chu rulers until the Kingdom of Yue collapsed in 334 B.C. Thus, it would be appropriate to situate the date of the tomb after that point, although its interest would not be diminished in any form.

Although Tomb Number 1 at Tianxingguan was looted at various times throughout the centuries before excavations began in 1978, this enormous wooden structure (length — 8.20 meters; width — 7.50 meters; height — 3.16 meters), consisting of nine chambers or compartments, contained 2,500 exceptionally varied items: weapons that reflected the exploits and rank of its occupant, bronze bells, elegant elbow-rests and seats with lacquer in multiple hues, and a drum hanging between the necks of two lacquer phoenixes resting upon two recumbent tigers. A vast assortment of texts written on bamboo — which are now being deciphered and interpreted — should cast considerable light upon literary activities within the Kingdom of Chu.

The characteristics of the tomb of Zeng Houyi, a prince within the realm of Zeng, are an even greater source of astonishment

54

Inner coffin. Lacquer. Warring States Period (475 B.C.–221 B.C.). Discovered in the tomb of Zeng Houyi at Leigudun, Suixian (Hubei) in 1978. Height: 132 cm. Length: 249 cm. Width: 127 cm.

This inner coffin, which was placed within a large wooden sarcophagus (219 x 320 x 210 cm.) contained the remains of Zeng Houyi, who had been swathed in a silk shroud. Like the nobleman's body, the shroud had almost entirely decomposed by the point at which it was discovered. The artisans had decorated the outer surface of the coffin with yellow lacquer, upon a background of black and red lacquer. The interlacing motifs and figurines appear to reflect a general principle of geometric representation, but they also reveal an astonishing assortment of deities with human bodies and animals' heads. The "arabesques" and vermiculate decoration are stylized variations upon ancient serpent and dragon themes.
Cf. *Wenwu*, 1979, 7, p. 15.

55

Double vessel. Bronze. Warring States Period (475 B.C.–221 B.C.). Discovered in the tomb of Zeng Houyi at Leigudun, Suixian (Hubei) in 1978. Height of the *zun*: 33.1 cm. Waist diameter: 14.5 cm. Base diameter: 15 cm. Height of the *pan*: 24 cm. Diameter: 47.3 cm. Diameter of the base: 15 cm.

This double container consists of a *pan* basin where a *zun* vessel could be set. In addition to musical instruments, Zeng Houyi's tomb contained 140 bronzes; the majority were piled in the center room containing the carillon. Although some of these bronzes appear to have been produced by the *cire perdue* method, most of them, including this specimen, were produced by the most conventional method which relied upon multiple molds. The baroque quality of its ornamentation, consisting of masses and clusters resembling the type of open-work which was characteristic of the Spring and Autumn Period required a considerable number of molds for casting all of the decorative items. It appears that the *cire perdue* method may have been used for these complex portions, whereby the beauty of the final product would have been derived from a combination of the two methods.
Cf. *Wenwu*, 1979, 7, p. 48 and pl. 7, no. 3.

than are Wangshan or Tianxingguan. Excavation of this tomb at Suixian[26] took place from September, 1977 until March, 1978. The somewhat unusual layout consisted of a square possessing two sides that were prolonged until they intersected and the total surface area was 220 square meters. The depth of the tomb was more than thirteen meters. It had been ingeniously set upon a stone foundation coated with three different layers of materials: clay (20 to 40 centimeters), wood (10 to 30 centimeters), and a type of yellow clay. Slabs of various dimensions rested upon this composite foundation; although some were obtained from the immediate vicinity of the tomb, others appear to have originated from quarries located more than a hundred kilometers away from the tomb. A fine layer of clay was placed upon the slabs located at the upper entrance to the tomb and upon the burial vault composed of heavy planks. The vault, consisting of four compartments (north, east, center and west), possessed the appearance of an enormous sarcophagus containing subdivisions to accommodate the deceased and his burial furnishings. The latter category included more than 7,000 items,

56

Map of Pingshan (Zhaoyutu) Mausoleums. Bronze. Warring States Period (fourth century B.C.). Discovered in the former kingdom of Zhongshan (Tomb Number 1) at Pingshan (Hebei) in 1978. Height: 48 cm. Length: 94 cm. Thickness: approximately 1 cm. Hebei Provincial Museum.
For Chinese archeologists, this simple engraved bronze plaque represents the most astounding discovery from this exceedingly abundant tomb. It indicates the five principal tombs at the site, with numerical notations and distances. Unfortunately, the plaque was damaged by fire many centuries ago.
Cf. *Wenwu*, 1979, 1, pp. 5 and 24; pl. 8, no. 3.

57

Tiger capturing a fawn. Bronze with gold and silver inlaid work. Warring States Period (fourth century B.C.). Discovered in the former kingdom of Zhongshan (Tomb Number 1) at Pingshan (Hebei). Height: 22.5 cm. Length: 51 cm. Hebei Provincial Museum.
The two ferrules on the tiger's back, which are adorned with animals' mouths, suggest that there was a stand. When this piece was discovered two fragments of wood were still attached to it. The nature of the subject and the supple portrayal of motion suggest the closely related zoomorphic style of the steppes. After the Shang period, the art of border regions displays many analogies with the Siberian style which emerged in the area between the Qarasuk and Tagar rivers.
Cf. *Wenwu*, 1979, I, p. 8 and pl. 2, nos. 1-2.

58

Insignia in the form of a trident.
Bronze. Warring States Period
(fourth century B.C.). Discovered in the former kingdom of
Zhongshan (Tomb Number 6)
at Pingshan (Hebei) in 1978.
Height: 144 cm. Length: 80.3
cm.

This trident belonged to a
group of six. It consisted of
bronze leafwork with three tips,
enclosed within a hollow shaft
and fastened to it by means of
two rivets. While it is not possible to determine its symbolic
meaning, it is tempting to compare these items with the three-
pointed headgear of Siberian
shamans and with other typical
insignia of the Asiatic steppes.
It is also appropriate to add that
the trident reproduces the shape
of the *shan* ("mountain") character, which is the source of its
designation in Chinese terminology. A set of smaller but
heavier tridents was discovered
within Tomb Number 1 at the
same site. The handles still contain a few traces of the wooden
stakes which these insignias
must have been mounted upon
in order for them to be set in the
ground around the chieftain's
tent.
Cf. *Wenwu*, 1979, I, pp. 29, 31.

including exceptional zoomorphic figures in bronze that are strongly reminiscent of the Shizhaishan statuary produced in the small Kingdom of Dian in Yunnan during the Han Period. This is an unusual discovery; some Chinese archeologists interpret it as a verification of the creative prolixity of Chinese artisans who developed a zoomorphic genre that was entirely unrelated to the art of the Asian steppes. Nevertheless, it is also possible for more objective observers to wonder which ethnic groups may have inhabited the Kingdom of Zeng during this era.

In spite of a design that evokes a sarcophagus with multiple compartments, it is not actually possible to interpret Zeng Houyi's tomb as a typical Chu tomb. Specifically, it did not contain any swords even though swords have consistently been discovered in all of the tombs of dignitaries from this kingdom, the influence of which is otherwise so clearly visible.

The inscriptions provide evidence of Chu influence: one inscription engraved upon a bronze vessel indicates that it had been cast for Zeng Houyi at the request of the King of Chu, in approximately 433 B.C. Although no dates are given the same words appear upon all of the bronzes — *Zeng Houyi zuo,* "cast for Zeng Houyi" — or upon a knife found near the sarcophagus: "Zeng Houyi's dagger."

Because of this form of identification, the tomb shall henceforth constitute a point of reference for dating other items that possess generic similarities but offer no indications as to their origins. Indeed, the tomb has provided a fascinating series of inscriptions: on bronze, bamboo, musical stones and lacquer. In all there are more than 10,000 characters. These inscriptions recount the history of the principality of Zeng, and refer to the art of warfare, to astronomy — 28 constellations had been painted on the walls of the central chamber — and even to music.

Indeed, the tomb contained the largest collection of ancient musical instruments to have been discovered thus far. The most beautiful of these instruments is an extraordinary carillon consisting of sixty-four bells with truncated oval cross-sections. Although these bells weigh 2.5 tons, they were still hanging from heavy wooden crossbeams (7.48 meters × 3.35 meters) placed in an L-shaped pattern. These crossbeams supported the bells for more than 2,000 years, in two superimposed rows resting upon six bronze caryatids (three in the first series and three in the second series). Each of the bells contain musicological data — there are fifty-three inscriptions, and thirty-five are of an entirely unknown type — with strong indications of analogies with categories of music that existed in other realms, such as Chu, Qi, Jin or even in the court of the Zhou sovereigns.

59
Implements for setting up a tent. Bronze. Warring States Period (fourth century B.C.). Discovered within the former kingdom of Zhongshan (Tomb Number 6) at Pingshan (Hebei), in 1978. Length of stakes: 20 cm. Hebei Provincial Museum.
These bronze implements — a roof mounting and attachment stakes — were used to set up a tent made of hides. Some traces of the tent were present alongside the extremely lavish mortuary accoutrements within this tomb. Cf. *Wenwu,* 1979, I, pp. 1–52.

It is possible to cite an example of how archeology contributes to scientific knowledge. Since the discovery of the Suixian carillon, Chinese musicologists have used it as a standard for testing 117 comparable bells at the Shanghai Museum. Their efforts have already suggested certain conclusions: when one strikes the inner portion of a bell, the wave is propagated in a circular pattern, exactly as if the bell possessed a rounded shape. In contrast, the waves are segmented instead of circular when one strikes the bell near its edge.

Undoubtedly, two tones were already being used during the Middle Zhou Period. Carillons from the final phase of the Western Zhou dynasty included at least eight bells, so as to provide a minimum of three tones; hence, the range was greater than three octaves.

Whereas it has not yet been possible to discover cores used for producing bells under the Shang monarchs or under the Western Zhou rulers, fragments of an outside mold with several sections were discovered at Houma in Shanxi Province.

Bells were tuned by means of filing and by manual finishing procedures after they were cast. At Suixian, however, it. was possible to encounter specimens of bells that were unusable because of insufficiently careful techniques; there was no way of remedying defects in design or in metal-casting by hand. Another interesting aspect of the Suixian carillon apart from its luxuriousness and its beauty is that it contained inscriptions for two tones, *sui* and *gu*. Hence, it provides a reference point for studying bells that do not contain inscriptions.

The strong ties between the small Zeng realm and the Kingdom of Chu or its rulers in Nanling are demonstrated by many aspects of Zeng Houyi's tomb. The Chu monarch frequently sent gifts to the ruler of Zeng, and the delegation chosen to attend the prince's funeral included relatives and vassals of the king of Chu. The calligraphic qualities of the bamboo inscriptions; the script appearing on bronze items which was closely comparable to the script used for royal bronzework in Chu; types of weapons; the multi-hued appearance of lacquer-work; and the administrative terminology pertaining to officials, which closely resembled the terminology employed in Chu — all of these features appear to suggest that the larger kingdom had practically annexed its small neighbor.

Nevertheless, a riddle persists: this is not the first time that inscribed bronzes referring to the realm of Zeng — from the beginning of the Spring and Autumn Period until the beginning of the Warring States Period — have been discovered in the Suixian region or in the plains of Henan. On the other hand, the *Annals* of the Spring and Autumn Period mention two principalities with this name: one was located in Shandong and the other was vaguely described as existing south of Henan. Earlier texts did not furnish any indications and until now it did not appear that a principality known as Zeng, whatever its location may have been, would have existed during the fifth century B.C. Nevertheless, contemporary evidence indicates otherwise.

Could it be that after the Warring States Period this principality was given another name in historical texts written within the Great Plain, just as the realm of Sui was perpetuated as Suixian? Is it possible in this instance that the same principality may have possessed two distinct names? It must be acknowledged that the court of Zeng conducted ceremonies comparable to those intended for a Son of Heaven, if any significance is to be attributed to the discoveries at Sujialong in Hebei where there were many large bronze pieces and chariots. During a period when reverence for monarchs became fragmented, this circumstance is not surprising to any extent, although the silence of official texts with respect to such a well-organized political entity only becomes more puzzling. Does Zeng represent a unique situation? This would hardly seem plausible, and everything is unfolding as if current excavations were contributing to the rediscovery of the glorious past of many small realms that ancient texts had intentionally consigned to relative obscurity.

The Art of the Kingdom of Zhongshan

A similar situation arose with respect to the Kingdom of Zhongshan[27] in Hubei. During the Warring States Period this small state was represented by elegant bronze creations that always bore two simple and bold characters indicating the kingdom's name. Nevertheless, its origins are a mystery. Maybe it was established by a Zhou scion who had founded a Zhou colony in a region where the dynasty's authority had not been fully consolidated, as had been customary since the beginnings of this dynasty. Some sources have even named the legendary Duke of Huan, a paragon of princely virtues, as a possible founder. Or perhaps it resulted from the rise of local rulers and the introduction of civilization within a non-Chinese group such as the Di, who are cited in texts from the Spring and Autumn Period? The Di are described as "barbarians" whom the inhabitants of northern and western China feared on account of their periodic pillaging of these regions, although the Di subsequently sought refuge in their chosen homeland west of Shaanxi. It appears that, during the sixth century B.C., other western nomads displaced the Di, whom China's sedentary inhabitants were attempting to push northward at the same time. Thus, at the end of the fourth century B.C., the Di had finally settled in the Pingshan region with the consent of the Kingdom of Wei and became its vassals for a certain period of time. They remained in this region until 296 B.C. when the Kingdom of Yan invaded their domains and expelled them.

Chinese archeologists are now inclined to doubt the account given by ancient texts and they reject the claim that a barbarian kingdom arose within Chinese territory. Whether this viewpoint is correct or is a patriotic fantasy can perhaps be answered in part by recent discoveries.

60
Lamp with fifteen lampwicks. Bronze. Warring States Period (fourth century B.C.). Discovered in the former Kingdom of Zhongshan (Tomb Number 1) at Pingshan (Hebei) in 1978. Height: 84.5 cm. Hebei Provincial Museum.
In keeping with a style which was maintained for a long period of time in Chinese art, the lamp possesses a tree-like appearance, accentuated by the presence of monkeys and birds which appear ready to leap from one branch to another. Creatures which must remain on the ground, namely men and other animals, peer upward from the base.
Cf. *Wenwu*, 1979, I, p. 9 and pl. 1, no. 1.

Three excavation projects were undertaken at Pingshan from November, 1974, until June, 1978, at a site where peasants for the past forty years had already observed interesting vestiges of the past. These projects led to the discovery of five exceptionally lavish royal tombs.

One of the most astounding finds consisted of a bronze plaque buried within Tomb Number 1: the layout of a mausoleum [28] was drawn upon this plaque, which constitutes the most ancient architectural drawing to have been discovered in China. The five tombs are shown within this plan — which bore the title *Zhaoyutu* — and the draftsman had carefully indicated the distance between each tomb and the respective places of worship situated nearby. Comparison of the measurements indicated within the plan with distances measured at the site has made it possible to identify certain units of measurement that were used in the Kingdom of Zhongshan.

A ceremonial structure was erected above each of the tombs illustrated on the plate; there can be no doubt that this was a widely practiced custom during that era and efforts are now being undertaken to identify counterparts at other important Chinese tombs. These efforts have already borne fruit. As has been indicated, remnants of a superstructure have been identified at the tomb of Fu Hao at Yinxu and portions of a ceremonial pavilion were found on the top portion of a tomb at Guwei (Huixian) in Henan Province. Hence, it appears to have been demonstrated that, during the Warring States Period, monarchs' and princes' tombs were often adorned with similar structures, the origin of which can be traced to the era of the Shang rulers. This custom persisted for an extremely long period of time until the period of the Southern and Northern dynasties. Furthermore, a text entitled the *Mingdiji,* which appears in the *Hou Hanshu,* provides further evidence (as if such evidence were still truly necessary) that the custom of erecting places of worship and ceremonial pavilions upon the tombs of dignitaries was extremely widespread during the Han Period. Under the influence of Buddhism, other practices emerged after the Six Dynasties Period, but, at a much later point, on the fringes of the empire it is possible to observe a distant echo of ancestral customs in the Xi Xia tombs from the Song Period.

The origin of these monuments is no longer as mysterious as it initially appeared. It is undoubtedly necessary to seek links with the *mingtang* of antiquity which the scholars mention incessantly without ever furnishing a clear definition. Relying upon such texts as the *Li Ji* and the *Zuozhuan,* Henri Maspéro has interpreted these locations as "... the place where the monarch continued to conduct his usual religious activities. The ancient pattern consisting of four buildings symmetrically placed on the four sides of a central building survived because in each of these buildings it was necessary for the king during each month to perform the ceremony of clothing himself in the color representing the appropriate season, to eat food associated with that season, and to sleep in a room corresponding to the specific month."[29] Léon Vandermeersch has approached this topic on an abstract basis: "Within the expression *Mingtang, tang* means a palace and *ming,* which is usually an adjective meaning "luminous," must be interpreted as a transitive verb: the "*Palace of Light*" is the *palace which produces light* ... because of its role as the location from which royal power was propagated like radiant light the "*Palace of Light*" was the seat of the monarchy."[32] In this instance however, there is a departure from the funerary domain, that is undoubtedly the sole domain where these super-structures erected upon tombs existed. Thus, there would appear to be stronger links with shrines established inside dwellings in order to perpetuate veneration of the family's ancestors.

It is unlikely that the origin of these structures is solely attributable to the Warring States Period. Careful study of tombs at Anyang, Houjiazhuang, Xiaodun, or Dasigongcun has revealed several tombs where stones were consistently placed at the bottom of relatively deep holes. These supporting stones for columns demonstrate that superstructures had been placed above large tombs since the beginnings of kingly authority in China. It is probable that this configuration was soon incorporated into the design of tombs in order to create an imposing structure that would be especially suitable for the pageantry associated with veneration of the souls of the deceased. Moreover, some Chinese archeologists have introduced a hypothesis that initially appears to be somewhat attractive: the "tumuli" (*fengtu*) cited within the *Rituals of the Eastern Zhou* would presumably have emerged in southern regions where an abundance of water always posed a threat to human architectural feats. Confucius cited these primitive tumuli, and examples have recently been discovered at such locations as Dunxi in Anhui Province or at Gourong in Jiangsu Province. Thus, these tumuli may have been introduced as a necessary foundation for preservation of ceremonial structures and their origin may be attributable to the elementary need to safeguard the oratory (which had already existed since the Shang Period) from floods. In our opinion, this theory concerning the origin of tumuli is not

61
Ding tripod with lid. Gilded bronze. Warring States Period (end of fourth century B.C.). Discovered in the former kingdom of Zhongshan (Tomb Number 1) at Pingshan (Hebei) in 1978. Height: 51.5 cm. Diameter: 65.8 cm. Hebei Provincial Museum.

This bronze *ding*, whose shape is entirely conventional, is noteworthy on account of the presence of cast iron legs. In keeping with a common prac- tice during this era, the lid was adorned with three rings, which are vestiges of zoomorphic ornaments. These rings served as supporting legs when the lid was turned over. The decoration, which is placed around the waist, con- sists solely of a long inscription containing 78 lines with six characters and one line with a sole character. The text describes the King of Zhongshan's conflict with the Kingdom of Yan and allows a date of approximately 313 B.C. to be established for this bronze vessel.

62
Table stand. Bronze with gold and silver inlaid work. Warring States Period (fourth century B.C.). Discovered in the former kingdom of Zhongshan (Tomb Number 1) at Pingshan (Hebei) in 1978. Height: 37.4 cm. Length: 48 cm. Hebei Provincial Museum.
Four small stags, whose bodies are adorned with "plum blossoms," appear to be leaning against one another so as to support this bronze object. Four dragons and four phoenixes are intertwined above them on a stand. The "naturalist" portrayal of the stags emphasizes the magical image of the dragons, which are placed around the restrained but vivid image of the phoenixes, symbolizing unending life.
Cf. *Wenwu*, 1979, 1, p. 8, pl. 5, no. 2.

63
Triple lamp. Bronze and silver. Warring States Period (fourth century B.C.). Discovered in the former Kingdom of Zhongshan (Tomb Number 6) at Pingshan (Hebei) in 1978. Height: 66.4 cm. Hebei Provincial Museum.
A performer is holding a pole in one hand and a serpent in his other hand. A monkey is clinging to the pole. Bronzework of this type had already emerged during the Warring States Period. A similar specimen belongs to the Freer Gallery, for example. In this instance, however, the figures form a base for three lamps: one lamp rests upon the pole and two upon the serpent. The entire piece is composed of silver-coated bronze, except for the man's head which is made of silver.
Cf. *Wenwu*, 1979, 1, p. 12 and pl. 1, no. 2.

extremely convincing. During the Bronze Age, from Brest to Tokyo, embankments were created throughout Europe and Asia. Although small prayer altars may have been erected upon these high mounds their form may have been influenced far more by geomantic and religious elements than by requirements of a purely practical nature. In this instance all of the difficulties of interpreting archeological evidence are present. Which forces were more powerful, physical constraints or constraints that human beings willingly adopted for properly expressing their view of the world? After all, for many civilizations high places have been the preferred habitat for heroes and deities.

At this point it is appropriate to consider the inner portions of the tombs. The items that were found there would appear to suggest that, during the Warring States Period, several ethnic groups lived in Zhongshan, where specifically Chinese elements were combined with elements representing groups which differed from the inhabitants of the Great Plain.

For example, items associated with the everyday life of the deceased person were wrapped in large pieces of cloth, and jade ornaments resembling pins were fastened to burial apparel. In addition, there were impressive staffs resembling tridents, the ends of which possessed the shape of the *shan* (mountain) symbol. Six of these staffs, which were 1.44 meters high and 80 centimeters wide, were situated within one of the two niches beside the burial vault within Tomb Number 6. Remnants of a leather canopy and the necessary bronze items for assembling it were found nearby. Thus, the tridents were originally intended to be displayed as insignia around the tent of the chieftain or king. Within the tomb there were numerous ceramic, lacquered, and bronze vessels. Comparison of the bronzes with those which were discovered in the tomb of King Guo, who ruled the Kingdom of Zhongshan, suggests that Tomb Number 6 may be the sepulchre of a monarch whose reign would have ended nearly a generation earlier, or approximately between 290 B.C. and 280 B.C.

Each trident is divisible into two sections: leafwork for the tips and the fretted bends; and a hollow tube intended to be placed over the first section which would be secured by rivets. The tridents are not unique: a comparable set of smaller but heavier tridents was also found within Tomb Number 1.

The tridents — accompanied by other treasures such as a stand composed of four intertwined dragons or a statue of a tiger carrying its prey — suggest the proximity of Central Asia. In our opinion and in contrast to any form of Sinocentrism, it is necessary to take into account the links that may have existed between Zhongshan's rulers and nomadic cultures during the Warring States Period.

Kingdoms of the Great Plain

During the same period, progress continued in the kingdoms located within the Great Plain and it has been possible to discover evidence of the fundamental change embodied by the introduction of iron. At Xinzheng, the early capital of the Han domains, or at Yangcheng, another Han city, recent discoveries have included not only remnants of outer walls, but also traces of the inner city (for commoners) and of the palace complex. High proportions of iron tools were discovered at both locations. Indeed, urban development appears to have attained a particularly advanced level at Yangcheng; within a large palace in the northern portion of the city, a man-made lake was supplied by ceramic ducts that channeled excess water to less elevated areas in order to provide water for the inhabitants. Systems of this type had already been created at Zhengzhou or at Yinxu during the Shang Period, but, in this instance, significant improvements had been introduced.

North of the Yellow River in the former Kingdom of Jin, the ruins of Houma, which were discovered in 1956, also indicate the vitality of a region where the ways of the past were fading.

Excavations during 1969 and 1970 permitted discovery of a trench containing sacrificial relics (Maybe the ceremony actually took place in this same location): bones from cattle, horses, and sheep were found alongside pieces of jade. Nevertheless, the site was even more significant in terms of its many tombs from the Warring States Period, where exceptional zoomorphic bronzes have been discovered (since 1960), and in terms of the originality of written documents stored within these tombs. Indeed, it was possible to identify the subsequently famous text of a "friendship oath" adopted by the rulers of principalities mentioned within ancient chronicles, although there were no authentic specimens of such an oath prior to this interesting discovery.

64
Cylindrical vessel with unicorns. Bronze. Warring States Period (fourth century B.C.). Discovered in the former kingdom of Zhongshan (Tomb Number 1) at Pingshan (Hebei) in 1978. Hebei Provincial Museum.
This vessel, which resembles containers for brushes, even though their use has not been confirmed for this period, is noteworthy on account of the delicate interlaced motif which adorns the waist and on account of the fully traditional vitality of the fabulous creatures situated beneath it.
Cf. *Wenwu*, 1979, 1, pl. 8, no. 2.

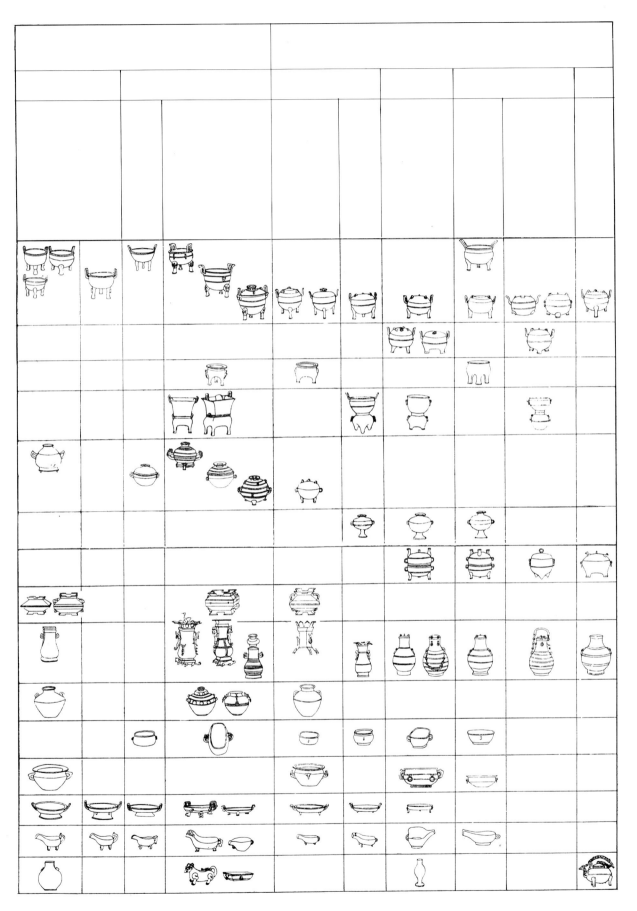

65
Chariot ornament in the form of a serpent's head. Bronze inlaid with silver. Warring States Period (475 B.C.–221 B.C.). Discovered at Xiejiayaicun, Yongji (Shanxi) in 1954. Length: 21.3 cm.
This chariot ornament containing geometric motifs composed of delicate silver inlaid work is highly typical of art from the Warring States Period. It is possible to observe the sets of "straight lines and curves" which would evolve into the *chokkomon*, one of the most widely used motifs in early Japanese art.
Cf. *Wenwu*, 1955, 8, p. 43.

Fig. 12   Bronzes of the Central Plain. Evolution of forms during the Spring and Autumn Period and also the Warring States Period. Reproduced from *Kaogu yu Wenwu*, 1981, 3, pp. 102–103.

The Chu Treasure

There is, however, no phenomenon as impressive as the prosperity of the Kingdom of Chu which has been the source of treasures without any counterparts in other regions.

In August 1974, two bronze vessels were unearthed at the western gate of the town of Gucheng[31] in Henan Province; there was a *ding* tripod containing eighteen triangular silver coins with a total weight of 3,072.9 grams and an urn containing 392 gold coins weighing 8,183.3 grams was found beneath the tripod. A pit which had been dug during the era of the Western Han was situated nearby but the bottom of the pit contained a round hearthstone from the Warring States Period. Thus, it is not impossible that coins from the Spring and Autumn Period or from the Warring States Period had been left there at the same time as the hearthstone — but the circumstances are a mystery. Was someone attempting to protect a treasure or to dispose of it? For what purpose? Is there actually a link between the position of the hearth and concealment of this treasure? It is still dif-

ficult to provide answers for questions of this kind, but the treasure itself has contributed some astonishing conclusions.

The triangular silver coins can be divided into three groups according to size and weight. In turn one can establish two categories for the gold currency: 195 flat pieces or slabs and 197 ingots. Both types contain inscriptions of the sigillary type.

If one relies solely upon information furnished by historical texts, the coins represent an enigma. Similar currency with a spade-like shape was indeed commonplace during this period, especially within the Kingdom of Yue, although this form of currency was produced from bronze. Of course, silver slabs were placed in circulation under the Han rulers. Nevertheless, these flattened ingots, widely used under the Eastern Han dynasty, always contained three symmetrically arranged punch marks or only one punch mark. In contrast, the number of punch marks appearing on the Gucheng currency varied and in some instances there were as many as six punch marks. Similarly, the gold coins and ingots do not correspond closely to prior descriptions of currency from this era. In *The Scales of Commerce (Ping*

chun) in the *Shi Ji,* Si Ma Qian stated that the golden coins minted during the reign of Han Wudi (*circa* 140–80 B.C.) were produced from white gold although they actually consisted of an alloy of gold and silver. Thus, the Gucheng currency, which consists entirely of pure gold or pure silver, is wholly inconsistent with this description. For clarification it is necessary to turn to archeology.

Not far from Gucheng, comparable currency was discovered at Niucun, at a site that has been indisputably attributed to the end of the Spring and Autumn Period or to the early Warring States Period. Furthermore, it appears that this type of currency was widely used throughout the Kingdom of Chu during the same period because specimens have been found in several tombs within the Changsha region, including Tomb Number 2 at Wangshan. Thus, it is possible that southern Henan had been entirely drawn into the orbit of the Chu rulers at this time; the Kingdom of Chu was practically the only kingdom capable of using pure gold.

To a certain extent, the periphery of the Kingdom of Chu (Anhui, Shandong, Jiangsu, Hebei, Shanxi) represented a belt of precious metals, as has been demonstrated by discoveries in 1979 at Shouxian in Anhui or at Qingzhou in Shandong. From the latter location, gold coins were soon introduced in Japan and this circumstance may constitute a remote source for the legendary description of the archipelago as "the Golden Realm." Such legends partially accounted for the Mongol emperors' efforts to conquer Japan in 1274 and in 1281.

Furthermore, during antiquity, the Kingdom of Chu acquired a reputation for gold-smelting that did not diminish over the centuries. The highest numbers of ingots are attributable to the period from 241 A.D. to 223 A.D., immediately prior to establishment of the Empire.

Was a portion of this region's gold ever exported as far away as Bronze Age Japan? There is no way of knowing at the present time but, in relation to the Chinese mainland, it is at least permissible to affirm that during the Warring States Period, regardless of the vicissitudes of warfare, the Chu civilization, represented by its currency, expanded into many provinces, gradually absorbing or conquering the Central Plain.

66
Hu vessel adorned with an eagle's head. Bronze. Warring States Period (475 B.C.–221 B.C.). Discovered in the former kingdom of Qi, at Cangjia-zhuang, Zhucheng (Shandong) in 1970. Height with (movable) handle: 47.5 cm.
The exceptional elegance of this vessel with a fluted waist is derived from the lid consisting of an eagle's head with a movable beak. The lid was fastened to the handle of the pitcher by two rings.
Cf. *Wenwu,* 1972, 5, p. 14 and pl. 5, no. 3.

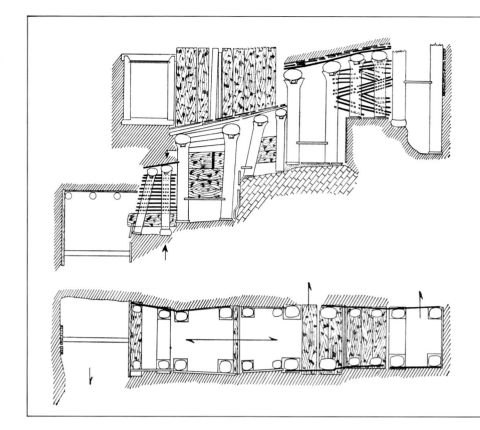

Fig. 13. Tonglushan mines: diagram and cross-section of tunnels. Reproduced from *Wenwu,* 1975, 2, p. 4.

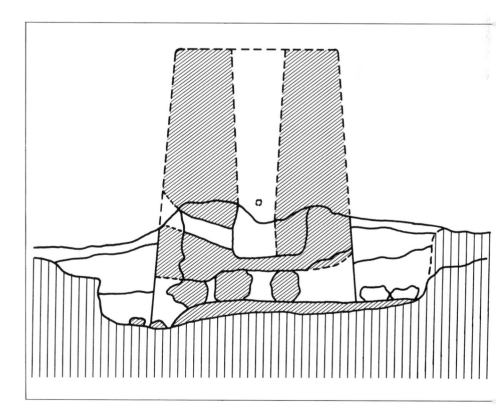

Fig. 14. Reconstruction of smelting furnace at Tonglushan. Reproduced from *Kaogu xuebao,* 1982, 1, p. 9.

Door-knocker. Bronze. Warring States Period (fourth century B.C.–third century B.C.). Discovered at Yixian (Hebei) in 1966, at the site of Xiadu, which was formerly the capital of the Kingdom of Yan. Length of mask: 45.5 cm. Diameter of ring: 29 cm.
This door-knocker fully captures the inventiveness of bronzesmiths during the vigorous Warring States Period: an ancient theme, namely the *taotie*, was still present but it was recreated by means of the spiral patterns of an exceptionally imaginative design composed of dragons, serpents, and birds of prey. The result was a creation which appears to be derived from a dream, although in daily life its presence was strongly audible.

Iron

As for general technological progress it is not probable that iron-working would have nourished other civilized areas whose creations were perhaps less splendorous but were clearly more influential in terms of life in China.

Since 1974, significant information from the site known as Tonglushan[32] in Hubei Province has contributed to understanding of metalworking and of ancient mining techniques in more general terms — although many uncertainties persist. Large-scale excavation in 1974 and then from 1976 until 1979 have permitted investigation of a copper mine that was worked from the Spring and Autumn Period and then from the Han Period — where the highest level of activity existed — until the Tang Period when the mining tunnels and the foundry located at this site appear to have been abandoned.

With tunneled pits, the mine extended several dozen meters beneath a mountain. The tunnels were supported by wooden slabs. During the Spring and Autumn Period there were mere trenches where it was necessary to crawl on hands and knees. During subsequent eras the miners built tunnels where a man of average size could stand at full height. In one of the most ancient sections of this mine, archeologists found carts and tubs that had been used to carry ore to the surface.

Professor Xia Nai and his colleagues have pursued efforts to reconstruct a furnace from ruins situated at the surface. The furnace appears to have consisted of a smelting hearth situated beneath a cover resting upon a relatively narrow chimney. Air circulation was provided by two small vents within the outer walls. In this way it was possible for air to travel through a T-shaped duct at the base of the hearth in order to accelerate combustion. Wood ashes were discovered within the hearth area. The entire furnace was coated with a layer of pebbles and clay, and the average diameter was 1.60 meters.

For the past thirty years the topic of the introduction of iron in Chinese civilization has inspired extensive research and a certain number of disputes.[33] On the basis of current studies and analyses, it appears that some items produced from iron, which is such a readily available element, were already being used at Banpo. It is probable that the ore was obtained by crude techniques which represented the only available method for a considerable period of time. It appears that production of slag from gangue containing iron ore for the purpose of obtaining iron did not become sufficiently advanced so as to permit creation of simple and small but usable farming implements until

68

Human figure supporting a lamp. Bronze with traces of lacquer. Warring States Period (*c.* fourth century B.C. — third century B.C.). Discovered in Tomb Number 5 at Shangcunling, Sanmenxia (Henan) in 1975. Height: 48.9 cm. Diameter of lamp: 23.7 cm. Zhengzhou, Henan Provincial Museum.

In keeping with a design which became conventional during the Han Period, this lamp consisted of three detachable parts: the kneeling human figure serving as a lamp-bearer, the leg of the lamp, and the lamp itself, consisting of a hollow bowl into which oil was poured. Traces of black and red pigments, which may have been lacquer, are observable in several locations. Thus, this creation belongs to the relatively rare category of painted bronzes: one of the most outstanding examples of this category was a painted mirror which was discovered at Hongmiaopo in Xi'an (Shaanxi) in 1963.

Cf. *Wenwu*, 1976, 3.

69

Helmet. Iron. Warring States Period (fourth century B.C.–third century B.C.). Discovered in Tomb Number 44 at Xiadu, Yixian (Hebei), the former capital of the Kingdom of Yan, in 1965. Height: 31 cm. Length: 29 cm.

This helmet consisting of iron plates arranged in strips around a centerpiece demonstrates the skills of armorers during the Warring States Period. All of the structural characteristics of Chinese armor had fully emerged. The basic design did not change over the centuries and it was imitated in Japan, where it was highly suitable for the needs of light cavalry forces.

Cf. *Kaogu*, 1975, 4, p. 231 and pl. 5, nos. 1–2.

the period preceding the Warring States Period. The earliest iron tools to have been discovered thus far, which have been attributed to the sixth century B.C., were found near Changsha in Henan, within Tomb Number 314 at Zhiziling, and at Luoyang in Henan, in a forge at Shuini. Once again, the Kingdom of Chu appears to have been a center of progress in a manner entirely comparable to the heart of the Central Plain. Clearly, this situation was more than coincidental.

After the Warring States Period, the number and diversity of iron tools expanded significantly within the "seven kingdoms," or the seven largest principalities of that era. The technical quality of early ironworking quickly reached an outstanding level. After the middle phase of the Warring States Period ironworkers mastered casting methods that were derived from technological advances in bronzemaking in China. Of course, the level of production was not the same in every kingdom. The central kingdoms, with abundant supplies of iron, produced a vast range of items for ordinary use or for funerary use, according to two distinct series. It appears that far less diversity existed in the outlying regions, although impressive foundries have been discovered at Lianhuabao (present-day Liaoning) in the Kingdom of Yan and at Linyi (present-day Shandong) in the Kingdom of Qi.

Development of casting techniques is represented by such sites as Dengfeng or Xinzheng in Henan but especially by Xinglong in Hebei, where seventy percent of the molds consisted of two sections — a right side and a left side — and permitted casting of several tools at once. These reusable cast iron molds with two surfaces represented a significant advance in relation to earlier earthen molds which were not durable.

During the Warring States Period strict regulations were not yet introduced to coordinate the activities of ironworkers. Nevertheless, the complexity of this type of activity and the high production costs only permitted a limited number of sites. Usually, there was only one large foundry for the domains of a given rule. The relative rarity of foundries tends to support hypotheses affirming that the use of iron, like the use of bronze during earlier eras, only transformed Chinese economic relationships in an extremely gradual form, while the majority of the peasantry continued to till the land with antiquated stone tools.

Nevertheless, knowledge of how to produce iron tools arose everywhere, with the exception of extremely remote regions such as Guangdong or Guangxi which imported iron tools from the Kingdom of Chu or from the realms within the Great Plain. In this way, farmers slowly began to dig their fields much deeper than in the past. As a result rice cultivation expanded significantly, especially in regions where natural conditions had not favored creation of rice paddies, such as Cheng, Wei or Qin. Philologists have indicated that the expansion of irrigated fields is confirmed by the fact that during the Warring States Period there were at least five distinct categories of dikes or boundaries identified by specific expressions.

This phenomenon indicates the extent to which irrigation techniques benefited from advances in metalworking, even though small farmers continued to use the same methods that their ancestors had employed during the earliest phases of the monarchy.

70

Human figure bearing a lamp. Bronze. Warring States Period (fourth century B.C.–third century B.C.). Discovered in 1964 at Yixian (Hebei), at the site of Xiadu, the former capital of the Kingdom of Yan. Height: 13 cm. Because of the simplicity of this sturdily designed human figure who is erect and is smiling discretely, this piece has a rustic charm which distinguishes it from more ornate lamps. A comparable, but larger lamp (Height: 28.3 cm.), portraying a man squatting on his heels, is owned by the Minneapolis Institute of Arts.
Cf. *Kaogu*, 1975, 4.

IV. CREATION OF THE EMPIRE

In 221 B.C., all of China was unified as a result of the conquests and authority of the ruler of the Kingdom of Qin. Henri Maspéro has affirmed: "During the same year, the ruler, in order to acknowledge these new conditions, adopted a new title, designating himself as "the Supreme Lord," or *huang-ti*. This title, translated as "emperor," was retained by China's rulers until the Revolution of 1911. The China of the past had truly disappeared forever, and a new way of life began to arise upon the ruins."[34]

If the concept of unity was inherent in the original monarchy long before establishment of the empire, the geographic dimensions of the empire constituted an innovation to a greater degree than did the centralization or unification of authority. Such a perspective has indeed emerged among contemporary historians in China, and it is most fully represented by the appearance of the significant publication known as *Lishi yanjiu* (*Historical Studies*). From their viewpoint, the empire constituted a fulfillment of ancient China and important changes in society emerged much later, during the third century A.D., when China was once again divided into three large territorial units and barbarians gradually settled within its borders.

Indeed, the Qin emperors, who ruled for little more than a decade (221 B.C. — 207 B.C.), were less an imperial dynasty than instruments of a destiny: the destiny of China for the next 2,000 years. Until recently, these emperors were only — or almost entirely — portrayed by the misleading mirror of the *Histories of the Dynasties,* with the dreadful image of having been rulers who dared to reject the "books" and teachings of antiquity. Was it not affirmed that the First Emperor and his minister Li Si, in 213 B.C., burned ancient texts and executed the stubborn scholars who refused to submit to the new order?

The Contributions of New Texts: Yunmeng

A recent and exceptionally abundant archeological harvest is now overturning many ideas that were repeated from one century to the next. For example, if one lends credence to the scholars' diatribes, it is possible to conclude that the First Emperor sought to establish a society that to a certain extent would be emancipated from the authority of texts. Now there is evidence of precisely the opposite. Indeed, it has been known since the writings of Si Ma Qian that *Qin Shi Huang* had ordered erection of a stele, a veritable model of an official text, within every district that he established. These stelae contained the countless legal texts of the era, whereby laws, weights and measures, and precepts for adhering to standards of behavior were disseminated throughout the empire. It is only in our era, however, that excavations have confirmed the existence of something that had previously appeared to be nothing more than an idea.

In 1975, at a site known as Xiaogan, in Yunmeng[35] north of Hankou, the tomb of a forty-year-old man who had died shortly after establishment of the empire was discovered. Around his remains there lay more than a thousand bamboo sheets containing texts written in *lishu,* the elegant official script of the Qin scribes, with each character having been placed inside a flattened square. Some sheets contained writing on both sides. The bamboo sheets were characterized by three different lengths (23.1 centimeters, 25.5 centimeters, 27.8 centimeters), while the width varied from 0.5 to 0.8 centimeters. In contrast to earlier text specimens of this type, there was a perceptible effort to conserve materials: the sheets were fastened together beforehand so as to form a "volume" that could be read from top to bottom, although not as a single text. Instead, it was necessary to follow the actual sequence of sentences. The first sentence appeared in the uppermost portion of each sheet and was followed by a second and third sentence below, in a sequence requiring continuous movement back and forth from one sheet to another. It is easy to envision the difficulties encountered by archivists when the passage of time destroyed the bamboo rings holding the sheets together. Furthermore, the various manuscripts were intermingled as a result of various disturbances and disruptions affecting the entire tomb. Possibly this purely practical discovery will oblige philologists to undertake protracted efforts to verify ancient texts whose composition may very well have been altered at an extremely early point in time.

The actual nature of the text paradoxically reinforces the physically derived concept of a fragile and not entirely coherent amalgam. Indeed, the initial portion of the bamboo sheets consists of an extremely arid chronicle of events that had occurred between 306 B.C. and 217 B.C. In terms of its content this chronicle is comparable to the extant portions of the *Bamboo Chronicles* (*Zhushu Jinian*) that appeared during the third century B.C., although doubts now exist with respect to establishment of an earlier origin for these *Chronicles*. Nevertheless, the document is followed by a long letter from a governor named Teng, describing the attributes that a loyal public official must demonstrate. Subsequently, one encounters unusual compilations of learned treatises concerning proper behavior in enlightened circles, mingled with proverbs of a popular nature and aphorisms. One of these aphorisms appeared in the *Laozi*, and another was found in the *Liji*. Finally, there was a long text describing the requirements to regulate economic activities in different areas. One had to inform the government of the actual status and composition of harvests, to maintain suitable health conditions for livestock, and also to notify the government if one of the horses entrusted to an official died. A set of rules was also provided for storing and inspecting grain, along with rules concerning use of certain objects or commodities of exchange, such as bolts of cloth. There were also regulations concerning markets administered or supervised by the government. Subsequently, there were a series of regulations pertaining to craftsmen who had to adhere faithfully to the government's instructions concerning the nature and quality of their goods, and abide by the official calendar defining suitable tasks for the winter and the summer. The various responsibilities of craftsmen with different qualifications — from apprentices to skilled workers — were likewise defined in precise terms: no details

were left to chance and this body of labor legislation appeared to have been extremely comprehensive. As the text continued, it provided a series of practical instructions concerning erection of tamped earth embankments, the roles of foremen and supervisors in producing goods or in connection with large public construction projects, distribution of military responsibilities and appointment of public officials. There were also rules for collecting unpaid debts, fundamental requirements for expediting correspondence, and rules for transmission of official documents in behalf of the government.

Future research will undoubtedly develop significant conclusions from this collection of regulations, but it is already obvious that these documents provide hitherto unexpected confirmation of governmental authority over life within the empire. Indeed, there is a basis for wondering when these theoretical prescriptions were put into practice. Taking into account the "unified multi-national Chinese empire" referred to by contemporary Chinese historians and sociologists, it is possible that because of local centralization within each small kingdom during the Warring States Period, a ready-made framework existed for the provinces and administrative divisions that emerged under the empire. Perhaps it was merely sufficient to issue orders to local potentates who then immediately became designated as public officials. One observation is inescapable: the government sought to regulate everything, from the appearance of standing grain and the quality of harvests to quantities of oil used for lubricating the axles of chariots. Nevertheless, it is interesting to observe that alongside these provisions reflecting the practical and efficient orientation of the lawgivers, the epistolary essay concerning the art of being a dedicated public servant possesses a distinctly Confucian tone. Perhaps the minister Li Si sought to eradicate every trace of the philosopher's teachings.

Contributions to Regional History

No less than official chronicles, archeological evidence confirms that Imperial precepts were readily adopted by populations that in some instances lived far from the seat of power. In Guizhou Province, two sites that have shed light upon the development of Imperial authority within the southernmost portions of China are Hezhang, discovered in 1976, and Weiningxian. These sites included more than fifty tombs containing the remains of persons who were members of the Han ethnic group. Most of the bodies were buried with bronze or iron weapons. These were weapons intended for warfare, not ceremony, as their owners had died in combat during a war or an insurrection. This hypothesis is confirmed by the fact that there are many nearby tombs of members of a local ethnic group. Indeed, Si Ma Qian had written that construction of the "five foot road" between Guizhou and Sichuan, which began under the Qin rulers and was resumed under Han Wudi in 129 B.C., had incited violent local upheavals. Nevertheless, there has never been a similar evocation of the conflicts that the authoritarian structure of the empire must have created in many other regions.

The First Emperor's Burial Army

The importance of written texts, military power, and elevation of centralization to a quasi-religious status — all of the cornerstones of Imperial power for the next 2,000 years had emerged during this period and excavations continue to provide confirmation. There is another aspect of the Qin civilization that has been revealed by excavations: the quality of its vigorous

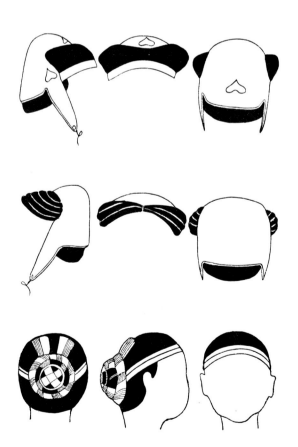

Fig. 15. Headdresses of warriors from Yangjiawan. Reproduced from *Wenwu*, 1977, 10, p. 11.

artistic endeavors, where there were affinities to art of the Warring States Period, although there was less concern with details except insofar as detailed work could contribute to understanding or to heightened admiration. At least, these attributes are suggested by the numerous figures comprising an "army of spirits": the impressive life-size army buried in the Imperial mausoleum, or the small army consisting of 3,000 figures of horsemen and foot-soldiers measuring 70 centimeters, which was discovered in a tomb in Xianyang, the capital city, at a considerably less ancient site known as Yanjiawan.

Clearly, it may be unnecessary to cite the existence of the vast life-size terra cotta horses discovered in 1974, inasmuch as the Chinese press and foreign publications have provided extensive descriptions. From one year to the next, however, excavations yield new discoveries. Thus, three trenches have been identified and excavated over the years, less than two kilometers east of the giant tumulus erected for the First Emperor. The imposing silhouette of this monument has dominated the neighboring plain of Xi'an for two thousand years. An impressive photograph of the tomb was taken by Victor Segalen a few months before World War I, capturing the image of Imperial subjects that the mausoleum offered to countless generations.

Since 1950 the Government has attempted to restore the original appearance of the tomb, as described within the *Shi Ji*. Today, its sides are covered with greenery so as to recreate the artificial mountain that they were intended to represent. According to Taoist mythology which had been widely adopted during the earliest centuries of the empire, mountains were the chosen abode of the immortal. Were the First Emperor and his tomb truly immortal? According to traditional accounts, Xiang Yu, a discontented rival of Liu Bang, founder of the Han dynasty, profaned the tomb only a few years after its completion, in 210 B.C. or in 209 B.C. Recent excavations in the immediate vicinity of the mausoleum have indeed uncovered indications of a conflagration. Did Xiang Yu, a clever but vainglorious southerner, vent his wrath upon the Emperor's remains and the underground palace? Perhaps future excavations will furnish the answer. At this point no officially sponsored excavations have located the founder of the Chinese Empire, and archeologists have only respectfully investigated the periphery of the sacred enclosure; too much is at stake to permit excessively hasty excavation.

Of course, past discoveries and the evidence that continues to emerge permit us to dream. Perhaps it will be possible some day to see the wonders described by Si Ma Qian in the *Shi Ji,*

71-72

Archer. Terra cotta, with traces of polychromy. Qin Period (221 B.C.–210 B.C.). discovered in 1977 in Trench Number 2, east of the First Emperor's mausoleum at Lintong (Shaanxi). Height: 122 cm. Lintong, Qin Statuary Museum.

This archer who is wearing a cuirass and kneeling on the ground belongs to a group of 120 warriors who are ready for practice or for actual combat. The question remains unresolved. Many Western archeologists, such as H. Brinker and R. Goepper (*Kunstschatze aus China*, p. 123), tend to believe that the warrior was preparing to bend his bow which is no longer present. Chinese archeologists, relying on historical texts, interpret the archer's position as a resting stance or as a stance preceding a drill, whereby the bow would have been placed around the archer's chest and he would have held his arrow in his hands. The relics discovered near the archers confirm the original presence of authentic weapons: arrowheads and fragments from wooden bows. Moreover, the occasional presence of swords and scabbards indicate that some archers also carried swords. It is possible to observe that the armor consists of an actual shell of metal and leather plates which are connected to one another by metal fasteners and strips of cloth. This type of armor continued to be traditionally preferred in China and during the era of the *samurai* in Japan. The sole of the right boot, which is not shown here, contains carefully reproduced rough spots, thereby indicating the degree of precision which the Qin sculptors sought to achieve.
Cf. *Wenwu*, 1978, 5, p. 9 and pl. 4, no. 1.

73

Warrior wearing a cuirass. Terra cotta, with traces of polychromy. Qin Period (221 B.C. – 210 B.C.). discovered in 1977 in Trench Number 3, east of the First Emperor's mausoleum at Lintong (Shaanxi). Height: 196 cm. Lintong, Qin Statuary Museum.

This warrior is wearing a cuirass extending across his chest and his abdomen. The cuirass was fastened in the rear by two overlapping leather straps which were fastened to a belt. Today, it is difficult to know what he held in his clenched right hand or in his open left hand. On account of the exceptional dimensions of this figure and on account of the ornamentation which is still observable on the straps of his cuirass, it is possible that this statue represents an officer (the height of the foot soldiers usually varies between 1.75 and 1.85 meters). Does the position of his left hand indicate an order? This possibility is suggested by comparison with the statues discovered in Trench Number 3.
Cf. *Wenwu*, 1979, 12.

translated by Edouard Chavannes at the turn of the century. "From the beginning of his reign, Che-hoang had ordered the digging and preparation of Mount Li. Later, when he had gained dominion over the entire empire, he sent more than seven hundred thousand workers there. They dug until water came forth, then cast bronze and prepared the sarcophagus. Palaces and buildings for every official function were erected there; splendid utensils, jewels, and rare items were brought to be placed within (the tomb). Artisans were instructed to make arbalests and swift arrows; if anyone attempted to dig a hole in order to enter the tomb he would have been fired upon immediately. A hundred bodies of water, the Kiang (Yangtze), the Ho, and the vast ocean made of mercury were created with contrivances allowing the flow back and forth from one location to another. All of the heavenly configurations were placed at the top, and the entire face of the earth was recreated below. *Jen-yu* (seal or whale) oil was used for torches that would, so it was believed, burn for a long time . . . Grass and bushes were

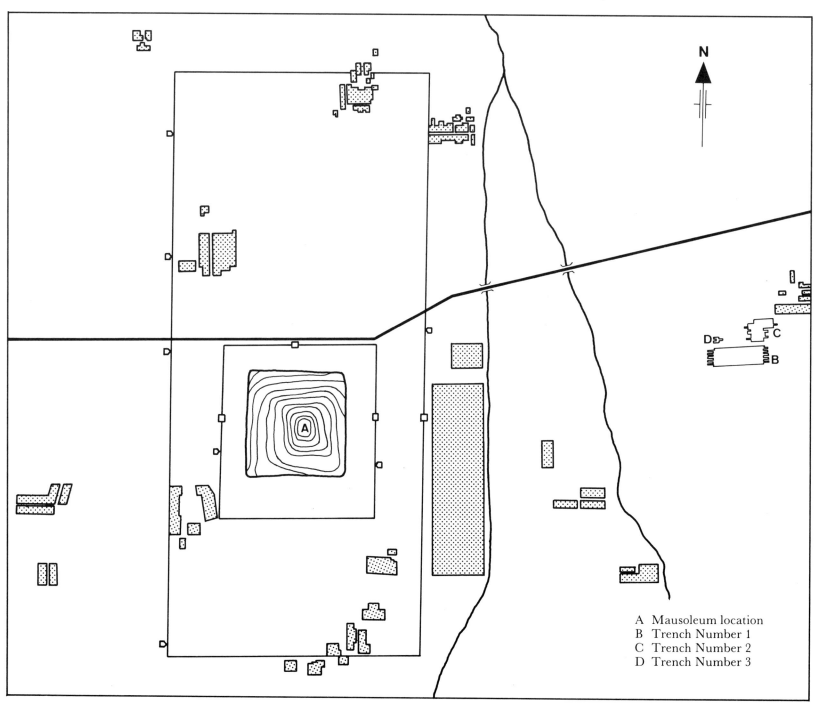

A Mausoleum location
B Trench Number 1
C Trench Number 2
D Trench Number 3

Fig. 16.   The First Emperor's mortuary retinue: locations of trenches containing statues. Reproduced from *Wenwu*, 1975, 11, p. 2.

74   Head of warrior

planted so that (the tomb) would resemble a mountain."[36]

Since 1974, three carefully planned trenches have been discovered near the tumulus. The first trench, with a rectangular shape, contained 6,000 foot-soldiers and horses. The second, with a surface area of approximately 6,000 square meters, was essentially T-shaped, with four layers of bricks resting upon pillars of calcinated wood that were supported by brick columns; and a group of more than 300 archers was found there. The third trench, with an area of 520 square meters, contained a chariot and warriors in armor. During the summer of 1975, several empty and unfinished structures were located in the same area. It is possible that these structures were intended for the major portion of the Emperor's army, whereas the other trenches contained only the three flanks in accordance with the order of deployment that has been described in treatises on the art of warfare based on the *Guanzi,* written by Guan Zhong during the fifth century B.C. It is clear that this complex was intended to be of far more extensive dimensions, but the death of the First Emperor and the serious unrest that ensued did not permit completion of the work.

Even before admiring the plastic or technical qualities of the statues that have been unearthed there, Chinese archeologists are perhaps most deeply impressed by the importance of this discovery since it sheds light on military strategy in ancient China.

The function of chariots during the era of the First Emperor continues to be one of the most frequently debated aspects. In earlier times, during the era of the kings, chariot warfare was subject to precise rules requiring the use of formations of five, ten, or twenty chariots. Within the First Emperor's tomb, however, the chariots are arranged in groups of four instead of five. This distinctive trait had been observed by the official chroniclers who wrote during the thirty-first year of his reign, in the *Annals of the First Emperor (Qinshihuang benji)*: "When the Emperor goes to Xianyang, four chariots accompany him and he departs at night." But while the group of four chariots has been archeologically verified, the Emperor's retinue offers other unique characteristics. At the end of the Warring States Period, chariots usually carried three armed men and were unaccompanied. In Trench Number 1 and in Trench Number 2, however, the chariots are accompanied by escorts in accordance with the ancient practices of the Shang and Zhou monarchs. This arrangement had fallen into disuse during the Spring and Autumn Period (770–475 B.C.). According to the *Zuozhuan,* new rules of warfare dividing the functions between chariot-borne forces and infantrymen were introduced in 541 B.C. This change was undoubtedly influenced by the wars that the rival kingdoms had waged in the heart of the Great Plain. In these vast expanses, the combatants mustered constantly increasing numbers of warriors and chariots, with the result that the principles of military strategy ultimately became diversified so as to allow placement of foot-soldiers on one side and teams of horses on the other.

In the distant western Kingdom of Qin, however, geographical conditions — such as a terrain that was often mountainous — and ideological factors — such as deep loyalty to Shang customs — accounted for a different mode of development. In this way, the characteristically complex Qin order of battle arose, as described at length by Ma Duanlin in the *Wenxian tongkao* in the thirteenth century. The First Emperor's funeral retinue now offers a striking counterpart. The chariots were placed in front of the foot-soldiers while squads of horsemen supported the charioteers' maneuvers. Archeologists have interpreted this innovation as evidence that cavalry, as an element of warfare, had already attained its maturity under the Qin rulers instead of during the Han Period. Although chariots were still used, their relatively reduced numbers in relation to concepts presented during antiquity indicate that the chariot had become an anachronism at this point.

It is also appropriate to observe that the three excavated retinues were arranged facing eastward. Is it possible that the mausoleum was completely surrounded by comparable detachments facing other possible attackers? The subterranean abode of the deceased was intended to offer an inverted but accurate image of their earthly abode, which would have been the luxurious capital of Xianyang on the banks of the Wei River in this particular case. Ancient texts indicate that three types of detachments existed within the capital: one lived on the palace grounds, the other was quartered outside, while a third protected the periphery of the city. The statues discovered approximately 1,200 meters east of the outer wall of the tomb appear to represent the third detachment. Furthermore, the exceptional number of statues should not be considered surprising: the three detachments garrisoned at Xianyang may have included as many as 50,000 men.

For all admirers of art these countless clay statues also permit scrutiny of terra cotta modeling techniques at the beginning of the empire, and provide extremely valuable information on a technique that had been regarded as being of considerably less ancient origin.[37]

The material is usually gray and it was fired at quite a high temperature after preliminary drying in the open air. Each statue is composed of two layers of clay: the innermost layer, from 3 to 10 centimeters thick, is relatively coarse, whereas the outer layer, measuring approximately 3 centimeters, was applied as a finish in order to conceal the joints where the various pieces were fitted together.

All of the statues were made of multiple parts, the number varying according to the complexity of the subject. Certain sections were hollow, whereas others were partially or entirely filled with clay. Some elements, such as the hands, were individually modeled or molded; the latter method gave the hands a rigid quality, with the four fingers extended and the thumb placed beneath them and set slightly apart as if to grasp something. The individually modeled hands, such as those of the officers, are significantly different. With recognizable suppleness, these hands were designed to portray all of the gestures of martial leadership.

The heads consisted of hollow front and rear sections that were created from molds and the two sections were joined at the ears or in front of the ears. An extremely thin surface layer never exceeding one centimeter was placed over these two sections which were three to five centimeters thick. There was a relatively small number of sections that appear to have been rough cast and then carefully reworked with chisels or knives before the clay mixture had completely dried, a procedure that seems to have been employed for producing the most clearly individualized statues. This phase of work and, in general, preparation of surface layers for the faces obviously required exceptional precision. A mixture of fine clay and water, or barbotine, was used for attaching multiple external components to the main piece. Thus it has been possible to identify twenty-four categories of mustaches and beards adorning the warriors' faces. The various headdresses and hairstyles also required a vast range of hollow or solid components which were directly molded on the head or were subsequently attached. Finally, the clothing and especially certain pieces of armor likewise required extremely delicate workmanship, where shapes were molded directly upon the torso of the figure, from an extremely thin layer, the thickness of which was only 0.5 to 2 centimeters.

Like the human figures, the horses were created by joining specially molded pieces together. The bodies and the heads consisted of a right and a left section, the two sections joining precisely in the middle of the belly in order to form the body. The belly was thicker (approximately 7 centimeters) than the back (from 2.5 to 4 centimeters). Among many of the equine statues, holes with diameters of 10 to 12 centimeters which were carefully sealed during finishing, are situated on the left flank or on both flanks. These holes were undoubtedly intended to allow the sculptor to reach into the statue in order to assemble its components. Or perhaps they were intended to facilitate the flow of air during firing of these large sections (154 × 70 centimeters) which were difficult to heat in a uniform manner. In turn, it appears that all of the horses' legs were produced by molds since the form hardly varies from one statue to another.

Subsequently, many details were added to the essential pieces: ears that were hand-finished from crude models; manes and forelocks; short tails (38 to 44 centimeters) for draft horses; and long tails (85 centimeters) for saddle horses. These items and all other parts of the horse's body were attached to the main piece by a barbotine, either before or after firing.

Polishing and painting constituted the final phase of the craftsmen's labors. For painting, a wide variety of inorganic pigments was available: various shades of yellow or ochre, green, vermilion, red, black, white, and purple. In this way it was even possible to reproduce the patterns of the five different materials representing the uniforms of low-ranking officers.

Although the splendor of this funerary army was unique, its composition was not. The statues referred to by archeologists as the "three thousand men and horses" that were discovered near Xianyang at Yangjiawan demonstrate the survival of this custom during the times of the Western Han rulers. It is probable that additional discoveries will soon provide other examples of distinguished warriors buried with similar martial ostentation.

Excavations around the First Emperor's mausoleum are continuing successfully. In the village of Shangjiao[38] east of the tomb, an important complex was discovered in 1976 and 1977; ninety-three trenches, essentially arranged in two rows, contained horses as well as statues. It has only been possible thus far to complete limited inspections of most of them but the twenty-eight that have been properly investigated provide an overall impression. One or more horses facing the Imperial tomb were buried in each trench. Each animal was accompanied by a clay figure in a squatting position with its hands resting upon its knees or concealed within its sleeves. The more or less oval faces of these grooms for the afterlife always display different expressions whereas their headdresses are generally comparable — with the hair arranged in coils. The horse skeletons found in these trenches belonged to relatively small steeds, undoubtedly ponies, 1.5 to 1.6 meters long, with a height of 1.4 to 1.5 meters up to the withers. Thus, they were precisely the same size as their terra cotta replicas.

The presence of real horses, instead of equine statues, is surprising insofar as it directly links the burial rituals conducted for Qin Shi Huang to the ceremonies of royal dynasties during the Bronze Age. In this way, it confirms the veracity of the *Shi Ji*'s description of sacrifices. "Eul-che (the First Emperor's son) said: 'The Emperor's wives who have not borne children should not be set free.' Thus, he decreed that all of these women would follow the Emperor to the grave and a great number were put to death. When the coffin had been lowered into the tomb, someone remarked that the laborers and craftsmen who had built these wonders and hidden many treasures knew where everything was, whereby the great worth of everything that had been buried would soon be known far and wide. When the funeral rites had ended and the central passageway leading to the tomb had been hidden and sealed, the door to the outer entrance for this passageway was shut and everyone who had worked as a laborer or artisan was locked inside with the treasures, and could not escape."[39]

Indeed, the deaths of the workmen were somewhat consistent with the horrifying logic of protecting the deceased ruler and his treasures. On the other hand, the deaths of the Emperor's concubines were theoretically a violation of the dynasty's own principles because "during the first year (384 B.C.) of Duke Xi'an, the custom of putting people to death during funerals was outlawed in the Kingdom of Qin."[40] Furthermore, precisely contemporaneous tombs located in the immediate vicinity of the mausoleum suggest that the Emperor's death may have been followed by the more or less voluntary suicides of certain family members and high officials. This aspect likewise links Qin society to the royal dynasties, and it at least partially supports the view of contemporary Chinese historians who have perceived the Qin and the Han less as creators than as organizers of a new world, namely as rulers who spurred the social order of antiquity to its highest stage of development.

New Information Concerning Pottery Production

It is now appropriate to leave the realm of the deceased and return to that of the living. Indeed, many items discovered near the First Emperor's mausoleum provide evidence about how work locations and production were organized during this era.[41]

For example, the production of pottery took place in two types of establishments whose functions appear to have sometimes overlapped; there were both government-owned and privately owned facilities. Specimens of pottery from this era often contain identifying inscriptions consisting of four to six characters which indicate their origin. Some inscriptions include a place name, identified as such by inclusion of the character *li,* for "village." There are also frequent references to "Xi'an" (yang) or to other large towns within the capital region.

Apart from palace names, the names of potters' kilns appear. They are usually identifiable because of their poetic suggestions even when an effort was made to disguise these names as geographic designations. An example is "the village in the willows," which has no ancient or recent counterpart among place names within this region. Finally, there are some specimens containing potters' signatures such as "*Xi,*" or "Joyful."

On account of the diversity of these markings, there is a tendency to attribute them to private kilns. Indeed, the pottery that was produced in government-owned kilns always bears an administratively precise indication of origin, by referring to the official who oversaw production: "Kongyin of the Right Department" (*Yousi Kongyin*) or "The Master Potter of the Left Department" (*Zuosi gaowa*). The official's name is often accompanied by purely administrative information, such as the regional rank of the production location: metropolitan, district, or municipal.

Indeed, currently available information would appear to indicate that the two types of ceramic production were intended for different needs. The private kilns seem to have produced commonplace items — ordinary crockery and various ceramic products for daily use among all of the intermediate or more humble strata of the population. From a typological viewpoint, these productions provide a link between pottery from the Warring States Period and pottery associated with the Han dynasty. These were simple and inexpensive wares that were sold in marketplaces. Their presence within the conventional channels of commerce clearly distinguished them from the creations of the government's kilns.

75
Horse. Terra cotta with traces of brown paint. Qin Period (221 B.C. — 210 B.C.). discovered in 1974 in Trench Number 1, east of the First Emperor's mausoleum at Lintong (Shaanxi). Height: 127 cm. Length: 205 cm. Lintong, Qin Statuary Museum.
This horse belongs to a group of twenty-four life-sized steeds harnessed to six chariots in teams of four. The chariots were discovered beside a group of foot-soldiers.
Cf. *Wenwu*, 1975, 11, p. 2 and subsequent pages.

The official kilns specialized in producing architectural items used to protect and adorn palaces or buildings intended for administrative functions. It appears that these kilns seldom produced ceramic items for conventional purposes. Undoubtedly, at the Court and in aristocratic homes, there was a preference for wares created from materials with considerably more tactile appeal than the coarse pottery of this period. For example, Han wares were usually coated with lacquer.

Discoveries within the vicinity of the First Emperor's mausoleum have confirmed the existence of at least nine different official production locations. Nine of the items found within Trench Number 1, situated east of the tomb, bore references to the "Capital Works Ministry" (*Dusigong*), which reappeared at a later point in the Han city of Changan. This prestigious production facility within the capital was undoubtedly responsible for producing the impressive funerary statues. Nevertheless, the majority of ceramic items or construction materials were produced as the "Right or Left Works Authority" (*Yousigong* or *Zuosigong*) whose inscriptions were often accompanied by the expression *shaofu* to further indicate their official production. Nearly all of the tiles within the mausoleum or within the Apang palace at Xianyang belonged to this category and the signatures of individual production foremen often appear beside the official seal. There are other items bearing the inscription *Dajiang,* "the Master Craftsmen" or "the Master Shop." According to the *Han Shu,* it would seem that this facility was not as large as the "Right and Left Works Authority," although it also produced high quality ceramic items.

Lastly there were the *sishui* inscription or other slightly different inscriptions where the character *si* was always present and must be interpreted as referring to "the Court." Insofar as can be determined at this time, this designation was used for items of exceptional quality, which originated from kilns specifically intended for producing tiles and other architectural items under the supervision of the Right and Left Works Authority.

There were also occasional references to the "Left Palace" (*Zuogong*) or the "Right Palace" (*Yougong*). According to the *Shi Ji, Zuogong* referred to a specific place instead of a division of the Court or of the government. Nevertheless, Chinese archeologists have once again disagreed with Si Ma Qian and believe that, because these items were produced for an official building, the term *gong* clearly refers to a government-owned kiln.

Excavations have also uncovered references that never appear within ancient texts: *Beisi,* "the Authority of the North" and especially *Gongshui,* "Palace Water," or *Sishui,* "Court Water." Undoubtedly, one might envision workshops that originally specialized in producing ducts for supplying water and for drainage. This possibility is suggested by other ceramic pieces with such markings as *Dashui,* "Vast Water," *Zuoshui,* "Left Water," or *Youshui,* "Right Water." Finally, there were certain inscriptions in a small seal (*xiaozhuan*) script which identify the intended destinations of ceramic items in relation to various buildings. For example, items originating from Shangjiao near the Emperor's mausoleum contain such references as "Central Stable," "Left Stable," "Palace Stable," "Third Stable," and "Main Stable."

New Knowledge Concerning Architecture

Excavations in the vicinity of the Imperial Mausoleum have shed significant light upon the organization of other building trades within the Qin Court. In 1973, for example, a large quarry and a stone-cutting location were discovered northwest of the outer wall. Extending more than 1,500 meters from east to west and 500 meters from north to south, this complex covered an area of 75 hectares. Interesting results have been obtained from the excavations completed thus far.

The western portion, where tiles, millstones and pottery were found, was undoubtedly intended for the dwellings of craftsmen and their families. In the south, there were tiles with inscriptions referring to administrative units that must have been located in this area. At the center, it was only possible to unearth fragments of boulders and large pieces of iron: this spot had undoubtedly been the center of the quarry where stones were cut according to the desired sizes. Lastly, the eastern portion contained many vestiges of hearths but no precisely identifiable signs of dwellings. On the other hand, there were large architectural components as well as unfinished sculptures, accompanied by stone tools and pottery. Thus, it appears that facilities for finishing work were performed in this section.

Two coins, three iron weights, and the use of simple curves and "cloud" motifs on tiles and on ornamental pieces clearly date the quarry area back to the Qin Period. Unfortunately, this vast complex, like the immense tomb whose construction it facilitated, was systematically destroyed after a short period of time. This was a significant loss because it is not unlikely that certain essential items for the Xianyang palaces[42] were produced here.

For the past ten years, intensive excavations have taken place in the vicinity of the palaces, as in the case of Palace Number 1 between 1974 and 1975 or Palace Number 3 in 1979. Today, nothing remains but a relatively narrow stratum (approximately 40 to 75 centimeters below the present surface) where Chinese archeologists have attempted to determine the structural characteristics of the palace buildings. Both palaces were destroyed by a fire, the traces of which are still starkly visible although it does not appear that both were burned at the same time. Despite the fury of relentless and seemingly unsparing destruction, there are touching signs of the presence of human beings: final traces of the activities that must have constantly endowed this site with life although devastating flames ultimately engulfed the palaces.

The oldest murals to have been discovered in China thus far were located on a side wall. These murals portray horses, chariots and human figures outlined in black, tinted with brown, and accentuated with red and green. In keeping with an arrangement that became conventional in Han paintings, the background was unpainted. The quality of these frescoes which probably adorned a long corridor confirms the ancient origins of a pictorial tradition that had emerged long before the rise of the empire.

Hence, it is possible to perceive the somewhat arid account of Si Ma Qian in a new light: "(*Qin Shi Huang-di*) brought one hundred and twenty thousand eminent and wealthy families to the palace from all parts of the empire. The various ancestral shrines, the Tchang Terrace, and the Chang-lin (forest) were all located south of the Wei River. Whenever Qin destroyed a noble rival, he copied the style of his palace and rebuilt it at Hsien-yang (Xianyang) on the north bank of the Wei. The Wei was the southern boundary for these palaces. From Yung-men eastward, as far as the King and Wei rivers, buildings, dwell-

ings, covered passageways and circular corridors were joined to one another. All of the beautiful women, bells, and drums which (*Qin Shi Huang-di*) had confiscated from the nobles were brought to his palaces until they were filled . . . Then Shi-huang, because the population of Hsien-yang (Xianyang) was so large and the palace of the kings who had preceded him was too small, said, 'I know that King Wen of the Zhou dynasty maintained his capital at Fong and that King Ou's capital was at Hao. The lands between Fong and Hao are the domain of emperors and kings.' Then he built a palace for his audiences, south of the Wei River in the middle of the Chang-lin enclosure. He began by erecting the front hall beside the capital; it measured five hundred paces from east to west and fifty *tchang* from north to south. There was enough space for ten thousand men in the upper portion, and the banners of five *tchang* could have been placed at the bottom. A circular pathway for horses formed an overhead road. From the bottom of the pavilion it was possible to proceed in a straight line to the Southern Mountain, and a triumphal arch was erected on the peak of the Southern Mountain as the main entrance. From Ngo-pang, a covered road extended across the Wei River as far as Hsien-yang (Xianyang), symbolizing the T'ien-ki road that crosses the Milky Way and reaches Ying-che (a constellation). . . Then more than seven hundred thousand men who had been castrated were sent to build the Ngo-pang palace and the tomb on Mount Li (the Emperor's mausoleum). A stone sarcophagus was brought from the northern mountains and timber from the realms of Chou and King was floated along the rivers." A few years later, however, "Hiang Yu led his soldiers westward and put the inhabitants of Hsien-yang (Xianyang) to death by the sword. He killed Tse-yng, the Ch'in (Qin) king, who had surrendered, and he burned the Ch'in palaces. The fires continued for three months without ceasing. Then Hiang Yu seized their treasures and their women and returned to the east."[43]

V. THE HAN DYNASTY

The authority which the First Emperor established within about ten years was to be consolidated and reinforced by the Han dynasty whose power endured for four centuries (210 B.C. — 220 A.D.) in spite of countless upheavals and changes of capitals.

Vestiges of the Han Period are abundant in every region of China and, notwithstanding local differences, they provide a series of common features that confirm the long-standing belief that the Han were the first rulers to achieve both administrative and cultural unity throughout China. Their reign also represented the earliest period during which China's inhabitants, perceived as a unified group, came into direct contact with their turbulent nomadic neighbors: the Xiongnu in the north, the population of the Xiyu region in Xinjiang, the Donghu in northeastern China, and the tribes of southwestern China. These purely bellicose relationships which arose from the constraints of proximity gradually led the Chinese to discover regions "beyond the Western passes," far from their own agrarian and psychological environment. Thus, intrepid travelers from the Chinese Empire undertook sea voyages to Malaysia, to Burma, and even to the shores of India, while Zhang Qian (third century A.D.), who made his way across central Asia for military reasons, unwittingly created the famous "Silk Road."

As for what archeology has furnished in terms of understanding a dynasty that has been abundantly represented by texts and artifacts for many centuries, and has been extensively and carefully studied by scholars from every nation — archeology has essentially provided a sufficient quantity of evidence within specific categories to allow compilation of statistics or identification of clear patterns of development.

Tombs and Treasures

During the past thirty years, more than twenty thousand Qin and Han tombs have been identified. Although excavations have not been undertaken at all of these tombs — many, indeed, remain unexplored — the extensive endeavors that have taken place, along with evidence provided by historical texts, have allowed certain broad categories to be defined.[44]

After the demise of the Western Han, precise regulations for burial rites were established and these regulations are presented in Ban Gu's *Han Shu* as a dialogue concerning suitable accoutrements for tombs. In other words, burials were no longer pure formalities but important social obligations governed by ceremonial rituals that underwent significant changes during the two thousand years of Imperial rule.

Under the Han, whose tombs were carefully planned, the wooden burial chamber that had predominated during the Warring States Period was replaced by a subterranean structure consisting of engraved and carved stones or even specially designed and reinforced bricks.

Large hollow bricks were appropriate for erecting an essentially rectangular tomb which often resembled a house with a double-pitched roof. Long bricks (160 × 120 × 32 centimeters) were used to build the floor and to provide walls and partitions within the tomb while triangular bricks marked the front portion. In some instances long narrow bricks covering the tomb like a roof were carefully designed according to their intended positions and were numbered at a workshop so that they could be properly arranged after being hauled to the burial site. Under the Eastern Han rulers, however, small solid bricks that could be handled with greater ease gradually replaced large, fragile and cumbersome hollow ones. This new variety of brickwork was coated with a surface layer of fine clay which lent itself to decorative painting. In this way it has been possible to obtain the only remaining evidence of the previously unsuspected development of painting at the beginning of the empire, as a direct continuation of specimens now attributed to the Qin dynasty. Whereas examples of Han painting once consisted solely of a few painted bricks displayed at the Freer Gallery in

76
Five musicians leading a procession. Terra cotta. Western Han Period (circa
179 B.C.–141 B.C.). Discovered at Yangjiawan Xianyang (Shaanxi) in
1965. Height: 48 to 48.5 cm. Xianyang, Municipal Museum.
These musicians marched at the front of a formidable detachment of terra
cotta soldiers, consisting of more than 2,000 men. Their instruments, which
were undoubtedly made of wood, have disappeared but they are still leading
foot-soldiers and horsemen in accordance with the order of battle for armies
during Antiquity.
Cf. *Wenwu*, 1966, 3; 1977,10.

77
Detachment in battle formation. Painted terra cotta. Western Han Period (*c.* 179
B.C.–141 B.C.). Discovered at Yangjiawan, Xianyang (Shaanxi), in 1965.
Height: 48 to 70 cm. Xianyang, Municipal Museum.
A petty officer is at the head of the procession to set the cadence. Immediate-
ly behind him there is a row of five musicians, and ten soldiers wearing in-
completely depicted cuirasses and undoubtedly carrying lances which
ultimately disappeared. They are followed by eight horsemen.
Cf. *Wenwu*, 1966, 3; 1977, 10.

Washington (D.C.) or at the Nezu Museum in Tokyo, the
number of examples is now sufficient to permit research and
comparative analysis in relation to general trends in Chinese
painting.

From the famous Mawangdui banner or two paintings on silk
that were discovered at Zidanku near Changsha, in 1973, to the
banquets and feasts portrayed upon the walls of Mixian in
Henan Province, human figures from the Western and Eastern
Han realms were drawn with deft, calligraphic, and rapid
brushstrokes, conveying a playful and often caricatural quality.

Drawn upon a rectangle of yellowish silk (28 × 37.5 centimeters) with lively brushstrokes, the man from Zidanku is
carried heavenward by a vigorously portrayed dragon, thereby
representing a theme that was frequently evoked by poets such

78

Cavalryman. Painted terra cotta. Western Han Period (*c.* 179 B.C.-141 B.C.). Discovered at Yangjiawan, Xianyang (Shaanxi) in 1965. Height: 70 cm. Xianyang, Municipal Museum.

The cavalryman is restraining his horse which is ready to dash forward. Like all of the animals discovered at Yangjiawan, this horse is characterized by a vigor which the peaceful steeds of the First Emperor's retinue do not display. Does this difference merely represent variations in style, or, as H. Brinker and R. Goepper (*Kunstschatze aus China*, p. 149) have suggested, does it represent a new breed which was descended from Bactrian horses and was significantly different from the ponies of ancient China?
Cf. *Wenwu*, 1966, 3; 1977, 10.

79

Measuring pot (zhong) in the form of a wine jug. Bronze inlaid with gold and silver. Western Han Period (second century B.C.). Discovered in the tomb of Liu Sheng at Mancheng (Hebei) in 1968. Height: 59 cm.

This bronze measuring vessel, which possesses the same shape as a *hu* wine jug with a lid, is adorned with clouds formed by gold scrollwork. Beneath the base, there is an inscription consisting of eighteen characters arranged in five rows. The inscription indicates that this vessel originally belonged to a ruler of the Kingdom of Chu.
Cf. *Kaogu*, 1972, I, pp. 10-11; pl. 5, no. 2.

80
Ram lamp. Bronze. Western Han Period (2nd century B.C.). Discovered
in the tomb of Liu Sheng at Mancheng (Hebei) in 1968. Height: 18.5 cm.
Length: 23 cm.
The lid was lowered over the ram's head so that it would rest upon the horns,
in order to form the lamp bowl.
Cf. *Kaogu*, 1972, 1, p. 12 and pl. 6, no. 4.

as Qu Yuan (340 – 278 B.C.), during the Warring States Period.
This protagonist is wearing a sword with a flat, round pommel
of the type forged in the Kingdom of Yue. His clothing is disar-
rayed in an evocation of the wind and a journey to the land of
the Immortals or into the world of the dead, beyond the sea and
beyond the clouds.

The tomb of Pu Qianyu near Luoyang contains the oldest
polychrome murals to have been discovered within a tomb.
These large stone slabs from the first century B.C. are adorned
with a dragon, tiger, and phoenix at the cardinal points and also
human figures whose elegant clothing is accentuated by purple
hues.

Somewhat later, remarkable bucolic scenes were created at
Pinglu in Shanxi; oxen and farmers are portrayed tilling fields
amid landscape that is evoked in a simple form by curved lines
and stylized foliage of trees. These scenes would truly seem
primitive compared to the splendid compositions of subsequent
periods, but it is equally true that they represent an initial
Chinese perception of landscapes, prior to the extensive presence
of Buddhist influence that was formerly regarded as the source
of natural themes in Chinese painting.

At Wangdu in Hebei Province, there were paintings of
officials, where each figure is accompanied by an inscription
indicating his rank in civilian or military life. The processions

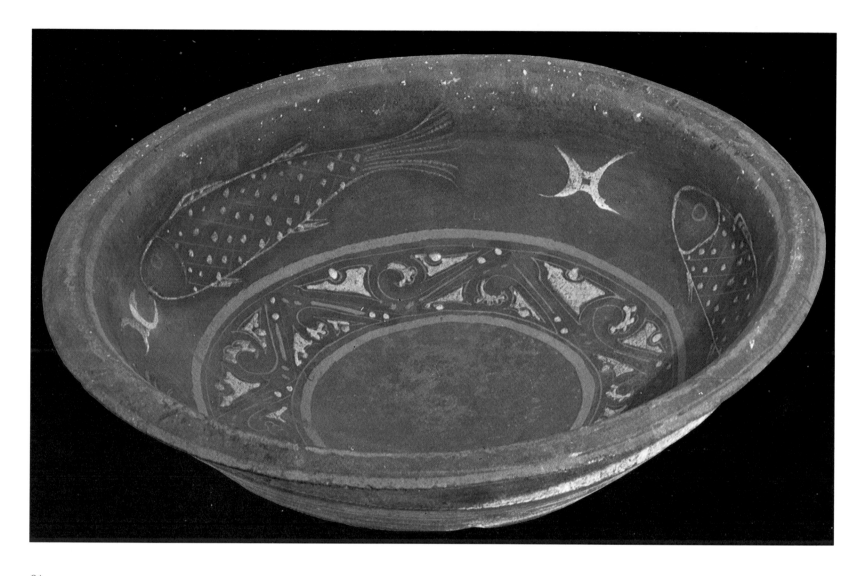

81
Pan basin. Terra cotta painted black, red, and white. Western Han Period (second century B.C.). Discovered in the tomb of Tou Wan at Mancheng (Hebei) in 1968. Height: 14.7 cm. Diameter: 55.5 cm.
The colors and motifs imitate the effects of lacquer, a costly material which was often replaced by other products, even in extremely lavish tombs. There is another piece which was suspended from this one, but aviform ornamentation replaces the fish pattern.

and banquet scenes of Holingol in Mongolia are counterbalanced by the funeral banners discovered at the opposite end of China, at Jinqueshan and Yinqueshan in Shandong Province. Although these silk banners appear to have been painted rapidly and without the exceptional precision displayed by the creators of the Mawangdui banner during the third century B.C., they still reflect the persistence and universality in every part of China of a repertoire whose common source of inspiration transcended local images and styles.

The same universality appears in the design of coffins or *guan,* which always possessed a rectangular shape. Boards were fastened together with tenons and mortises and the coffin was

then sealed with a coating of lime or lacquer. Any conceivable adornment could be added to the basic design. Thus, within Tomb Number 167 at Fenghuangshan (Jiangling, Hubei Province), the sarcophagus — which contained the nearly intact remains of a man embalmed in an antiseptic fluid in 167 B.C. — was covered with a simple layer of cloth and woven bamboo, whereas Tomb Number 1 at Mawangdui contained four sarcophagi placed inside one another. From the outside it was only possible to observe a large chest coated with black lacquer (2.95 × 1.5 × 1.44 meters). In contrast, there was an astounding array of colors inside this chest. One sarcophagus was decorated with golden clouds, animals, birds and mythological figures

82

Jade shroud with silver attachments. Jade and silver. Western Han Period (middle of second century B.C.). Discovered at Tushan, Xuzhou (Jiangsu) in 1970. Length: 170 cm.

It is probable that this jade shroud was intended for the remains of a relative of the ruler of Peng. It had 2,600 jade wafers sewn together with silver thread (800 grams). Its beauty and its state of preservation render it comparable to the jade shrouds of Mancheng (Discovered in 1968. cf. Illustration 83), or to those of the ruler of Zhongshan and his wife (discovered in 1978). The other shrouds contained gold attachments, however, because they were intended for members of the imperial clan. This shroud represents a different situation because silver was consistently used to attach the jade wafers.

83

Jade shroud with gold attachments. Jade and gold. Western Han Period (second century B.C.). Discovered in the tomb of Touwan at Mancheng (Hebei) in 1968. Length: 172 cm.

Along with the shroud of Liu Sheng, the husband of the princess buried in this shroud, this specimen, consisting of 2,156 jade wafers sewn together with gold threads (703 grams), is the first fully preserved jade shroud to have been discovered. When the tomb was opened, however, the jade garment was lying perfectly flat, because the body which had turned to dust had decayed in spite of the protective properties which the Chinese traditionally attributed to jade. Unlike the prince's shroud, his wife's shroud in the upper portion resembles a jacket where the jade wafers are wrapped with gold threads. It is appropriate to observe the *pi* disc which was used as a fastening point for wafers placed around the head of the princess, which rested upon a bronze pillow.

Cf. *Wenwu*, 1971, 1, pl. 2; *Kaogu*, 1972, 1, p. 15 and pl. 3, no. 2; *Kaogu*, 1972, 2, pp. 39–47.

84–85
Sarcophagus. Painted black lacquer. Western Han Period (second century B.C.). Discovered in Tomb Number 1 at Mawangdui, Changsha (Hunan) in 1972. Hunan Provincial Museum.
This sarcophagus contained the remains of the Marchioness of Dai, whose body was so well preserved 2,000 years after her burial that it was possible to determine the causes of her death. The sarcophagus contained two in-

ner coffins with one placed around the other. One coffin had a red lacquer bottom and the other was adorned with brocade attached to the sides. The outer sarcophagus contained painted decorative motifs: flying animals and winged divinities appear amid the spiralling clouds, creating the impression of creatures which are leaping as they travel from one location to another on the rushing winds.
Cf. *Kaogu*, 1973, 4, pp. 247–254 and pl. 4–5.

upon a black background. Another contained dragons, tigers, phoenixes, stags, and stylized gnomes upon a red background, while the innermost coffin was coated with satin embroidery enhanced by a decorative feather design.

Nevertheless, in comparison with the models adopted by the wealthy and by government officials, there were many variations attributable to regional or social factors. In the Luoyang region, for example, commoners often buried the dead between two large semicylindrical pieces of tile so as to create a tubular tomb. Bronze coffins were used in Yunnan (at Xiangyun), and stone coffins were used in Sichuan (at Wanghui).

Even emperors varied their burial arrangements from one reign to another. Thus, the splendor of the tombs of Qin Shi Huangdi or of the Han Emperor Wu (141 – 81 B.C.) differs significantly from the simplicity of Baling, the gravesite of Emperor Wen (179 – 157 B.C.), who was famous for his frugality. Historical texts indicated that no precious metals were placed within his tomb and that a tumulus was not erected, making it impossible to identify the gravesite with complete certainty. Perhaps Emperor Wen was buried at Renjiapo on the eastern periphery of Xi'an.

Certain regions, such as Shandong or Sichuan, acquired long-lasting reputations for the quality of their mortuary carvings. For example, there are the famous terra cotta bas-reliefs of Sichuan, the engraved slabs of Wuliangxi, and the tombs of the Guo family in Shandong which Edouard Chavannes studied at the beginning of this century. Recent excavations have uncovered an abundance of comparable monuments in various regions. In particular, it is appropriate to cite Xuzhou in Jiangsu Province, where there is an abundance of Han tombs with stone sculptures.

One example is the tomb of Baiji, discovered twenty kilometers northeast of Xuzhou in 1965. The narrative content of the bas-reliefs adorning its walls can be divided into two principal series of themes. One series is inspired by life on earth with traditional images of banquets, music, dancing and the arrival of processions and chariots. The other series illustrates a legendary cycle that originated during or after the reign of the Eastern Han Emperor Shun (126 – 145 A.D.). The motifs, which were hollow-engraved with polished surfaces upon a striated background, appear to float and palpitate gently upon the surface of the stone in a manner that was unique to the Eastern Han. They provide certain interesting details concerning the titles and the position of the deceased man, and offer an illustration of how the burial rules set forth in the *Treatise on Chariots and Apparel* (*Yufuzhi*) in the *Hou Han Shu* were interpreted. Indeed, this text indicates the proper number of stones to be used in erecting a tomb and provides strict rules concerning the number of chariots to be portrayed within bas-reliefs. Officials from the intermediate level were entitled to less than four hundred stones arranged in a precisely defined pattern. The anteroom of the tomb was decorated with welcoming motifs. In turn, the *mingtang,* as the burial vault was called in that era, or the *qianwansui shi,* "the ten million year room" or "the room for

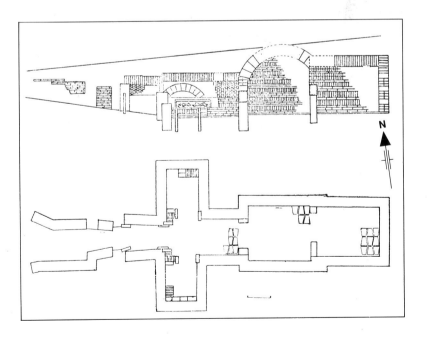

Fig. 17.   A Han tomb with engraved slabs from Xuzhou: diagram and cross-section. Reproduced from *Wenwu*, 1980, 2, p.44.

eternity," was adorned with banquet scenes expressing the joyful atmosphere that naturally reigned on these occasions. The two wings contained images of fully armed bodyguards and soldiers while the rear wall was decorated with two phoenixes presumably symbolizing the love uniting man and wife.

Carving of stone slabs was performed in several stages. Initially, stones had to be cut according to their positions within a tomb and then polished. In the second stage the designs were lightly traced in ink or soot, with or without use of rough models. Subsequently, the basic design was obtained by lightly carving the background portions. At times, a brown or vermilion coating was applied to the background and traces of these hues are still visible in certain parts. Apart from the bricks and bas-reliefs used in Sichuan, all of the ornamental work for Han tombs appears to have been encompassed by three techniques selected according to types of surfaces: painted decoration, carved or engraved decoration, and a combination of painting and engraving. The three methods are linked by the fact that each was more closely associated with drawing than with sculpture. In a general sense sculpture appears to have been curiously absent from the official Chinese repertoire and its use seems to have been confined to the burial rites. The splendor and striking individuality of items discovered during the past fifteen years, such as the spectacular jade shrouds, should not mislead anyone; all of these creations actually originated outside the context of art and belong solely to the ritual domain.

The jade shrouds, fitted around the remains of members of the Imperial family or certain aristocrats during the Han Period, are frequently mentioned in ancient texts.[45] Nevertheless, a fully preserved specimen of one of these burial garments was not discovered until 1968 at Mancheng.

It is undoubtedly necessary to conclude that the jade shrouds were derived from materials used for wrapping the dead during the reign of the Eastern Zhou when jade wafers were sewn into these fabrics. These early precursors of the jade shroud were suggested by the discovery of several pieces of jade from the end of the Spring and Autumn Period at Zhongzoulu in Henan Province in 1954 and 1955. The jade wafers corresponding to various portions of a human face contained small holes which permitted them to be fitted together or to be more conveniently sewn onto a piece of fabric intended for use as a shroud.

It is also possible to assume that the jade shrouds originated as a particularly lavish transposition or an enhanced version of the pieces of cloth that were customarily used for wrapping various portions of the corpse. Because pieces of jade were often

86-87
Coffin. Painted vermilion lacquer. Western Han Period (second century B.C.). Discovered in 1972 in Tomb Number 1 at Mawangdui, Changsha (Hunan). Length: 180 cm. Changsha, Hunan Provincial Museum.
This coffin adorned with painted vermilion lacquer was placed inside the black lacquer sarcophagus (Cf. Illustrations 84–85) and it contained another coffin with brocade decoration attached to the sides.
Cf. *Wenwu*, 1972, 9.

88
Ding vessel with painted decoration. Painted pottery. Western Han Period (second century B.C.). Discovered in Tomb Number 1 at Mawangdui, Changsha (Hunan) in 1972. Height: 18 cm. Diameter: 21 cm. Changsha, Hunan Provincial Museum.
This vessel is a *ding*, or a pot used for heating food. It is actually a painted ceramic imitation of traditional bronze models. The decoration seems to have been painted on hastily, as often occurred in the instance of mortuary pieces.
Cf. *Wenwu*, 1972, 9.

placed directly upon the corpse in order to seal the mouth, eyes and all of its orifices, or upon its burial garments, it is probable that the jade shroud is attributable to a combination of these two customs. Nevertheless, the stages of development remain obscure and, on the basis of discoveries thus far, the Mancheng shrouds (113 B.C.) continue to be the earliest fully preserved specimens.

It seems that the use of jade shrouds was generally a rarity, a circumstance that is hardly surprising. Only twenty-two have been discovered thus far: eleven from the Western Han domains and eleven from the Eastern Han. None of these shrouds predates Emperor Wen. Perhaps it should be concluded that no

89

Pan platter. Lacquer. Western Han Period (second century B.C.). Discovered in Tomb Number 1 at Mawangdui, Changsha (Hunan) in 1972. Height: 2.9 cm. Diameter: 18.4 cm. Changsha, Hunan Provincial Museum.

After the Warring States Period, lacquer was used for all "dishes" intended for the Court and for the aristocracy. This light and flame-resistant material, which was also pleasing in terms of tactile qualities, was so prized that the "Comments on Salt and Iron" (*Yanjielun*) in the *Hanshu* state that ten bronze goblets were necessary in order to purchase a single decorated lacquer goblet. Tomb Number 1 at Mawangdui contained 180 lacquer items, including thirty-one other *pan* platters comparable to this one. In the center of the platter, there is an inscription consisting of three characters: "*jun xing shi*" — "food for the Prince's enjoyment".
Cf. *Wenwu*, 1972, 9.

other shrouds existed or that the others were destroyed. The *Shi Ji* for the reign of Emperor Wu, as well as the *Huai-nanzi* and the *Lu Shi Chunquiu,* refer to the "jade garment," or the *yuyi*. It appears probable, as ancient texts indicate, that the significant economic expansion that occurred at the beginning of the empire led to a sudden and prolific increase in aristocratic wealth during the reigns of the emperors Wen (179 – 157 B.C.) and Wu (141 – 87 B.C.). For this reason Chinese archeologists are inclined to affirm that jade shrouds had not existed during the Warring States Period and that they are a creation of Imperial China.

Thus, a precise description of the jade shrouds with their gold, silver, or copper threads — depending upon the social rank of the deceased person — only appears at the end of the Han Period in the treatise on rituals in the *Hou Han Shu*. It is not clear whether the rule pertaining to threads was followed during the reign of the Western Han rulers. Among the eleven shrouds from that period, five are fastened together with gold, but only three provided thorough protection for scions of the Imperial family who were related to the rulers of Zhongshan. Although the other two cadavers may have belonged to members of the same family, as the name *Liu* suggests, it is possible that, during the reign of the Western Han sovereigns, all jade shrouds were sewn with gold threads regardless of the rank of the deceased. In fact, the *Han Shu* does not mention any distinctions comparable to those of the *Hou Han Shu* as far as the hierarchical status of different types of thread.

In general terms, the techniques for producing these extraordinary burial garments continue to be a mystery. For example, the wafers comprising the shroud of Princess Dou Wan, wife of Liu Sheng, contain decorative elements that demonstrate that these wafers had previously been used for other purposes. Even the wafers for Liu Sheng's shroud appear to have been cut from other larger pieces. Moreover, if one considers the variety of holes drilled in order to allow insertion of threads into the wafers, it is obvious that thread of the same size was not used for every portion of the shroud. Hence, it is tempting to assume that creation of jade shrouds, which were extremely rare by definition, did not become the source of a specific craft. Instead, this type of work appears to have existed within the framework of the usual activities of jade carvers. According to the *Hou Han Shu*, jade ornaments were created at the *Dongyuanjiang* in the Imperial Court. Indeed, archeologists are still attempting to interpret the *"Zhongshan"* inscription appearing on the rear surfaces of the Dingxian wafers. Does this inscription mean that jade carvers at the Court had saved the wafers for the Prince of Zhongshan's shroud, and that these wafers were subsequently sent to Zhongshan to be fastened together?

Furthermore, how were the shrouds fitted during this final phase of production? How was volume determined? Undoubtedly, the craftsmen began by creating cowls, gloves and footwear similar to items found at Linyi in Shandong Province. Subsequently, it would ostensibly have been easy to produce armlets, leggings, and breastplates — or essentially all of the components of the durable iron armor that had been introduced in Yan (later known as the "Realm of Zhongshan") at the beginning of the third century B.C., as the *Lu Shi Chunqiu* indicates. Naturally, it is possible to compare techniques for assembling iron plates for armor with the method of fitting together jade wafers for the

90 (a) and (b), 91
Figurines with woven clothing. Wood and silk. Western Han Period (second century B.C.). Discovered in Tomb Number 1 at Mawangdui, Changsha (Hunan) in 1972. Height: approximately 50 cm. Changsha, Hunan Provincial Museum.
In addition to its extremely sumptuous furnishings, the tomb contained a set of 162 wooden statuettes. Eighteen relatively large statuettes (approximately 50 cm. high) are dressed in realistic apparel. Items suggesting a banquet, such as a lacquer table and a platter containing food, were found beside them. These figurines undoubtedly represented female singers whose duty was to entertain during their mistress' meals. An embroidered silk cushion situated near the figurines appeared to be intended for her. The statuette wearing a hat is a male.
Cf. *Wenwu*, 1972, 9.

shrouds. An appropriate example is an iron helmet discovered in Tomb Number 44 at Xiadu (Yan). In designing and completing burial headgear or warriors' helmets, artisans arranged small plates around a ball or a tubular bead at the peak. The only difference in design is derived from the fact that burial masks did not contain large openings for the nose and the mouth because there was no need to allow for breathing.

Although the use of jade shrouds was an exception, the Han tombs as a whole are distinguished by the abundance and diversity of their bronze, lacquer, ceramic, and terra cotta mortuary accoutrements. Admirers of Han creations have known this fact for a considerable period of time, but recent finds have provided certain fascinating insights. The most noteworthy find, which has been briefly cited heretofore, was the discovery of Han painting; like the sculpture of that period, it was the continuation of traditions fully developed during the Qin Period, although certain other discoveries have also yielded astonishing and sometimes shocking technical novelties.

One of the curious items that deserves to be cited is a large, jointed wooden figure which is 193 centimeters high. It was discovered in 1978 at Daishu[16] in a tomb laid out in the so-called Chu style. In other words the tomb was compartmentalized, covered with a thick layer (more than 50 centimeters) of ashes and brick to prevent water from entering. A tomb discovered at Yangzhou in Jiangsu Province in 1977 was noteworthy on account of the shards of glass scattered throughout the sarcophagus. Undoubtedly, these were fragments of ornaments that had been set or sewn on the burial garments, and must have fallen when the body was placed in the tomb. Han texts referring to Xi Yu (*Han Xi Yu Zhuan*) allude to glass. And this discovery offers an example that illustrates the dissemination of this new product in China at the dawn of the empire as well as its use in the form of round or rectangular pieces attached to garments. We don't know whether this practice was reserved solely for the dead or it was also widespread among the living.

For the past several months the Yangzhou region has inspired admiration because of the discovery of the tomb of Liu Jin, Prince of Guangling during the era of the Eastern Han. Liu Jin rebelled against the empire and was forced to commit suicide

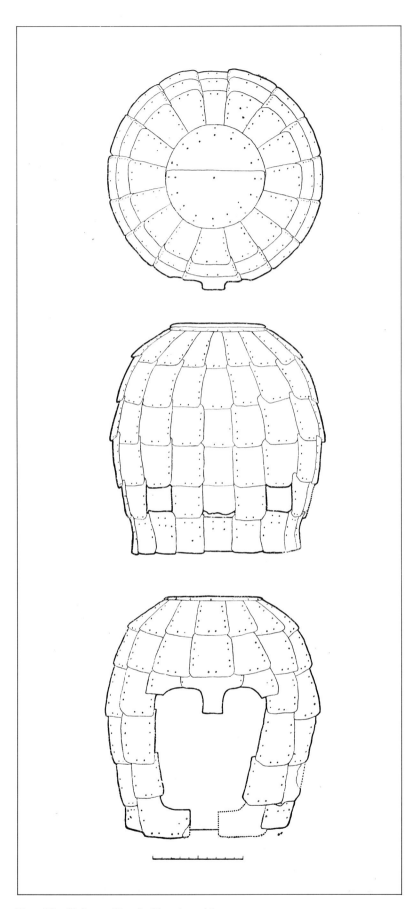

Fig. 18. Helmet Tomb Number 44 at Xiadu. Reproduced from Kaogu, 1975, 4, p. 231.

in 67 A.D. Aside from the usual burial accoutrements, his grave contained a marvelous bronze lamp inlaid with silver. The lantern set upon the back of a bull permitted control of the direction and intensity of its light. At the top, an elegantly decorated pipe trapped the smoke and channeled it toward the animal's body, so as not to pollute the room. Furthermore, the components of the lamp were detachable to allow easy cleaning.

Lastly, another amazing find consists of a small gray pottery vessel from a tomb in Guangzhou (Guangdong Province): this item from the first century A.D. is a model of a ship's rear rudder! Indeed, one of the constants suggested by contemporary discoveries is that an extremely long period of time appears to have elapsed between revolutionary innovations capable of wholly transforming transportation or industry in China and actual widespread application of these technical advances. Thus, the stern rudder only became a common feature in seagoing vessels during the Song Period, sometime around 1000 A.D. Yet it is fascinating to wonder whether this ingenious system was already being used by fishermen and pilots in the Guangdong region (Canton) during the Han Period.

A fuller comprehension of the Han Period can be obtained from painting, from palace construction techniques closely

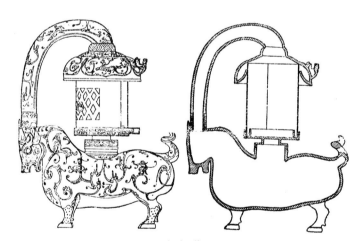

Fig. 19. Bronze lamp in the form of a bull. Discovered in 1980 in Tomb Number 2 at Ganquan (Jiangsu). Han Period. Reproduced from Wenwu, 1981, 11, p. 5.

92
Fang hu vessel. Lacquer. Western Han Period (second century B.C.). Discovered in Tomb Number 1 at Mawangdui, Changsha (Hunan) in 1972. Height: 60 cm. Changsha. Hunan Provincial Museum.
It is difficult to know whether the elegance of the diagonally arranged scrollwork or the astonishing state of preservation of this vessel deserves greater admiration. In the presence of the slightest lack of moisture, lacquer surfaces become wrinkled like dried hides and they subsequently peel and decompose into dust.
Cf. *Wenwu*, 1972, 9.

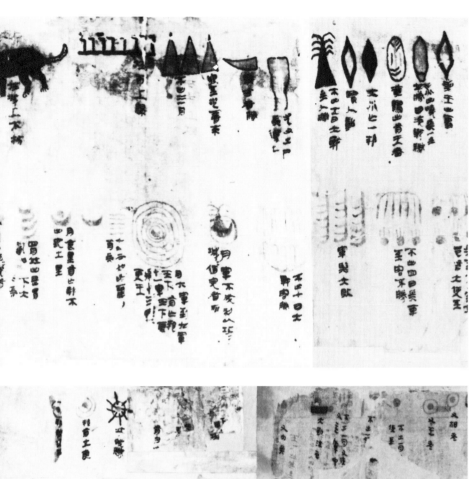

93-94

Predictions concerning five planets, Wuxingzhan *(detail).* Ink on silk. Western Han Period (second century B.C.). Discovered in Tomb No. 3 at Mawangdui, Changsha (Hunan) in 1973. Changsha, Hunan Provincial Museum.

This treatise on the stars and the constellations represents a significant contribution to the history of scientific thought in China. It is the oldest treatise on astronomy to have been discovered thus far. The text indicates the positions of five planets during the first seventy years of the Empire, as well as containing computations concerning their respective revolutions and a description of the principal comets.

95-96

Instructional painting, Daoyintu *(detail).* Ink and colors on silk. Western Han Period (second century B.C.). Discovered in 1973–1974 in Tomb No. 3 at Mawangdui, Changsha (Hunan). Changsha, Hunan Provincial Museum. This didactic painting consists of images explaining the principal steps — approximately forty — in a series of exercises intended to ensure optimum physical well-being. The clothing and appearances of the individuals vary from one illustration to another because the painter undoubtedly wished to depict individuals of different ages and occupations. In general terms, Tomb No. 3 at Mawangdui was abundantly endowed with medical manuscripts.

Cf. *Wenwu,* 1975, 6, pp. 6–13.

resembling those of the Qin Period, which are represented by the ruins of Ganquangong[47] in the Xi'an region (discovered 1978–1979), from an innovation in navigation, and from the splendid craftsmanship represented by countless creations discovered in Han tombs. The discovery of texts that had previously been lost or ignored is more recent and perhaps even more astounding. Along with technical innovations, these texts permit greater understanding of the general level of knowledge under a dynasty that oversaw establishment of the first Chinese university during the reign of the Emperor Wu (124 B.C.).

The quest for written evidence, like the search for artifacts, is continuing on the floors of tombs. For example, there is Dingxian,[48] in Hebei Province at the center of the former kingdom of Zhongshan. At the beginning of the empire, the rulers of Zhongshan and dignitaries from the empire were buried close to the walled town of Dingxian. Chinese archeologists have recently completed their investigations within Tomb Number 40 in this vast complex, after having discovered the entrance to the tomb in 1973.

Despite the harmful effects of the wind, rain and farmers' labors during two millenia, the tomb retained an imposing mound with a diameter of about 90 meters, surrounded by a rectangular wall (145 meters from north to south and 127 meters from east to west). The actual tomb included a southward-facing corridor that led to a slightly larger compartment—an antechamber—and then to a square burial vault. The length of the entire tomb was 61 meters.

97

Map of military garrisons, Zhujuntu *(detail).* Ink on silk. Western Han Period (second century B.C.). Discovered during 1973–1974 in Tomb No. 3 at Mawangdui, Changsha (Hunan). Changsha, Hunan Provincial Museum. This map of military garrisons, along with two other documents discovered within the same tomb (map of southern Hunan and a map of a town), represents the oldest specimen of Chinese cartography to have been discovered thus far. The inscription *"Xudujun,"* or "Xudu garrison," appears in the upper left portion, inside a geometric motif. A river is depicted at the bottom, and, in the middle, there are palm-leaves which realistically depict a variation in altitudes. Unfortunately, the document had deteriorated considerably.
Cf. *Wenwu,* 1976, I, pp. 24–27, insert, and pl. 1.

98

Chest for cowrie-shells. Bronze. Western Han Period (second century B.C.–first century B.C.). Discovered during 1956–1957 in Tomb No. 13 at Shizhaishan, Jinning, Yunnan. Height: 39.5 cm. Neck diameter: 40 cm. Base diameter: 45.6 cm.
This drum-shaped chest was intended for storing cowrie-shells which were used as a form of currency. It was found in one of the tombs from the Kingdom of Dian which were discovered during 1955–1960. The history of this small kingdom which was established in 334 B.C. by a general from the Kingdom of Chu whose victories in western regions were interrupted by an advance by the Qin army, is recounted in chronicles. The official existence of the Kingdom of Dian was acknowledged in 109 B.C., when the Han emperor Wu (140 B.C.–87 B.C.) gave the ruler of Dian a golden shield (discovered in Tomb No. 6) which bore the inscription "The King of Dian's Shield."
The artistic creations of the Kingdom of Dian are characterized by originality where forms typical of southeastern Asia—the drum, for example—are combined with a style reflecting the preferences and influence of art from the steppes, which is observable in zoomorphic art. The Shizhaishan discoveries have been complemented by discoveries in the twenty-seven tombs at Lijiashan (Yunnan) in 1966. Tomb No. 24 at that location contained an extraordinary set of bronzes depicting a tiger and two bulls, whose form is reminiscent of the water-buffalos being led in an endless procession by the human figures on this chest.
Cf. *Kaogu xuebao,* 1958, 3; *Kaogu,* 1963, 6; *Wenwu,* 1975, 2, pp. 69–81.

99
Detail from chest for cowrie-shells. Ill. 98.

In the left wing of the antechamber, which had formerly been divided into three narrow corridors by a set of frames, there were the remnants of a chariot, a large number of gray potsherds, and a few fragments of black lacquer. The right wing contained far more significant treasures: three chariots and thirteen horses with trappings made of gilded bronze, iron, and even silver in accordance with the requirements of burial regulations.

The smallness of the burial vault did not diminish the hopes inspired by the antechamber. The vault, which measured 11.5 meters from north to south and 11.4 meters from east to west, with a total height of 3.3 meters, had been dug 60 centimeters deeper than the antechamber. The entire vault was covered by a thick carpetlike layer of debris where ashes were mingled with ceramic fragments. This was the resting place for the intricately designed sarcophagus. On the outside, six layers of mulberry bark formed a protective carapace and, within the sarcophagus, two partitions revealed three parallel compartments. The coffin was in the middle compartment and contained five coffins enclosed within one another. The innermost coffin, which contained the body, was made of red lacquer and was surrounded by four coffins of black lacquer. A silk cloth had been placed around the three outermost coffins and the entire set of coffins had been wrapped in red silk.

The tomb's occupant, who was wrapped in a jade shroud with golden threads, lay with his head facing northward and his feet southward. The jade shroud had 2567 wafers. Although the bones had decomposed long before the tomb was discovered, the funerary offerings were still present; mirrors had been placed at the head and feet and were accompanied by headdress clasps, swords, gold "horse's hoof" and "deer's hoof" currency, gold coins, a lantern, and jade and bronze items.

The splendor of the tomb does not permit any doubts concerning the rank of its occupant: he was a ruler of Zhongshan. It is obvious that he died subsequent to the date

100
Chest for cowrie-shells. Bronze. Western Han
Period (second century B.C.–first century
B.C.). Discovered in Tomb No. 10 at
Shizhaishan (Yunnan) during 1956–1957.
Height: 50 cm. 25.3 cm. x 21 cm. Yunnan
Provincial Museum.
This extremely beautiful chest for cowrie-
shells depicts a horseman who appears to
be protecting the four water buffalos which
the two tigers seem ready to attack.
Cf. *Kaogu xuebao,* 1958, 3; *Kaogu,* 1963, 6.

101-102
Ornament in the form of a mirror. Gilded bronze. Western Han Period (second century B.C.–first century B.C.). Discovered in Tomb No. 6 at Shizhaishan (Yunnan) during 1965–1967. Yunnan Provincial Museum.
Ten monkeys are arranged in a playful circle around this ornament in the form of a mirror. At the center a red stone (agate?) constitutes a knob.
Cf. *Kaogu xuebao,* 1958, 3; *Kaogu,* 1963, 6.

103
Aviform lamp. Bronze. Western Han Period (late first century B.C.). Discovered at Hepu (Guangxi) in 1971. Height: 32 cm. Length: 41 cm. The small bowl for the oil rested upon the back of the bird—a phoenix whose large open beak appears to be holding a hood. In this way, the smoke flowed into the body of the lamp and accumulated there without polluting the atmosphere. The neck of the bird is removable in order to allow cleaning. The surface contains finely carved decoration, but it is difficult to recognize it today.
Cf. *Kaogu,* 1972, 5.

mentioned on the bamboo sheets buried with him. In other words, this monarch died after the tenth day of the fourth month of the second year of Wufeng's reign (36 B.C.).

Nevertheless, the many texts on bamboo sheets which the tomb contained are even more interesting than its sumptuous furnishings.[49] These texts provide fascinating information that significantly enriches comprehension of the development of ideas during this period.

The manuscripts met with a truly unfortunate fate, for it appears that they were burned shortly after completion of the tomb. Today, they exist as disordered fragments that cannot be easily arranged in a logical sequence. Nevertheless, the patient endeavors of philologists and paleographers have permitted identification of eight separate groups of texts.

One of these groups consists of texts from Confucius' *Analects* (*Lun Yu*). Indeed, nearly half of the entire work had been transcribed. Although this is not the oldest version of the *Lun*

Yu, it is the longest in spite of the missing portions. It is also the most original version, abounding with expressions that often differ from those used in previously discovered versions. Accounting for these variants and determining which forms most fully represent tradition from one find to another, archeological discoveries challenge ephemeral certainties on the history of ancient texts.

Dingxian has prolifically contributed new evidence. One text entitled the *Rujiazhiyan* presents distinctly Confucian ideas— sincerity (*zhong*), filial piety (*xiao*), reverence (*li*), and trust (*xin*)—but an archaic outlook predating the attitudes of the Eastern Han is prevalent. There is even contemplation of human nature (*ren*) or virtue (*de*), which are said to have been fundamental preoccupations during the times of Da Yi, the first Shang ruler, and Wen, the first Zhou ruler. This curious combination which perfectly represents the scholars' cherished dream of a Golden Age would appear to be questionable, except for the

irrefutable fact of discovery of the tomb. It therefore becomes necessary to mistrust certainties even when they are derived from ostensibly sound premises. The manuscript demonstrates the astonishing continuity of Chinese thought during periods when China was nevertheless being transformed under the influence of significant political and economic changes.

Other texts confirm this impression, although the links between them are not always obvious. Examples include: the *Tai-gong,* whose thirteen sections refer to rules of good government, rituals, and prohibited activities; and the *Wenzi,* which is cited within the bibliographical treatise (*Yi wenzhi*) in the *Han Shu.* The *Wenzi* contains maxims attributed to Laozi, Confucius, and King Ping of the Zhou dynasty. In the form of a dialogue, it also provides a treatise concerning "human nature" (*ren*), fairness (*yi*), diligence, worthiness (*gong*), virtue (*de*), and the path to heaven (*tiandao*).

Another unusual text discovered at Dingxian is the *Liu'an-wangzhao Wufeng ernian zhengyue qiju ji* (*Account of King Liu'an's Voyage during the First Month of the Second Year of Wufeng*), which is attributed to the Han emperor Xuan (73 – 48 B.C.). This fragment, which is unique in relation to both its era and to current knowledge, describes the experiences of a monarch from an outlying region during his visit to Chang'an, the Han capital. The anonymous author carefully recorded everything that the royal visitor observed, as well as the names of localities along his route. This text is a priceless revelation of the life of the aristocracy during the Western Han.

The abundance of manuscripts is not limited to Dingxian. One of the major objectives of current excavations pertaining to the Han Period is to establish a collection of manuscripts that will significantly enrich our vision of literature and science at the dawn of the empire.

The tombs at Mawangdui near Changsha were widely publicized and the press offered extensive reports concerning the tombs' occupants and its burial accoutrements. In 1972, it was possible to disinter the remains of a woman (Tomb Number 1) in a perfect state of preservation, because of the reddish embalming fluid in her coffin and the depth of the hermetically sealed tomb. Less emphasis was granted to the extremely important manuscripts stored in her husband's tomb (Tomb Number 2), discovered in 1973, or in her son's tomb (Tomb Number 3), discovered in 1974. These manuscripts consisted of texts transcribed on high-quality raw silk in long and narrow scrolls (48 centimeters or 24 centimeters wide). One unusual aspect is that even though a few "volumes" had been placed upon

bamboo or wooden rollers, most of the manuscripts had been folded and stored in rectangular lacquer boxes.

Thus, Tomb Number 3 at Mawangdui contained the oldest version of the *Laozi*[50] to have ever been discovered. The manuscript was prepared at the beginning of the second century B.C., and was buried with the remains of a young man who was the son of Li Cang, Marquis of Dai, who was an important official at Changsha (who died in 186 B.C.). The occupant of the tomb had died in 168 B.C. and, for this reason, it is possible

104
Lamp-bearer. Bronze. Western Han Period (second century B.C.–first century B.C.). Discovered in Tomb No. 13 at Shizhaishan (Yunnan) during 1956–1957. Height: 56.5 cm. Yunnan Provincial Museum.
This kneeling human figure must have held the base of a lamp in his hands. It should be noted that he is wearing a mirror-like waist ornament.

to establish an approximate final date for preparation of this copy of the *Laozi*. The manuscript consists of two sections which do not appear to have been transcribed at the same time. According to whether or not the taboo concerning the name of Liu Bang (Han Gaozu, founder of the Han dynasty: 206 – 194 B.C.) is respected, it is possible to conclude that one section was transcribed before 206 B.C. and that the other was transcribed somewhat later during the reign of Liu Bang. This conclusion is supported by paleography because one section is written in "privy seal" (*xiaozhuan*) calligraphy and the other in the official Imperial script (*lishu*).

The text itself is divisible into two sections: one pertains to the *Dao* (the Way) and the other to *De* (Virtue). The fact that the latter section appears first suggests the greater importance attributed to the political and social content of the text than to its metaphysical content (*dao*). This particular order is consistent with the structure of the chapter within the *Han Feizi* entitled "Commentary upon the Laozi" (*Jie Lao pian*). Some scholars regard this as evidence of the earliness of the Mawangdui version discovered in the tomb, because pragmatic concerns and a sense of the practical worth of ideas received far greater emphasis than metaphysics during the Warring States Period. It appears that the order was not reversed until later and perhaps not until the era of the Eastern Han when philosophers were seeking new

105

Zhuo halberd. Bronze. Western Han Period (second century B.C.–first century B.C.). Discovered at Shizhaishan (Yunnan) during 1956–1957. Total length: 26.5 cm. Length of animal figure: 3.2 cm. Yunnan Provincial Museum.
This halberd with a long pike, which was mounted within a socket, is typical of weapons from this region. As always in Yunnan, the bovine appearing here is a water buffalo.
Cf. *Kaogu xuebao*, 1958, 3.

ideas by giving spiritual meaning to ancient precepts. At this juncture, philologists must complete the task of comparing these ·texts with those of Wang Bi (226 – 249 A.D.), which have been regarded as the cornerstone of the Taoist tradition for 1,700 years. The fact that the Mawangdui version is more ancient does not necessarily mean that it is more faithful. Two traditions may have coexisted throughout antiquity, whereby it would not be possible to decide arbitrarily that one is more authoritative than the other.

The same tomb contained other equally fascinating manuscripts. There were medical manuals accompanied by a chart portraying gymnastic poses and by a volume containing 52 formulas (another codex of this type, written on thin wooden tablets, was discovered at Wuwei in Gansu Province in an Eastern Han tomb). There were also illustrations of comets and clouds, accompanied by notes indicating how celestial phenomena were interpreted during this period. Indeed, these phenomena were perceived as omens or divine responses to men's questions and were used for divination. Lastly, the tomb contained three maps: a topographical map of the southern portion of the Changsha region where mountain chains are represented by level curves; a military map; and a map indicating walled cities. Thus, Chinese cartography was thought to have started at the end of the Eastern Han dynasty, but must be placed five hundred years earlier. Archeologists have been especially intrigued by the military map, whose title in large characters is "The Map of Billeted Armies" (*Zhujuntu*).[51] This map is a silk rectangle, 98 centimeters long and 78 centimeters wide; three colors — red, black, and green — were used. It shows the southern portion of the Changsha region (*guo*) as well as the northern boundaries of regions located further to the south which had not yet been fully incorporated into the empire. An orthogonal projection had been adopted, and the surface of the map was evenly divided into squares. Military encampments are indicated for each of the zones demarcated in this manner, whereas the middle portion of the map contains an image of a triangular walled city filled with armed soldiers.

The origin of this priceless military document is unknown. From the beginning of the empire, between the third century B.C. and the second century B.C., or from Qin Shi Huangdi to Han Wendi, there were only two campaigns in this region. Both took place during the reign of the Empress Lu (Gaohou, 187 – 179 B.C.), in response to expansion of the kingdom of Nan-Yue. These campaigns are described in the chapter of the *Shi Ji* on Nan-Yue (*Nan-Yue liezhuan*), where it is indicated that

106

Ornamental plaque. Bronze. Western Han Period (second century B.C.–first century B.C.). Discovered in Tomb No. 10 at Shizhaishan (Yunnan) during 1956–1957. Height: 9.7 cm. Length: 15.6 cm. Yunnan Provincial Museum.
This plaque, whose robust composition evokes the vigor of full-relief carving, is a magnificent example of a theme which frequently appears in zoomorphic art from the steppes during the first millenium before Christ: namely a struggle between beasts, or, even more frequently, a peaceful domestic animal being attacked by predators or serpents. The Kingdom of Dian produced other comparable pieces, such as this boar being attacked by two tigers, which was exhibited in Paris and in London in 1973.
Cf. *Kaogu xuebao,* 1958, 3.

the Kingdom of Changsha was severely defeated by that of Nan-Yue. Nevertheless, the Kingdom of Nan-Yue was unable to take advantage of its victory and its troops, loaded with spoils, promptly withdrew. The second attack took place at the end of the reign of Empress Lu and southern China was not truly pacified until the reign of Emperor Wen. Thus, the map corresponds to this phase in expansion of the empire.

The wording of the title, as well as the terminology used in captions for the map, provides a precise indication of the nature of the forces stationed in the area because the term "army," or *jun,* is used. During the Han Period this term referred to a unit of about 5,000 men. Thus, the map shows an expeditionary force of at least 20,000 men. On the other hand since the population of the Changsha region did not exceed 25,000 households during this era, it appears improbable for such a large army to have been mobilized locally. It is more likely that Imperial troops were sent to reinforce the lord of Changsha who represented Imperial authority in his conflict with the unruly southern inhabitants. Thus, at a later point, the priceless secret map of the encampments of the Imperial forces was buried with the dignitary whom the central government had sought to assist.

There were other treasures buried within the famous Tomb Number 3 at Mawangdui. Other manuscripts on silk included: a *Treatise on Horses* (*Xiang ma jing*), treatises on astronomy, a *Treatise on the Planets* (*Xingjing*) written by Gan De and Shi Shen, who were astronomers during the Warring States Period, and a series of *Predictions concerning the Five Planets* (*Wu xing zhan*). There were also some fragments of the *Yi Jing,* as well as a copy of the *Compilation on the Warring States* (*Zhanguoche*), which was used by Si Ma Qian to compose the history of the principalities appearing in the *Shi Ji.* Thus, a single site has contributed a broad panorama of Chinese literature in the form in which it existed during the earliest phase of the empire.

Nevertheless, this treasure was not unique. A comparable collection of texts was discovered in 1972 at the site called Yinqueshan at Linyi (Shandong Province), in two tombs from the beginning of the Han dynasty. This same site is also famous in the history of Chinese art because one of the tombs contained a banner comparable to that of Mawangdui although it was of an inferior quality.[32]

The manuscripts on bamboo sheets that were stored at Yinqeshan included two interesting historical texts: the *Springs and Autumns of Yanzi* (*Yanzi chunqiu*) in Tomb Number 1, and an almanac entitled *The Calendar of the First Year of the Yuangnang Era of the Han* (*Han Yuanguang yuannian lipu*) in Tomb Number 2.

These manuscripts also included a copy of the works of Mo Zi (Tomb Number 1) and certain texts that had long been considered to be apocryphal or to have been composed much later than the beginning of the empire, such as the works of Guanzi or Wei Liaozi. Today, however, Chinese archeologists attribute the greatest importance to the treatises on military science and strategy that were found at this site: the *Six Tactics* (*Liu tao*), *Master Sun's Art of Warfare* (*Sunzi bingfa*), and *Sun Bin's Art of Warfare* (*Sun Bin bingfa*). These treatises had disappeared at a very early point, undoubtedly as many as two thousand years ago, and scholars had wondered whether Si Ma Qian's references to these works were erroneous, with one text having been attributed to two different authors. Other scholars have adopted the hypothesis that the *Sun Bin bingfa*, mentioned in ancient bibliographies, truly represented the experience of military leaders who, from the end of the Spring and Autumn Period until the end of the Warring States Period, on repeated occasions had to contend with constantly reinvigorated adver-

107
Hu flask with handle. Bronze. Western Han Period (Second half of first century B.C.). Discovered in 1971 at Hepu (Haopi) in Guangxi Province. Height: 43 cm. Neck diameter: 12.4 cm. Waist diameter: 18.4 cm.
Hu flasks were intended for beverages. A handle in the form of a pair of dragon heads from which two small chains extend to the waist is situated above the lid. The finely incised petal motif which covers the lid, the neck, and the base of this vessel is typical of the Late Western Han Period. Some collections, such as the Musée Cernuschi's collection, contain similar specimens discovered during excavations in Tonkin between 1935 and 1936.
Cf. *Kaogu,* 1972, 5.

saries. Nevertheless, the same scholars refrained from giving opinions on the *Sunzi bingfa* and even tended to doubt the existence of Master Sun.

108
Gui bowl with handle. Bronze. Western Han Period. (Second half of first century B.C.). Discovered in 1971 at Hepu (Guangxi). Height: 10.6 cm. Diameter: 24.2 cm.
This vessel is a *gui* which was used to store food although the dragon's head handle endows it with the appearance of a cooking pan. Like all of the bronzes found in this tomb, it also contains the finely engraved ornamentation which is characteristic of this period and of specimens found not only in Hunan (Changsha) but in Tonkin (Thanh-hoa).
Cf. *Kaogu,* 1972, 5.

109
Wine flagon. Gilded bronze. Western Han Period (26 B.C.). Discovered in 1962 at Dachuancun, Youyu (Shanxi). Height: 24.5 cm. Diameter: 23.4 cm.
The ornamentation includes two rows of wild animals situated amid a mountainous landscape. The inscription upon this bronze reads: "24 *jin* flagon for warm wine, completed in the third year of the Heping era (26 B.C.) in Zhongling in the town of Hu (now Youyu)."
Cf. *Wenwu,* 1963, 11, page 5, figs. 4–6 and pls. 1–2.

The recently discovered text of *Sunzi bingfa,* consisting of 2,300 characters, only represents approximately one-third of the version which was compiled and printed during the Sung Period, although it does contain the same thirteen chapters. Furthermore, this text cites some other works by Master Sun that have been lost or whose existence had been entirely forgotten.

Sun Bin's treatise on warfare consists of 11,000 characters, with the text divided into two sections of fifteen chapters apiece. The author scrutinizes the various causes of victory and defeat and places considerable emphasis on the concept of psychological cohesion that should join the soldiers to one another and to their leader. Sun Bin also develops the concept that indissoluble loyalty between soldiers and generals can unfailingly lead armies to victory. This same theme had previously been expressed by philosophers during the Warring States Period, who regarded "the human spirit" that must govern proper relationships as the principal virtue of soldiers. In this sense and in spite of the violence of an especially turbulent history, Chinese civilization appears to have always retained an official fealty to a model of society based upon the preeminence of the individual civilian. The fabulous discovery that the Yinqueshan manuscripts represent will be able to inspire research and discussion in this domain for many years. Thus far, Chinese historians have affirmed that these manuscripts, to a certain extent, reflect the rise of the land-owning classes. Even more than artifacts, the texts inspire not only conflicting ideas, but a collision among current ideologies.

110

Miniature house. Bronze. Han Period (206 B.C. — 220 A.D.). Discovered in a large tomb with a vault (Tomb Number 1) at Wuzhou (Guangxi) during 1975–1976. Height: 33.3 cm. Length: 40 cm. Width: 31.4 cm. Height of legs: 12 cm. Wuzhou, Municipal Museum.

This miniature house is noteworthy for its elegance and quality of workmanship. This is a building mounted upon pilings, which is a type often found in damp regions, such as southern China. The miniature house may have been used as a larder but at the time of its discovery its contents had decomposed to such an extent that it was impossible to determine their composition. All of the items found at this site in Wuzhou were of excellent quality and they confirm the strong bonds existing between southern regions and the civilization of the Great Plain. A comparable house without pilings had already been discovered in 1971 at Hepu, in the same province.

Cf. *Kaogu*, 1972, 5.

Cf. *Wenwu*, 1977, 2, page 71 and pl. 3, no. 3.

111

Liubo players. Glazed terra cotta. Eastern Han Period (middle of second century A.D.). Discovered at Lingbao (Henan) in 1972. Height: 24.2 cm. Length: 19.2 cm.

The game of *liubo*, a form of backgammon, had already existed in China since the Warring States Period. According to the *Zhanguoci* it originated in the Kingdom of Chu. During the Han Period, similar figures often appear in the bas-reliefs adorning tombs and on so-called "TLV pattern" mirrors. Full-relief versions, such as this one, are less common. Despite many literary references, the rules for the game of *liubo* remain largely unknown. To date, it is only known that the players used six sticks, along with dice and twelve small dominoes which constituted markers, as is shown in the rear portion of the board. (With respect to the rules for this game, consult the *Harvard Journal of Asiatic Studies*, Vol. 9, 1945, pp. 202–206 and Vol. 15, 1952, pp. 124–139.)

112

He pouring pot. Bronze. Eastern Han Period (middle of second century B.C.). Discovered at Tushan, Xuzhou (Jiangsu) in 1970. Height: 14 cm. Neck diameter: 7.3 cm. Waist diameter: 12.7 cm. Base diameter: 7.7 cm. This pouring pot was used for serving fermented beverages. A canine figure forms the handle while a bird appears to be perching upon the spout. This pot was found in the tomb of an aristocrat, who was wrapped in a jade shroud with silver threads (Cf. Illustration 82).

113–114

Three-story watchtower. Glazed terra cotta. Eastern Han Period (middle of second century A.D.). Discovered at Lingbao (Henan), in Tomb Number 3. Height: 130 cm. Length: 44.5 cm. Width: 44.5 cm.

This particular tomb provided an abundance of architectural models such as this watchtower. These items provide a basis for recognizing the elegance of the structures which must have existed in the central plain, which was the heart of ancient China. On each floor, sentinels can be seen keeping watch and it is possible to observe archers in the corners, with buglers and look-outs between them. The corners of the roof contain star-shaped ornaments and the silhouette of a phoenix crowns the entire structure. Cf. *Wenwu,* 1975, 11, p. 76 and pl. 13, no. 2.

115

Palace complex. Mural. Han Period (third century B.C. — third century A.D.). Discovered at Holingol (Inner Mongolia).

This mural which had been seriously damaged reveals the customary austere color scheme of paintings from the Han Period. It is interesting because of the vast architectural complex which it depicts. This was undoubtedly a palace, and the painter, by means of inscriptions, attempted to identify various portions (for example, "doorway to official's quarters"). The painting depicts the activities of officials and servants, while cavalrymen and color-bearers appear in many locations. The artists adhered to the same technical conventions as the creators of painted bricks in Sichuan, for example. It is already possible to observe overhead "birds' eye" views which the artists who created the cave paintings of Dunhuang developed into a complete system of perspective.

The Statue of Li Bing

Lastly, in 1974, the discovery of the stone statue of Li Bing, who was the Prefect of Shu (Sichuan) during the reign of the First Emperor, has simultaneously revealed technological and artistic aspects of the Han civilization.

Li Bing contributed to the development of a vast irrigation system by using water from the River Min. Water was conveyed to the plains of western Sichuan by a cleverly constructed series of diversion canals. Nevertheless, the statue of Li Bing was not erected until much later. An inscription appearing on the sleeves of the stone figure actually reads: "On the twenty-fifth day of the intercalary month of the third moon, during the first year of the Jianning period of Emperor Ling of the Eastern Han dynasty (168 A.D.), Cheng Yi, supervisor of irrigation and protection of rivers and canals, with his assistant Yin Long, erected statues of the three deities to safeguard and preserve the water forever." Another inscription on the front of the robe refers to "the late Prefect of Shu, Li Bing."

The history of the Dujiangyan irrigation system, associated with Li Bing, is significant because it indicates the durability of human endeavors through the centuries and generations. During the Warring States Period the rulers of Shu had already established the initial components of an irrigation system. Nevertheless, a series of major projects was not truly started until after the conquest of Shu by the Qin (277 B.C.) and the establishment of the empire (221 B.C.). In archives and historical texts, it is possible to discover the contours of gigantic embankments dug from the hillsides (terracing perhaps) and to learn that the sides of the canals were protected by a layer of oval stones. For two thousand years the principal components of the dams and diversion channels have remained the same. China's current government takes pride in having restored the creations of the First Emperor's official to their former extensiveness and economic importance.

The allusion to the "three deities" appears even more astonishing. It also occurred in a text from the period of the Eastern Jin (317 – 420 A.D.), but the practical aspect is most fascinating. The statues are said to have been erected at a location where "the water at its lowest level does not reach their feet, and never rises higher than their shoulders when it is at the highest level." Parisians, who admire the "Zouave of the Pont d'Alma," are familiar with this type of measuring arrangement. Today, however, it has not been reliably determined whether the statue of Li Bing at Dujiangyan, not far from the famous

Anlan chain bridge, is truly the one mentioned in the *History of the Eastern Jin* or whether the statue merely represents one of the portrayals of this dignitary who was exceptionally popular and was more or less worshipped by local people whose lives he had helped improve.

The statue, 2.9 meters high and 96 centimeters wide, weighs four tons. It was cut from grayish sandstone, with a hollow portion having been provided at the base in order to accommodate a wooden tenon to secure the statue on its base.

The figure, wearing a robe with broad sleeves and an official headdress, is quite typical of statues from this era: the somewhat

116
Parinirvana (Death of Buddha) scene. Cliff carving. Han Period (206 B.C.–220 A.D.). Kongwangshan cliffs, east of Xuzhou (Jiangsu).
The Kongwangshan cliffs had already been cited in the *Historical Recollections (Shiji, Chronicles of the First Emperor)*. Undoubtedly, this location had been used for religious ceremonies since an extremely remote point in Antiquity: initially for local rituals, and later for Confucian rituals. An unusual aspect, however, is that archeologists have also discovered rock-carvings such as this one where Buddhist themes appear. Buddha is portrayed in a reclining position, surrounded by disciples and worshippers, whose presence is indicated solely by depiction of their faces, in accordance with a conventional procedure among artists during the Han Period.
Cf. *Wenwu*, 1981, 7, pp. 16–19 and pl. 1, no. 2.

flat shape of the body suggests the style of the oldest *mingqi* and the modeled face, with its joyful smile, is reminiscent of the officials, so amusing with their officious gestures and their affable demeanor, as portrayed on the walls of the tomb of Wangdu.

This statue is exceptionally important in many respects, but its greatest significance is to the domain of the history of art. Han sculpture, in fact, continues to be a relatively unfamiliar domain, represented by bas-reliefs or by marvelous molded ceramic creations, but rarely by full-relief creations in stone. This statue, indeed, is a rare example of nonmortuary sculpture.

Discovery of the Most Ancient Buddhist Cliff Carvings in China

Undoubtedly, the number of discoveries of this type will increase. This prospect is at least suggested by the interest recently inspired by a rupestrian complex in northern Jiangsu, namely the Mount Kongwang[53] site, not far from the coastal town and sea resort of Lianyungang. One hundred and ten human figures, carved in low-relief and reflecting rather rudimentary workmanship, appear upon a cliff in a section about eight meters high and seventeen meters wide. Near the same location two large stone animals carved in full-relief, namely an elephant and a toad, appear to be guarding the site. The presence of the toad, which appears so frequently in traditional Chinese iconography, as well as the presence of human figures presenting gifts or dancing, had led to premature classification of these figures within the series of Han bas-reliefs illustrating Confucian themes. Nevertheless, the elephant theme, which is closely associated with Buddhism, has drawn the attention of scholars during recent years. Having studied the forgotten cliff more closely, they discovered incontestably Buddhist figures; there are many seated Buddhas, as well as a reclining Sakyamuni surrounded by his disciples, thereby constituting a *paranirvana* scene.

This new perspective confirms the current belief that Buddhism entered China at an extremely early point, at the time of the Western Han rulers. Nevertheless, it is astounding that a cliff shrine of this type would have existed under the Eastern Han during the first or second century A.D. on the eastern edge of China. This shrine is much earlier than the midfourth century when the earliest grottoes were created at Dunhuang in the western portion of the empire (Traditional date: 366 A.D.). It would seem difficult to deny a geographic and chronological trajectory for the large cliff temples in northern China, from Dunhuang to Longmen, but the problem must be entirely reexamined with respect to southern China. As Paul Pelliot has suggested, images and ideas may have been transmitted more rapidly by sea than by land.

VI. THE THREE KINGDOMS AND SIX DYNASTIES

The Collapse of the Han Empire

At the beginning of the third century A.D. the Han empire collapsed, caught in the turmoil of a moral and economic crisis that would affect Chinese civilization for several centuries. The period known as the "Three Kingdoms Period" (220 – 280 A.D.), the brief reunification of the empire under the Jin (265 – 316 A.D.), and the period of the Northern and Southern Dynasties (*Nanbeichao*, 317 – 589 A.D.), when barbarian ethnic groups and rulers overran northern China and established short-lived kingdoms while six local dynasties successively held power in the south (222 – 589 A.D.), convey an impression of decomposition, weakness, and misfortunes, accentuated by wars whose echoes appear endlessly in the *Dynastic Histories* and folk tales. Nevertheless, these somber years represent one of the most constructive phases of China's history. Today, Chinese historians emphasize two predominant trends emerging at this time; ideas, religions such as Buddhism, and technical knowledge were imported from Central Asia and India, as well as from the Mediterranean World, whereas the culture of the central plains spread more vigorously than ever to outlying regions. Chronicles have primarily emphasized the wars, migrations, and carnage of this period, and at the end of the third century there were allusions to a certain depopulation of China, or at least of regions adjacent to the central basin of the Yangtze River, where the armies of Wei, Wu and Shu were locked in combat. The literature and poetry of this era clearly reflect the malaise of a morally and physically divided nation on the brink of exhaustion. A study of artifacts and techniques reveals another facet: during this same period, the Chinese invented the waterwheel (*jiligu*), gunpowder (*liandan*), and the compass, while cultivation and consumption of tea became widespread. Similarly, sixth century merchants, instead of transporting ready-made silk fabric to Byzantium, introduced for the first time the necessary items for producing silk — eggs from silkworms and mulberry plants.

The Diversity of Archeological Discoveries

Nevertheless, archeological discoveries do not convey a clear impression of this cultural expansion, unless a phenomenon which is likely to intensify with the passage of time ceases to exist beyond our own era; even when abundant archeological evidence is available, it contributes less to discovery of China's past after the establishment of the empire than to understanding of pre-Imperial periods. It may be necessary to conclude that the remarkable contributions of such discoveries are somewhat overshadowed by the weight of historical documents that, for many decades and, indeed for centuries, have influenced us and prepared us for these finds. Although the results of excavations may be indispensable for the history of techniques, they do not dazzle the eye like a jewel gleaming in the dark, as in earlier periods.

Today, Jiayuguan, which was discovered in Gansu Province during 1972 and 1973, is regarded as the most spectacular site from this era. It consists of a complex of eight tombs erected between the third century and the beginning of the fourth century. Six of the tombs were decorated with numerous murals painted on bricks, and there are more than 600 of these creations.

With a style similar to that of Han painting, these works which radiate liveliness and a sense of humor were drawn with deft brushstrokes and any form of retouching would have been impossible. A few bursts of color—especially the reds—within the bold outlines impart the scenes with a feeling of gaiety and vivacity. Certain features, however, distinguish these frescoes from those of the Han. The fluid brushwork, with free use of upstrokes and downstrokes, differs significantly from the regular iron wire strokes of Han artisans. Lastly, it is possible to observe that the trees in a mass of mulberry boughs are portrayed with a fan-like shape of the type found on the walls of the Buddhist grottoes at Dunhuang during the fifth century. Once again the elements of landscape painting appear to have been present within the tombs long before the flowering of Buddhist painting.

117

Vessel in the form of a winged lion. Protoceladon stoneware with green glaze. Western Jin Period (265 A.D.–316 A.D.). Discovered at Danyang (Jiangsu) in 1966. Length: 17.5 cm.
This leonine pouring vessel exemplifies the quality of the wares produced by southern Chinese potters during this period. It is possible to observe that the decoration, which represents a type whose use is of extremely ancient origin, consists of a combination of incised motifs beneath the glaze with a barbotine overlay. This same technique was continued with great success by Tang and Song potters.

118

Warrior. Terra cotta. Northern Wei Period (386–534). Discovered at Huhehot (Inner Mongolia) in 1975. Height: 39 cm. Museum of Inner Mongolia.
In 1975, excavation of a Northern Wei tomb which had been identified and studied in 1955 and in 1961 led to discovery of a collection of thirty-four terra cotta figurines. These figurines have provided evidence which permits fuller comprehension of life in this peripheral region where the peoples of Central Asia exercised a highly significant influence, extending as far as the center of the Great Plain. There are two warrior figurines. Both were created in several sections, with the head and the arms having been added subsequent to completion of the body. It is possible that this smiling soldier's hands held a bow, the typical weapon of hunters and of every inhabitant of the steppes. He may also have been a sorcerer or an exorcist intended to dispel evil spirits.
Cf. *Wenwu*, 1977, 5, p. 39 and pl. 5, no. 2.

119

Pouring pot in the form of a ram. Glazed protoceladon stoneware. Period of the Southern and Northern Dynasties (fourth century). Discovered in Tomb Number 7 at Xiangshan in Nankin (Jiangsu) in 1970. Height: 12.4 cm. Length: 15.5 cm.
This tomb whose occupant was a member of the Imperial family which ruled in Nankin contained an extensive collection of mortuary furnishings consisting of ceramic articles of this type, which were produced at southern Chinese kilns in northern Zhejiang and southern Jiangsu during this particular period. Tomb Number 7 at Xiangshan was the tomb of Emperor Wu of the Eastern Jin Dynasty (317–420), who died in 392.
Cf. *Wenwu*, 1972, 11.

120-121

Seated Maitreya Buddha (front and rear views). Sandstone. Northern Wei Period (471). Discovered at Xingping, Xi'an (Shaanxi). Height: 86.9 cm. Width: 55 cm. Xi'an, Shaanxi Provincial Museum.

This stele depicts Maitreya, the future incarnation of Buddha. The half-closed eyes, full cheeks, and smiling face are characteristic of the Northern Wei style prior to its development into an elongated style which is typical of the Longmen sculptors. On the other hand, the statue's garments reflect the style of the Longmen sculptors. It is possible to recognize the forward positioning of the body and especially the linear appearance of folds which develop into "birds' wings" at the ends. The Buddha's hands express "joy of knowledge" *(dharmacakrapravartanamudra).* His feet are resting upon the hands of a standing deity extending upward from the pedestal. At the base of the halo, animals' legs appear to support this deity. Thus, the pedestal is of the so-called "lion seat" *(shizi zuo)* type. On the rear side of the halo, twenty-five escutcheons arranged in seven rows contain light relief-work depicting various scenes in a true-to-life form, including scenes from Buddha's life. A lengthy inscription appears at the bottom. Although it is unfortunately incomplete, it nevertheless allowed a date to be established for this statue, which was provided as an offering in 471 by a follower of Buddha who desired a peaceful afterlife for the soul of a deceased family member.

122-123
Buddhist stele (front and rear views): Sakyamuni preaching. Stone. Northern Qi Period (550–577). Discovered at Linzhang (Hebei) in 1958. Height: 72.6 cm.
This stele portrays Buddha seated amid six disciples, in a pose indicating absence of fear *(abhayamudra)*. The pedestal contains lions and tutelary kings intended to protect the Jewel of Buddhahood, while flying genies *(apsara)* enhance the arborescent halo, which was carved with open portions (Illustration 122). On the rear side (Illustration 123), holy figures sitting in lotus positions replace the *apsara*.

Thus, certain economic and artistic transformations took place during the Six Dynasties Period. Historians have enthusiastically investigated this intriguing period, marked by a widespread military, economic, spiritual and political crisis, when the various regions of China began to create the essential factors which would merge to form the brilliant Tang civilization. Jacques Gernet has contrasted the specific problems of northern regions—the process of sedentarization of nomadic populations, centralizing trends, and military expansionism—with such uniquely southern problems as the slow and difficult assimilation of aboriginal populations, a massive but gradual influx of various waves of "settlers" fleeing the north, weakness of centralized authority, and the power of aristocratic families. This traditional perspective is accompanied by a long-established belief that southern China was relatively impoverished, unaffected by significant trends in commerce, and that progress in agriculture was somewhat delayed. But, as indicated before, it is appropriate to wonder whether the results of excavations may partially alter this evaluation, thereby restoring to the regions of central China a degree of vitality that is known to have existed before the empire and whose signs are clearly observable during the zenith of Imperial power.

124

Two bodhisattvas. Carved stone wall. Northern Wei Period (386–435). Discovered at Longmen, Luoyang (Henan) in 1978. Height: 160 cm. and 170 cm. *In situ.*
These two bodhisattvas are situated within the middle row, near the central entrance to the Bingyang Cave. The style suggests that they were carved during the reign of the Northern Wei Dynasty. The entire wall had disappeared after modification of the cave during the eighteenth century. Cf. *Wenwu,* 1980, p. 1 and pl. 2, no. 3.

125

Handrail urn. Sandstone with green glaze. Northern Qi Period (550–577). Discovered at Dingxian (Hebei). Height: 70 cm. Beijing, Palace Museum. This urn with a greenish glaze is indicative of the quality of wares from northern China prior to the Tang Period. Apart from the fineness of the clay and the sheen of the glaze, it is possible to admire carved or superimposed elements — in imitation of Sassanid goldsmiths' creations. This type of ornamentation subsequently accounted for the charm of Tang wares.

Nanjing, capital of southern China, is famous for the tombs of the Liang emperors (502 – 557 A.D.), but other traces of the past have also been uncovered, such as the walls built around Nanjing in 221 A.D. and 229 A.D. and the walls of the southern Qi capital (479 –502 A.D.). Through the research of Professor Cheng Te-k'un, it has been known that the Changsha region was undoubtedly the birthplace of celadon wares. Recent discoveries have furnished extensive confirmation. For example, three kilns, discovered in 1975 in the Nanshan region of Jiangsu Province at Dasigongyan, Liushitou and Mapigu, were situated within enclosures measuring 1,500 meters by 400 meters. Outfitted with sophisticated accessories, the kilns operated at temperatures between 1160° C. and 1260° C., thereby representing a noteworthy advance in relation to the decadent techniques of Han potters. To comprehend the importance of this discovery, it should be kept in mind that baking of sandstone, the raw material for celadons, took place at approximately 1100° C. to 1200° C., whereas white porcelain was baked at 1300° C. to 1350° C. In other words, the Nanshan crafstmen had developed the essential means for completing a transition from simple pottery to stoneware.

Development of Glass Production

It is hardly surprising that all of the crafts using fire were affected by similar advances during this period. Glass, for example, initially imported from Hellenistic nations, was first introduced in

126
Pilgrim's flask (bianhu). Yellow-glazed pottery. Northern Qi Period (550–577). Discovered at Honghecun, Anyang (Henan) in 1971, in the tomb (attributed to 575) of Fan Zui, the Governor of Liangzhou. Height: 20.5 cm. This ceramic flask imitates not only the flat shape of comparable leather items, but the *repoussé* ornamentation of Sassanid goldsmiths' creations. The figures consist of a group of foreign performers wherein four musicians provide accompaniment for a female dancer. This pilgrim's flask which predates the Sui Dynasty confirms the ancient origins of the influence of West Asian styles, which affected Tang art to such a significant extent. Cf. *Wenwu,* 1972, 1, p. 49 and pl. 7.

China during the Warring States Period, as the fragments discovered at Jincun near Luoyang, or at Changsha have confirmed. Apart from being prized for its beauty, glass, which was as uncommon in China as jade and served as a substitute for jade,

was considered priceless by the rulers of that era on account of its rarity. Under the Han dynasty, glass was imported from Syria which filled specific orders for the Chinese market. Its use increased rapidly. Indeed, glass was used to produce jewels and inlaid work for belt plates or bronze mirrors. Sometimes it was substituted for jade in the form of small plates that were inserted into the mouths of corpses. Authors even wrote admiring poems to praise this extraordinary substance.

Nevertheless, production of glass in China did not develop until the Six Dynasties Period, through the efforts of men from other lands. At the beginning of the reign of the Northern Wei rulers (386–534 A.D.), a certain Yuezhi established a glassworks at Pingcheng near Datong. The *Wei Shu,* or the *Wei Chronicles,* cited this fact, pointing out that the fascinated Emperor ordered erection of a glass palace that would be large enough to accommodate one hundred persons. This account is undoubtedly exaggerated, but archeology from time to time has yielded interesting specimens. For example, the tomb of the Feng family at Ding in Hebei Province, discovered in 1957, contained two glass bowls. One of these was blue and the other was of a bluish-gray, with a diamond-shaped decorative motif. Even the tale of the glass palace appears to possess some validity; glass was used for windows in Pompei in the first century A.D. Were the Chinese aware of this fact, or were they satisfied with imitating the splendor of glass with tiles and terra cotta decorations covered with a thick lead glaze (*liuli*) which glittered in the sunlight and provided multicolored reflections? In any case, the existence and properties of glass appear to have haunted the imagination during the Six Dynasties Period. Two tales from the sixth century describe it in magical terms. Thus, the *Hanwu Gushi* tells how Han Emperor Wu had built a temple with transparent glass doors to honor the deities. In turn, the *Xijing zaji,* or "Miscellany concerning the Western Capital," describes the extravagance of Han Emperor Cheng (32 B.C.–6 A.D.), who built a bath-house with thick windows of green glass for his consort Zhao Feiyan. Thus, it can be ascertained that glass, a rare and priceless material, which legends associated with the world of ancient sovereigns and princes, was actually introduced on a much broader scale during the Six Dynasties Period, as literary sources suggest and as archeological discoveries have gradually confirmed.

VII. THE SUI AND TANG DYNASTIES

The Sui Dynasty (581–617 A.D.), established at Chang'an by a general who had subjugated the Wei Valley and the eastern portion of Gansu, has been burdened with a poor reputation throughout Chinese history because the next two rulers successfully pursued an intensive public works program. These two sovereigns contributed to the long-term economic prosperity that emerged in China at the beginning of the Tang Period. Even today the Grand Canal built during these times continues to serve as a link between the northern and southern portions of the vast Chinese mainland. Nevertheless, unfavorable memories of the Sui Period persisted because the populace was burdened with forced labor and high taxes, and the authors who compiled the history of the Sui emperors shortly thereafter cleverly exploited these fears while praising the greatness of the Tang.

Grain Silos: A Vestige of Ambitious Projects

On various occasions contemporary excavations have uncovered certain examples of these highly diversified public works projects. In January, 1974, four granaries from the Sui and Tang Periods were discovered in the western portion of the ancient walled city of Luoyang. This fortuitous discovery took place during construction of embankments and was followed by two excavation projects during 1974 and 1975.[54]

The existence of facilities for storing grain can be traced to antiquity; in Neolithic villages, for example, there were silos with pear-shaped trenches and later, public granaries, as described by the historian Si Ma Qian. These granaries were intended to provide food for the inhabitants in the event of shortages or to stabilize grain prices in case of overabundant harvests. In addition, there were granaries for storing grain collected through taxes, which was used to defray the government's expenses and pay civil servants.

The *Miscellaneous Notes on Great Works (Daye zaji)* indicates that during the year of his accession Yangdi (605 – 617 A.D.) erected sixty large-capacity granaries in Luoyang.

Tiles and coins found adjacent to the recently discovered trenches in Luoyang appear to indicate that these storage facilities — one held 20,000 *piculs (shi)* and another 8,000 *piculs* — were set up by Yangdi. With a depth of 4 to 5 meters, a diameter of 6 to 7 meters at the bottom, and 9 to 10 meters at the surface level, these large pits were lined with thick boards, curved in a barrel shape, and were then arranged horizontally around the entire silo. The floor was made of planks extending like spokes from a wooden hub. In the middle portion of one trench were two holes for pillars (diameters of 10 and 12 centimeters) at the bottom of a rectangular hole (44 × 26 × 70 centimeters). The base of a center post intended to support the thatched roof undoubtedly rested upon these pillars. At the bottom of one pit, a layer of debris 5 centimeters deep, actually suggested the presence of a thatched roof but current knowledge does not permit definitive conclusions. These granaries appear to have been destroyed at a very early point, indeed no later than the reign of Wu Ztian (690 – 705 A.D.). Moreover, it has been extremely difficult to identify any related work at the surface level, such as roofing and entrances.

The significant architectural transformations that took place in the capital city reflect its prosperity under the Tang rulers. The scope of these changes — foundations for outer ramparts, gates, and terraces; establishment of the Furong Park; or completion of the renowned Nine Streams Pond (Qiujiang),

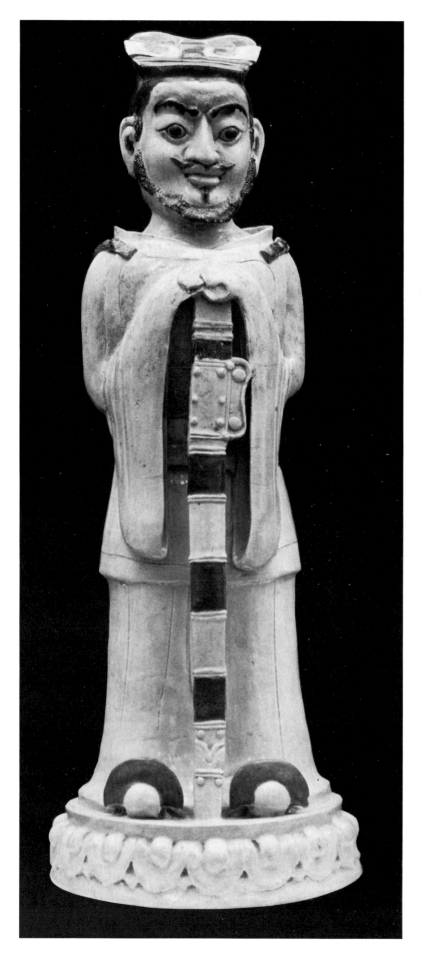

127
Military leader. Glazed white pottery with black ornamentation. Sui Period (595). Discovered in the tomb of Zhang Sheng at Anyang (Henan) in 1959. Height: 72 cm.

Zhang Sheng was a military leader who died in 595 and was buried alongside his wife, who had died earlier. The mortuary furnishings within their tomb consisted of 192 items, including 95 statuettes and 52 specimens of pottery. The statuettes were produced from an extremely white clay. Many of them portray female servants performing their daily tasks (Cf. Illustrations 128 and 129). These are simple pieces which are usually unglazed. On the other hand, six of the statuettes had been glazed, and this military leader standing upon a pedestal adorned with lotuses, belongs to that category. His strongly accentuated features, his exaggerated eyes, and his full beard express the martial vigor of a valiant warrior. Furthermore, he is leaning upon a sword which symbolizes his duties.
Cf. *Kaogu,* 1959, 10.

128
Woman with a flat basket. Painted terra cotta. Sui Dynasty (595). Discovered in the tomb of Zhang Sheng at Anyang (Henan) in 1959. Height: 23 cm. This figurine which belongs to an extensive collection (Cf. Illustration 127) containing 95 mortuary statuettes depicts a female servant using a flat basket intended for gathering dirt or grain.
Cf. *Kaogu,* 1959, 10.

where formal banquets were held to honor candidates who had passed the examination for "eminent scholars"—is fully indicated by excavations at such palaces as Daminggong. Discoveries of this type have been cited in reports concerning excavations undertaken since 1958.

129
Three female attendants. Painted terra cotta. Sui Period (595). Discovered in the tomb of Zhang Sheng at Anyang (Henan) in 1959. Height: 22 cm to 22.5 cm.
One of the servants is carrying a basin for water, and the other is carrying an urn, while the third has a lamp. All three belong to the collection of 95 mortuary statuettes found in the tomb of Zhang Sheng (Cf. Illustration 127). Cf. *Kaogu,* 1959, 10.

Wall Paintings

Excavations have continued from one year to another and the most noteworthy discoveries have consisted of three magnificent tombs erected in 706, namely the tombs of Yong Tai, Zhang Huai, and Yi De. Whereas the first tomb was excavated between 1960 and 1962 excavations at the latter two took place during 1971 and 1972.

Thus far, foreign publications have furnished extensive coverage of these rediscovered wonders. Apart from their inherent sumptuousness, however, these three tombs are not structurally different from tombs of the Han Period and they do not truly convey the magnitude and geometric perfection of

130
Small box. Gilded bronze. Sui Period (603). Discovered at Dingxian (Hebei) in 1969. Height: 19.5 cm. Length: 23.3 cm. Width: 22.8 cm.
This box was discovered in a treasure hidden within the foundation of a Northern Song pagoda which had been dedicated in 977 at the Qingzhisi in Dingxian. With "the third year of the epoch of Renshou" (603) indicated as a date, the box was already an "antique" and was hidden along with other rare and ancient objects dating from the Northern Wei Period (453) to the end of the Tang Period (889).
Cf. *Wenwu*, 1972, 8.

131
Double amphora. Sandstone with cream-colored glaze. Sui Period (608). Discovered at Xi'an (Shaanxi) in 1957. Height: 18.6 cm. Beijing, Historical Museum.
This double amphora was included among the mortuary furnishings of a nine year old girl, Li Jingxun, who was the granddaughter of the Northern Zhou emperor Xuan (557–581).
Cf. *Kaogu*, 1959, 9.

rituals which had attained a zenith. Nevertheless, these underground monuments, which had been erected in order to assuage the guilt of an emperor who had failed to save his children from the criminal vengeance of a power-hungry empress, have yielded an irreplaceable link in the history of Chinese art. From these tombs, it is possible to obtain an image of how advanced Tang painting must have been. It is widely known today that, apart from the remote site of Dunhuang where Buddhist grottoes were adorned with marvelous frescoes, hardly any specimens of secular or religious painting have survived from the Tang Period. The creations of Tang painters vanished in flames like their palaces or temples, or they were lost with the belongings of scholars sent into exile or in the turmoil of insurrections, whenever the passage of time had not reduced paintings on silk to mere tatters. Few Tang paintings have been preserved throughout the world — only the *Han Gan* at the Musée Cernuschi, a specimen at the British Museum, another at the Palace Museum in Taipei, and a few more!

The three tombs of Yong Tai, Zhang Huai and Yi De contained 800 square meters of Tang paintings. The style—

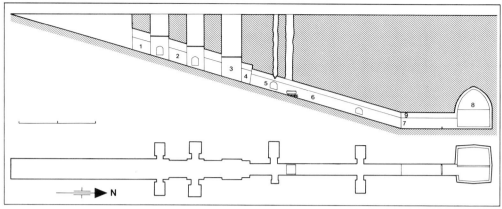

Figure 20. Diagram and cross-sections from Li Feng's tomb, near Xi'an. Reproduced from *Kaogu,* 1977, 5, page 314.

Figure 21. Arrangement of murals in Li Feng's tomb, near Xi'an. Reproduced from *Kaogu,* 1977, 5, page 315.

132-133
Camel-driver and his camel. Pottery with green glaze and traces of polychromy. Tang Period (703). Discovered at Hongqingcun (Shaanxi) in the tomb of Dugu Sizhen (built in 703) in 1956. Height: 84 cm. Beijing, Historical Museum.
This set of statuettes depicts a camel-driver and his animal. The fleshy lips, the large nose, and especially the curly hair of this camel-driver clearly indicate his non-Chinese origin. The technique employed for these pieces is typical of *mingqi* from the late seventh century and the early eighth century. The figures were produced from polished monochrome ceramic materials and were painted with cold pigments after firing.

134
Women with fans. Mural. Tang Period (706). Discovered in the tomb of the Prince Yi De in Xi'an (Shaanxi) during 1971–1972. Height: approximately 160 cm.
The murals from the tomb of Yi De (682–701) which was erected in 706 are among the most beautiful specimens of this genre. They shed new light upon the lavish decor of imperial or aristocratic palaces during this period. Cf. *Wenwu,* 1972, 7. p. 28 and pl. 3, no. 2.

flat tints set off by bold contours, brushstrokes of the "iron wire" type — clearly demonstrate the extent to which techniques for depicting human figures advanced during this period, as is confirmed by theoretical treatises and by the works of such painters as Gu Kaizhi (345–411 A.D.). Although techniques had become more sophisticated, the murals in the tombs also represent a direct continuation of Han art. Indeed, the landscapes seem only somewhat more detailed than those of Pinglu. Nevertheless, the extremely varied repertoire offers an incomparable illustration of life in the capital city at the height of the Tang dynasty, amid the full triumph of medieval China. It is therefore possible to encounter the customary female attendants and maidservants whose graceful and radiant images had already been captured

by *mingqi* figurines. At the same time there were more animated scenes, such as the famous "polo match," where twenty horsemen wearing boots and jerkins are galloping after a ball that five of the players are attempting to strike with their sticks. Two camels with pack-saddles appear in the background; these beasts were undoubtedly carrying provisions or other items required for the polo match. This history of polo, which was undoubtedly invented in Persia at least two thousand years ago, is indeed unusual. The term "polo" is probably of Tibetan origin. It is said that the Arabs became devoted to the game and that Harun al Rashid was the first caliph to play it. Later, the Byzantine emperors became ardent polo players. In China, the game was introduced under the Tang emperors, as the discovery of Zhang

Huai's tomb has confirmed. Its popularity, which endured through centuries and through upheavals, lasted until the end of the Ming dynasty when polo was introduced in India. Then, during the nineteenth century, the British encountered this previously unfamiliar sport and the first polo match in Britain took place in 1871.

In composition, the polo-playing scene strikingly demonstrates the painstaking efforts of painters during the Tang Period to depict the movements of human figures within a natural setting. The landscape is represented solely by a few trees placed at regular intervals in the foreground, and in such a way that they almost obstruct the observer's view. Behind this barrier, the background is smooth and uniform, in a manner wholly reminiscent of paintings from the Han Period. Thus, the artist's imagination was restricted to creation of an expansive and even cumbersome foreground which nevertheless launches the observer on an imaginary journey. It is appropriate to regard this arrangement as a tentative and modest anticipation of techniques that were more fully developed later by such eminent Northern Song landscape painters as Fan Kuan (around 960 – 1030).

The structure of the painting on the opposite wall provides evidence of considerably more advanced geometric refinement. This painting depicts the beginning of a hunting expedition where nearly forty horsemen are shown joyfully traveling amid mountains and trees. The principal elements of true landscape painting are readily observable: trees, boulders, and semi-conical mountains, presented with significant attention to detail and density. Although realistic proportions were not maintained for horses, trees or mountains, an impression of vastness was created by arranging the elements on a diagonal with a "bird's-eye" view. In terms of the entire composition, it is possible to identify two transitional points where the eye must move in opposite directions to create a sense of movement. One of these points is located in the lower right portion where the joyful horsemen are traveling leftward according to lines prolonging those of the mountain chains. The other transitional point is in the upper midportion of the painting. There, the group of horsemen that had been boldly and sharply evoked on the right side diminishes to such an extent that it finally becomes a dot above the center of the painting. In this way one encounters a wholly unfamiliar facet of Chinese landscape painting. Upon contemplating Japanese counterparts to such creations, it is possible to imagine the countless treasures that have unfortunately disappeared over the centuries in China where, in spite

of veneration for the deceased, far too little of the past has been preserved.

Little is known about the artists who created these impressive paintings although the names of two who completed murals for Yong Tai's burial monument appear in a famous treatise on painting, namely the *Treatise on Renowned Painters (Lidai minghuaji)* by Zhang Yanyuan (around 810–880). These two painters are Yang Qidan and Zheng Fashi, although it is not known whether they were solely in the service of the Imperial Court or whether they were also commissioned to complete funerary paintings. Since paintings for tombs would hardly ever be seen or admired, they were often of a slightly inferior quality. Nevertheless, the murals from the three tombs and especially the murals discovered in Yi De's burial vault represent an outstanding level of skill and convey an extremely favorable image of the probable characteristics of nonfunerary painting under the Tang emperors.

The themes adopted for the tomb murals are also relatively interesting because they offer a broader perspective of the official repertoire of Tang painters. Whereas processions of elegant ladies and dignitaries are fully consistent with traditional themes in Han burial paintings, other depictions of palace life which we are tempted to characterize as "genre scenes," significantly enrich our vision of painting in the Imperial Court. The polo match or the hunting scenes belong to this category. The paintings referred to in Chinese as "courtiers and emissaries" scenes are even more instructive. In the foreground it is possible to observe three important Court officials or dignitaries who are wearing elegant headgear made of a fabric coated with black lacquer as a symbol of their rank, whereas three "guests" or emissaries from other nations stand slightly to the rear. Each emissary is wearing the typical garb of his nation. It is clear that the painters, in addition to identifying their subjects, were desirous of providing vivid anecdotal effects. In a manner similar to scroll paintings, the archetype of the ideal Chinese official,

135
Horse. "Three-color" *(sancai)* glazed pottery. Tang Period (706). Discovered in the tomb of Prince Yi De in Xi'an (Shaanxi) in 1971. Height: 72 cm. Length: 83.8 cm.
This extremely beautiful horse is an outstanding specimen of a spectacular category which is highly esteemed by collectors. It possesses all of the indispensable attributes of a steed from an Imperial stable: powerful muscles and well-formed legs. It is appropriate to observe the restrained elegance of the portions done in barbotine: the mane, the forelock, the saddle with a tight-fitting saddle-cloth, and the harness. The tail has been carefully braided.
Cf. *Wenwu*, 1972, 7.

136
Mounted musician. Painted terra cotta. Tang Period (706). Discovered in the tomb of Prince Yi De, in Xi'an (Shaanxi) in 1971. Height: 33 cm. Length: 30 cm.
The tomb of Prince Yi De (682–701), which was erected in 706, contained an impressive collection of more than 1,000 mortuary items as well as forty murals. Many of the terra cotta figurines consisted of horsemen and horses. The mounted musicians accompanied the army in order to establish its marching cadence.
Cf. *Wenwu,* 1972, 7.

137
Mounted hunter. "Three-color" *(sancai)* glazed pottery. Tang Period (706). Discovered in the tomb of Prince Yi De in Xi'an (Shaanxi) in 1971. Height: 36 cm. Length: 31 cm.
The hunter is wearing a quiver filled with arrows and he is holding a falcon which is ready to take flight, while an animal rests upon the cantle of the saddle.
Cf. *Wenwu,* 1972, 7.

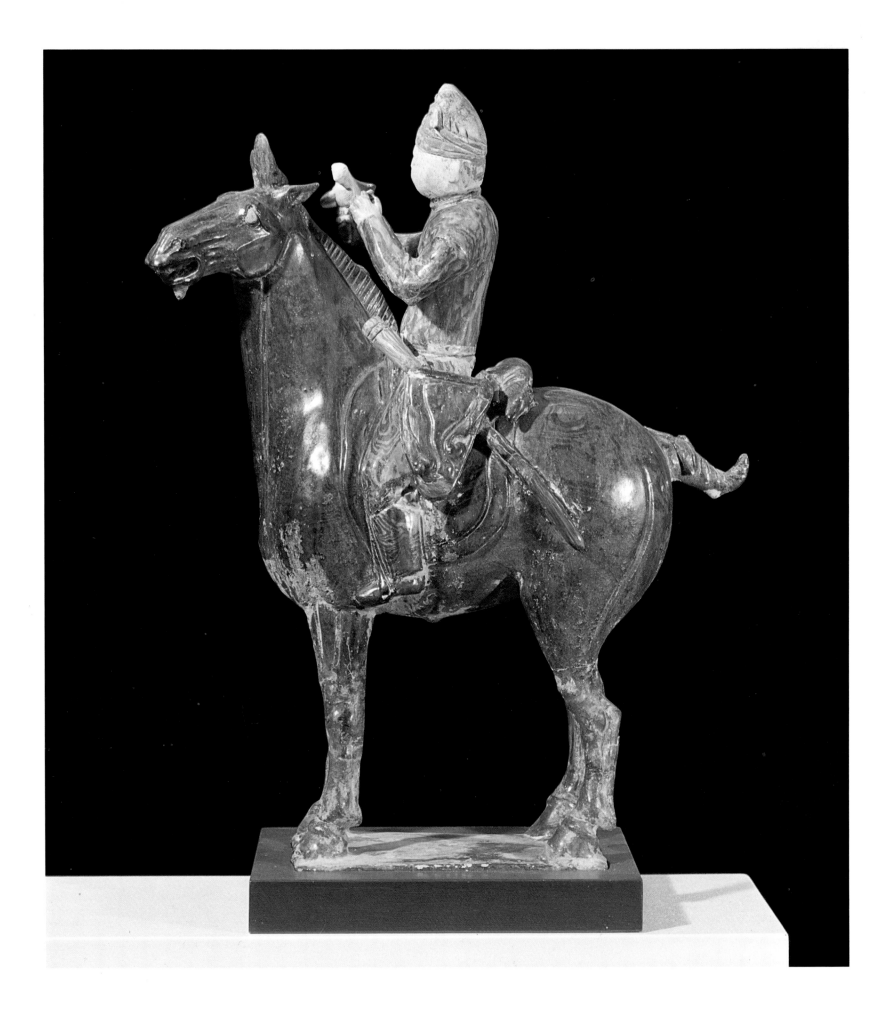

138-139
A military official and a civilian official. Painted and gilded terra cotta. Tang Period (718). Discovered in the tomb of Li Zhen at Xinglongcun (Shaanxi) in 1972. Height: 113 cm. Liquan (Shaanxi), Zhaoling Museum.
The civilian official and the military official constitute a pair, in accordance with a customary arrangement within the tombs of high-ranking persons during this period. The military official holds a pointed symbol of his authority in his hands whereas the civilian does not. The military official's bristling eyebrows, his resolute bearing, and his mitre-shaped headgear adorned with an eagle express the vigor of his martial sternness.
Cf. *Wenwu,* 1977, 10.

140
Horseman wearing a cuirass. Gilded terra cotta. Discovered in the tomb of Prince Yi De in Xi'an (Shaanxi) in 1971. Height: 34 cm. Length: 30 cm.
This horseman is wearing a gilded and lacquered cuirass, while his steed is wearing a skirted caparison. Comparable pieces had been created since the period of the Eastern Jin Dynasty (317–420) but no counterparts for the Tang Period had been discovered prior to opening of Yi De's tomb.
Cf. *Wenwu,* 1972, 7.

full of dignity and decorum, is counterbalanced by the baroque diversity of foreign faces. Although there are affinities to extant specimens of popular painting, such as a scroll by Yan Liben (seventh century) depicting "Bearers of Tribute," this particular encounter between members of the Court and foreign visitors possesses a distinct meaning. Within Zhang Huai's tomb, each side of the passageway leading to the burial vault contains two scenes dominated by this theme. Indeed, the foreigners appear to be facing the emperor's final resting place. These scenes undoubtedly were intended to portray ceremonies in honor of the deceased emperor, or one of the funerals so frequently attended by foreign travelers and ambassadors during the Tang Period when China's sphere of influence extended throughout Eurasia. A certain number of paintings on the theme of peaceful or hostile relationships with barbarians were formerly identified, but this particular discovery represented the first opportunity to observe a foreign delegation offering its condolences.

Certain paintings in the tomb of Yi De (Li Zhongrun) provide a basis for comparable observations. Indeed, two themes were reserved solely for Imperial tombs: the "Qiji halberdiers" and "palace escorts." A precedent for a comparable hierarchy existed in Han tombs where it is possible to observe processions of chariots wherein the number of chariots depended upon the social rank of the deceased person. Under the Tang emperors, regulations with a similar intent only permitted portrayal of Qiji halberdiers in the tombs of prefects or officials of at least the third level. The halberdiers were elite guardsmen who, like Roman lictors, headed processions of troops prior to the arrival of prestigious officials. Thus, in Yi De's tomb, the Imperial status of the deceased is indicated by two rows containing twenty-four halberds apiece, mounted on two racks.

Finally, these paintings are astonishing specimens of a type of art that was previously revealed solely by copies that are inevitably inferior to an original. Our understanding of ancient treatises on painting, such as the text cited heretofore, is significantly reinforced and enriched by these mortuary paintings. Thus, in the chapter on "landscapes, trees and cliffs" in the *Lidai minghuaji,* it is possible to read: "In the first years of our dynasty (the Tang dynasty)...Yang Qidan (and other painters) devoted their endeavors chiefly to murals for palaces and monasteries...When they portrayed rocks, they sculpted and carved them, to create the sharp edges of cut glass."

There is still the danger that the resurrection of these ancient murals will be temporary. A recent report (C. Allag, *CNRS,* 1981) has provided an extremely alarming technical assessment. The murals were painted on a relatively thick layer of lime (4 to 5 mm), which had been applied to a clay and straw coating over the brick walls. On account of the depth at which the murals were situated (7 to 17 meters underground), the prevailing humidity has produced changes in the clay substratum as well

141

Young groom. "Three-color" *(sancai)* glazed pottery. Tang Period (706). Discovered in the tomb of Prince Zhang Huai during 1971–1972. Height: 59.5 cm.

The mortuary accoutrements found within the tomb of Prince Zhang Huai (654–684), which had been completed during the same year as Prince Yi De's tomb (706), consisted of more than 600 items. The tomb was adorned with fifty murals. This groom's hair is divided into a double "bun," and he is wearing foreign attire. Like the horses which they were obliged to take care of, stable attendants usually came from Central or Western Asia. In figurines belonging to this category, foreign origin is often emphasized by depiction of faces with large noses and accentuated features.
Cf. *Wenwu,* 1972, 7.

142

Tutelary king. "Three-color" *(sancai)* glazed pottery. Tang Period (end of seventh century–beginning of eighth century). Discovered at Changan (Xi'an, Shaanxi).

This warrior possesses the typical commanding appearance of a tutelary king of the type customarily placed at tomb entrances in pairs. He is distinguished by his gestures because he is drawing a bow even though his slightly tilted stance atop an animal — a ram in this instance — is consistent with conventional portrayal of tutelary deities. The beauty of the glaze and the delicate interplay of speckled portions of the cuirass captures the observer's attention.

143

Lokapala, tutelary king (tianwang). "Three-color" *(sancai)* glazed terra cotta. Tang Period (618–907). Discovered at Zhongbaocun, Xi'an (Shaanxi) in 1959. Height: 65.5 cm.

This tutelary king was suspended from another similar figure, and both were preceded by tutelary monsters of winged quadrupeds with human heads which possessed pig-like ears and pairs of horns (one large and one small). The four creatures were situated just beyond the entrance of a tomb.
Cf. *Kaogu,* 1960, 3, p. 35 and pl. 10, no. 1.

144
Reclining bull. Pottery with brownish-red glaze. Tang Period (seventh century–eighth century). Discovered at Qinan (Gansu) in 1965. Length: 46 cm. This mortuary piece, which was executed in an extremely realistic form, was coated with a glaze whose colors crudely evoke the effects of "three-colored" wares.

145
Musicians riding a camel. "Three-color" *(sancai)* glazed pottery. Tang Period (723). Discovered in the tomb of the general Xianyu Tinghui at Nanhecun, Xi'an (Shaanxi) in 1957. Height: 58.4 cm. Length: 43.4 cm. Beijing Historical Museum.

This impressive camel is being ridden by a group of four musicians accompanied by a singer. The figures' long noses and luxuriant beards indicate their foreign origin. It is possible to recognize a lute-player *(pipa)* and a flautist (his instrument had disappeared). The same tomb contained another group of musicians riding a camel but the saddle-cover was decorated with a diamond pattern instead of stripes and the central figure was a woman. In 1959, another even more complex counterpart (ten musicians and a female singer upon a camel) was discovered at Zhongbaocun, which is also located in Xi'an. This piece is reminiscent of a famous musical instrument *(pipa)* preserved at the Shosoin in Nara (Japan). The latter instrument contains a painting depicting a small group of musicians placed upon the back of a white elephant.
Cf. *Wenwu*, 1978, 4, pp. 74–80.

as decomposition of the surface layer. The continuing deterioration has led Chinese authorities to remove the corridor paintings and display them at the Xi'an Museum; and they have placed glass over the paintings inside the burial vaults. Nevertheless, this particular measure may be more harmful than the original problem. Even when glass is used to protect the murals, greenish discoloration has continued to appear on the surface of the painted layer. For this reason, emergency preservation measures are considered with the long-term aspiration of performing a thorough cleaning of the underground portions of each tomb or of relocating the murals to a better environment. In any case, Chinese authorities may soon have to close the splendid tombs which were originally open to the public: the dead do not easily tolerate intrusions by the living.

Ceramics

All connoisseurs of Chinese art are familiar with the highly esteemed ceramic creations of the Tang Period. In particular, one of this era's most brilliant accomplishments is represented by "three-colored" pieces. During the past thirty years an abundant and superb harvest within this category has been obtained through tomb excavations. Although it may be inappropriate to pursue an extensive discussion of ceramics here, it may be useful to cite certain tentative conclusions based on finds, the origins of which are known with respect to locations and dates.

For example, Chinese archeologists have begun to develop interesting data on proportions.[55] In comparison with the sumptuous ceramic objects that have been cited and preserved by connoisseurs, approximately 70 percent of the ceramic funerary offerings discovered during the last thirty years are ordinary unglazed pieces that were painted after firing. These items of mediocre quality were produced rapidly but with exceptional variety of form. They were not intended for ordinary use and merely represented simulations of conventional items. At the same time there were certain pieces with a green or brown lead-based glaze; these were extremely similar to Han wares and protracted interment gave them a varicolored and somewhat lustrous appearance. As a result, some ceramic pieces of commonplace origins were transformed into rare curios.

These wares with monochromatic glazing return us to the world of the living. Today, it has been confirmed that, since the pre-Imperial epoch in China and indeed since the Shang dynasty, Chinese potters who had become highly skilled in every aspect of baking knew how to create "proto-porcelain" and were capable of producing partially vitrified wares with impermeable glazes. It is not yet possible to determine the fate of the ancient potters' secret, no doubt very carefully protected as it was transmitted from fathers to eldest sons; but it finally vanished. Yet, the potters' efforts continued, and during the Han Period they developed brown pottery with a ferrous oxide glaze as well as green wares with a cupric oxide glaze. For the latter type, a considerably stronger flame was required. Depending on the degree of exposure under firing, it was possible for portions of a single urn to display a broad range of shades—from bright green to yellowish green along with clear or somber intermediate hues.

Recent research has indicated that even at the beginning of the Tang Period, potters normally used clay with a high iron content (approximately 2 to 3 percent) so that the glaze appeared a rather bright greenish gray. As the Tang Period drew to an end, improvements in kilns permitted potters to reduce the iron content of their clays. On the other hand, the technical attributes of "green pottery" always varied significantly from one kiln to another on account of differences in materials. For this reason the Tang poets incessantly lauded regional "specialties." A mere allusion to the famous "Yue greens" was therefore sufficient to evoke an image of refined revelry and Wang Renyu, in *Events and Recollections of the Times of Kaiyuan* (713-741) *and Tianbao* (742-755), stated that in the court of Xuanzong (712-756) there were hardly any festive occasions that were not enhanced by the colorful sheen of Yue goblets which rang out like musical instruments.

In the Xi'an region or the central plain craftsmen wanted to match their southern counterparts' accomplishments. At Anyang or Gongxian, for example, there were several kilns that produced "green" pottery, although efforts to produce white wares were ultimately more successful in the north.

Development of white ceramic pieces clearly seems to have been one of the most ancient ambitions of Chinese potters because specimens have been discovered in the Longshan strata from the Neolithic Age. Dazzling white pottery was also created during the Shang Period, although the secret of how it was produced also appears to have been lost. There are actually several methods of producing white pottery. It is possible, for example, to retain the actual color of the clay; potters who used kaolin, for example, were able to eliminate the effects of any impurities by coating their work with a glaze containing soft iron. If the potter only had darker clays at his disposal, the natural color had to be concealed under a thick white coat over which a white slip was applied, and finally, a glaze. But as long as potters were unable to use high temperatures, their products retained a slight greenish tint. In certain situations it was only possible to obtain pure white pottery by using very high temperatures.

It has been ascertained that in the vicinity of Xi'an, approximately 30 percent of the luxurious ceramic items placed in tombs of the Tang Period consisted of white wares. This fact,

146
Bleating camel. "Three-color" *(sancai)* glazed pottery. Tang Period (eighth century). Discovered in the tomb of Qi Siming at Xianyang (Shaanxi) in 1970. Height: 82 cm. Length: 60 cm.
This mortuary statuette constitutes an especially admirable portrayal of these animals originating from other regions. At the beginning of the eighth century many camels were observable in Changan, which was a point of arrival and departure for the large caravans plying between China and Western Asia along the Silk Road.

as well as an inscription appearing upon the neck of a vase at the Palace Museum (Gugong) in Beijing, provides a basis for assuming that mass production of white pottery became possible during the seventh century.

Next to Xi'an, the other important center for producing "white pottery" was Henan where the Anyang kilns created the famous "dragon bowls." The Anyang kilns, like those of Shaanxi further west, often produced white pieces with a slight yellowish tinge. Thus, they began to specialize primarily in colored funerary pieces, such as the famous turquoise wares.

Notwithstanding earlier affirmations to the contrary, southern China, the source of the best green wares, also produced the most beautiful white ones, included under the general designation *xing*. The leading role of southern China had already been established during the Six Dynasties Period. In Jiangxi Province, the Nanchang kilns (whose fame would later be enhanced by Jingdezhen) produced such exceptionally white urns that their merits were praised in the *Old History of the Tang Dynasty (Jiu Tang Shu)*, where it is recorded that Emperor Xuanzong (712-756) especially admired them. It is true that for an extended period the quest for pure whiteness became an obsession among master potters in southern China. A few relatively crude specimens have been found in Hunan as early as the end of the Eastern Han dynasty. In contrast, even pieces with comparable flaws did not appear in northern China in the vicinity of Anyang until the Bei Qi Period (550-577), three hundred years later.

Lastly, a significant result of recent excavations is confirmation of the existence of decorative underglazes since the Tang Period. These underglazes became exceptionally popular at Cizhou (Hebei) during the Song dynasty. The 1973 and 1974 excavations at Yaozhou[56] in Shaanxi, which was famous throughout the Song Period for the quality and variety of its products, demonstrated that an extremely diversified output originated during the Tang Period. Wares with black or white glazes predominated, but yellow or green glazes were also used. There was also an abundance of ordinary unglazed pottery. At this site excavations have even revealed urns with a so-called belt decor where the color of the belly contrasts with that of the neck and base. It has likewise been determined that during the Tang Period the Yaozhou potters began to apply green tints

beneath milky, whitish glazes, although their products, baked with a moderate flame, appear to be inferior to similar wares produced in the Changsha region whose preeminence appears unchallenged.

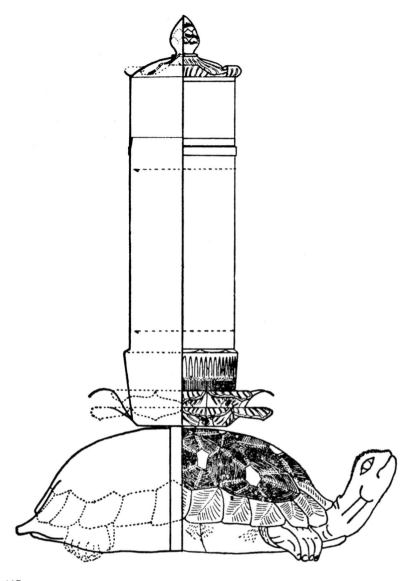

147

"Lunyu yuzhu." Gold and silver. Tang Period (618–907). Discovered at Dingmaoqiao (Jiangsu) in 1982. Height: 34.2 cm. Length: 24.6 cm. Reproduced from *Wenwu*, 1982, 11, p. 17.

A cylindrical vessel where the four characters *Lunyu yuzhu*, "priceless *Lunyu* candlestick," are inscribed within a scroll rests upon a lotus petal base which is supported by the back of the tortoise. The entire surface of the cylinder is decorated with an extremely dense scrollwork pattern. Other gold objects (these include lavish "dishes") from the same source also contain an allusion to the *Lunyu* (Confucius' *Analects*). Is it appropriate to regard this phenomenon as representing a style influenced by the Confucian renaissance which emerged under the Tang rulers and especially during the latter portion of the Tang Period?
Cf. *Wenwu*, 1982, 11, pp. 16, 24; pl. 1.

148

Phoenix head ewer. "Three-color" *(sancai)* glazed pottery. Tang Period (eighth century). Discovered at Luoyang (Henan) in 1961. Height: 32.2 cm.
This flat pouring vessel in the form of a phoenix' head is a ceramic reproduction of shapes and motifs which are typical of goldsmiths' creations. The short side therefore contains, in the form of a barbotine relief, a barbarian horseman who is aiming a "Parthian arrow" as he faces rearward.

186

Research at the Tongguan[57] kilns in the Changsha region of Hunan Province since 1957 and 1959 has actually permitted this site to be defined as the birthplace of ceramic wares with a glaze placed over painted decoration. Excavations were resumed nearly ten years ago, and many new finds have come to light.

The Tongguan kilns extended nearly six kilometers along a watercourse in a pattern resembling a string of beads. The size of these kilns varied greatly. Nearly all of their output can be attributed to the Tang dynasty (from the time of Yuanhe, 806-820, to the time of Dazhong, 847-859). Since 1974, more than 2,000 items have been unearthed, including three un-adorned pieces of stoneware resembling porcelain and several hundred porcelain-like stoneware items with a glaze applied over the decoration. Usually, decoration consisted of simple brown, green, blue or red spots beneath the glaze. There were, however, more than 200 urns containing motifs of human figures, animals, flowers and birds drawn with a lively and unerring brush. Fifty-four of these pieces even contained poems and songs. Thus, the Tongguan discoveries brilliantly confirm the vitality of decorative underglazes within this region beginning with the Tang Period.

This aspect represents one of the most important clarifications, but it is of special interest to both specialists and connoisseurs. In turn, the general public is most deeply impressed by the picturesque and dazzling quality of the famous "three-colored" items (*sancai*) which excavations have consistently unearthed during the past twenty years. For example, there are the Zhongbaocun collection that came to light in 1959 in a western suburb of Xi'an, or specimens from the tombs of Yong Tai, Yi De, and Zhang Huai, whose exceptional murals have been described heretofore.

This vast assortment of ceramic—even though many obviously belong to categories that have been recognized for a long time—now permits delineation of a general history of the development of the *sancai,* whereas thirty years ago, it was not possible to determine clearly the rise and disappearance of these items nor their role other ceramic burial accoutrements.

149
Guan vessel with handle. Gilded silver. Tang Period (eighth century). Discovered at Hejiacun, at Changan (Xi'an, Shaanxi) in 1970. Height: 24.3 cm. Neck diameter: 12.3 cm. Base diameter: 14.3 cm. Waist diameter: 20 cm.
This engraved gold-plated vessel contains elegant ornamentation where parrots are depicted inside a scroll with a floral motif. This type of decoration was extremely popular in the Imperial Court at Changan. To a certain extent this combination suggests themes typically adopted by the weavers who created the lavish brocades of this period.
Cf. *Wenwu,* 1972, 1.

On the basis of evidence gathered thus far, it therefore appears that the Sui tombs always contained ceramic items, even though Tang tombs do not consistently indicate the existence of this custom. Although some of the Sui pieces were glazed, they were usually unadorned.

According to a study of tombs in the Xi'an region, 87 percent of the tombs beginning with the Tang Period or the seventh century contained ceramic items that were usually small pieces intended solely for funerary purposes. At the same time, however, the famous "three-colored" pieces with delicate shading began to appear and at some locations, occasional floral motifs have been observed.

Throughout the eighth century, the number of commonplace wares in tombs appears to have diminished whereas uniquely funerary pieces increased Ninety-one percent of the tombs attributed to this period contained ceramic items from the golden age of "three-colored" wares. These were specifically intended for the afterlife. Their proliferation was short-lived, however. A century later the quality of burial accoutrements declined significantly and this trend was not counterbalanced by the introduction of life-sized ceramic substitutes for items from daily life. Whereas ceramic objects within the latter category were distinguished by essentially geometric patterns and designs, lavish decorative motifs were adopted for objects intended solely for funerary use. At this point the "three-colored" pieces disappeared or became extremely rare, even though their use continued under the Yuan and Ming dynasties, as one of the mortuary statues at the Musée Cernuschi demonstrates.

In this case, the discovery of splendid specimens, the dates of which can be accurately defined is a far more significant contribution of contemporary archeology than the exposure of a widely recognized and widely discussed phenomenon. As a result, it has been possible to develop a chronological framework for the apogee of the *sancai* — namely the first half of the eighth century—and to undertake a rigorous analysis of their composition.

An acceptable *sancai* was produced from extremely pure white clay, which was obtained by a lengthy process of cleansing, hardening and powdering raw clay. Baking consisted of two stages: an initial firing (at 1000° C. to 1100° C.) permitted hardening to take place, and colors were added after cooling; then the piece was returned to the kiln for a second baking at 900° C. It was necessary for potters to apply extremely precise knowledge and control of chemical transformations in order to

150

Footman bearing weapons. White marble, with traces of polychromy and gold overlay. Tang Period (740). Discovered in the tomb of Yang Sixu at Dengjiapocun, in Xi'an (Shaanxi) in 1958. Height: 40.3 cm. Beijing, Historical Museum.

This statuette depicts a hunter's servant instead of the hunter himself. The servant is carrying all of the weapons which his master may need: a sword, sabers, a bow and a quiver. Indeed, this piece is actually a counterpart to another, namely a statuette of the same dimensions, material and style, depicting a hunter who bears fewer weapons than his footman (nevertheless, the hunter does carry a saber, a sword, a quiver, and a club). These two extremely lavish pieces have been regarded as exceptional items thus far. The man whose tomb they adorned was Yang Sixu, buried in 740. Yang Sixu had been a loyal general under the Tang emperor Xuanxong (reign: 712–756).

Cf. *Wenwu*, 1961, 12, inserted plate.

151

Pan basin with ornamental phoenixes. Gold-plated silver with *repoussé* work. Tang Period (end of eighth century). Discovered west of the Daminggong at Changan (Xi'an, Shaanxi) in 1962. Diameter: 55 cm. Xi'an, Shaanxi Provincial Museum.

This silver basin was undoubtedly offered to Emperor Dezong (reign: 780-804) by an official from the Office of Rituals. During the Tang Period, gold and silver work, which had become popular during the period of the Northern and Southern Dynasties, thrived to an unprecedented degree, at least until An Lushan's revolt (755) which heralded the decline of the Tang Dynasty. Silver imported from Persia became the center of an extremely important branch of commerce, but mining of silver in each of China's principal regions — south of the Huai, south of the Yangtze, and in Lingdao — began during the Tang Period. In this instance, the *repoussé* ornamentation at the center of the multiple-lobed section consists of two phoenixes whereas the basin and the inner fillet contain a floral motif.

Cf. *Wenwu*, 1972, 1.

152–153

The Manjusri bodhisattva. White marble, with traces of gold overlay and polychromy. Tang Period (760). Discovered in 1959 at the site of the Anguosi, a temple in Xi'an (Shaanxi) that has disappeared. Height: 74 cm. This statue of Manjusri, a deity representing wisdom, clearly illustrates the zenith of Tang art: the renewed influence of India is observable in the fleshy outlines of the face, in the flowing quality of the robes, and in the careful depiction of the deity's jewels. This particular statue is comparable to a white marble Guanyin (Avalokitesvara) which was discovered in 1952 in the ruins of the Xingqinggong at Changan (present-day Xi'an) (Cf. Item Number 153 from the 1973 Tokyo Exhibition). Lastly, it is possible to recognize in this Manjusri a feminization of the deity which already foreshadows the art of the Song Period.
Cf. *Wenwu,* 1961, 7.

produce various colors. The quality of a *sancai* allowed little room for mere chance.

Any item that essentially fulfills these criteria can be regarded as a *sancai* by definition. Accordingly, the Tang tombs have yielded not only dishes, bowls and ewers but also human and animal figurines representing a throng of mortuary images, well-known among collectors. These pieces are the most outstanding specimens of *mingqi,* or substitute-offerings, and represent a remote echo of the bloody sacrifices of the Bronze Age.

But glazed human figurines of this type did not originate with the Tang dynasty. During the early 1970s specimens were discovered in a Northern Wei tomb at Simajinlong, near Datong in Shanxi and 484 has been established as the date. These figurines whose green lead-based glaze is comparable to glazes used during the Han Period, emerge as distant ancestors of the *sancai* figurines found in Tang tombs, even though a certain number of significant differences are identifiable: monochromatism, use of the red or gray hue of the clay for the body of each figurine, use of coarse glazes, and a perceptibly lower baking temperature.

However, production of glazed *mingqi* expanded rapidly during the period of the Southern and Northern Dynasties—a phenomenon suggested by the discovery of Bei Qi pieces that closely resemble *sancai*, in the vicinity of Anyang. Thus, tombs at Fancui and Puyang (the tomb of Luo Yun) in Henan Province contained white clay ceramic pieces coated with a white glaze or in tones of pale yellow and green tints against a deep green dark band that encircled the entire object. Indeed, these specimens can be legitimately regarded as an initial version of "three-colored" wares.

At what point it is truly permissible to speak of *sancai* has been partially answered by recent discoveries. Excavations that began in 1972 at the tomb of one of Emperor Taizong's famous generals, Cheng Rentai, who was buried within the perimeter of the Imperial mausoleum at Zhaoling in 664, led to the discovery of 466 statuettes. Whereas some of these statuettes possessed a yellow glaze and others a white one, various colors always applied to the glaze after baking. Indeed, this method produced ceramic pieces with an extremely attractive appearance highlighted by more than three colors although this form of coloring still lacked the durability of pigments which are mixed with a glaze and hardened by fire. The fragility of these hues undoubtedly explains why this spectacular technique was so promptly abandoned, even though archeologists tend to regard it as the initial phase of the *sancai*.

One year later, in 1973, excavations at another site, namely the tomb of Li Feng, who was the fifteenth son of Li Yuan, allowed identification of a new link. The tomb is located in Shaanxi Province near the mausoleum of Gaozu. Li Feng had died in 674, ten years after Cheng Rentai's death, and his tomb was completed during the following year, subsequent to the interment of his wife, a member of the Liu clan. Li Feng's tomb contained several authentic specimens of *sancai*, consisting of dishes, figurines and fragments. Hence, there is a reliable basis for concluding that *sancai* possessing all of the attributes of this particular genre were introduced no later than 675.

Beyond this point in time, examples become abundant. Sites which have offered the greatest numbers of pieces of this type include the tombs of Yong Tai (706), Zhang Huai (706), and Li Zhen (718), King of Yue. Subsequent to the Tianbao era (752-756), *sancai* became far less common, as if production were disrupted by the dramatic consequences of the revolt of An Lushan.

Evidence from various regions of China corroborates discoveries in the vicinity of the capital city, with additional confirmation of the three periods that have already been established for the history of *sancai*: an initial phase beginning during the reign of Gaozong and continuing until the period of Wu Zetian, namely from the middle of seventh century until the initial years of the eighth century; a culminating phase from the restoration of Zhongzong (706) until the end of Xuanzong's reign (756); and a final phase, from the middle of the eighth century until the end of the Tang dynasty.

The art of creating *sancai* spread throughout the empire. Although especially beautiful specimens have been found in large numbers at Xi'an and Luoyang, counterparts have also been discovered everywhere else. However, An Lushan's rebellion appears to have dealt a fatal blow to this craft. The *sancai* only continued in northern China under the encouragement of the Liao dynasty.

Thus, thirty years of excavations and discoveries with precisely defined criteria in terms of time and space suggest that under the Sui and Tang emperors, ceramic craftmanship, which was even more prolific than had been suspected, developed into a broad range of genres. One hitherto unexpected phenomenon is that a tendency toward unity prevailed in spite of a certain number of clearly affirmed regional trends. The artisans attempted to overcome local differences in order to arrive at a single type within each category: the most flawless. Thus, under the Tang dynasty, we encounter a fully established tendency that explains all of the exceptionally dynamic developments in porcelain production during the Ming and Qing dynasties. Today, it has become obvious that Western perception has given excessive emphasis to regional variations, despite the fact that the Chinese ideal specifically guided artisans toward acceptance of general canons in terms of form and quality. Although such a perspective may be valid for earlier feudal nations such as the European countries and Japan, it cannot be easily applied to China, where Imperial authority was never a meaningless concept, notwithstanding changes in power.

The Goldsmiths' Creations

During the Tang Period, admiration for colors and for bright, finely wrought materials naturally led to unprecedented appreciation for items of gold and pure silver. Historians and poets constantly cited the seemingly unrivaled sumptuousness of the Court in this era. In order to convey faithfully the extravagance that prevailed at this time, they often mentioned the priceless plates lying in heaps at the doors of rooms within the palace, entirely ignored by everyone. The *History of the Tang* recounts how Emperor Xuanzong lavished gold objects upon his concubine Yang Guifei and his barbarian general An Lushan, before An Lushan rebelled. As a result of his friend's betrayal, the emperor was forced to flee in humiliation, before An Lushan himself was finally murdered (757).

In 1970 a marvelous collection of these forgotten splendors came to light. The Hejiacun "treasure" was unearthed south of Xi'an, at the site where Xuanzong's cousin Li Shouli, Prince of Bin (who died in 741), had resided. Although it was entirely possible to envision such a find after previous discoveries in Xi'an during 1957, 1962, and 1963, the splendor of the newly-located treasure seemed incomparable. A silver urn and two large pottery jars contained more than 1,000 items: silver and gold vessels, precious gems, and samples of rare minerals traditionally used as medicinal substances in China, such as cinnabar, amethyst, litharge and rock crystal. In addition, there were many Chinese and foreign coins — Sassanian coins minted during the reign of Chosroes II (560-627), a Byzantine coin from the reign of Heraclius (640–641) and five Japanese silver coins minted in 708. This assortment of coins clearly demonstrated the cosmopolitan flavor of Chang An during the Tang Period.

It is likely that the treasure was hastily buried in a palace courtyard and abandoned during An Lushan's advance toward the capital city in 756. The son of Li Shouli may have attempted to hide his most beautiful possessions at that point. Yet this was

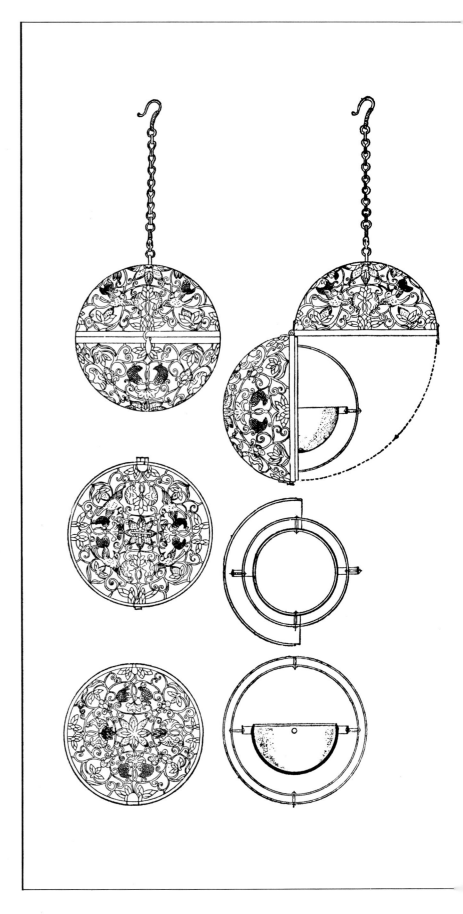

Figure 22. *The Hejiacun censer.* Reproduced from *Kaogu yu wenwu*, 1982, 1, p. 62.

a futile precaution; as in many similar situations neither the owner nor his descendants ever found their treasure again.

Nevertheless, this hoard has permitted contemporary archeologists to admire the most extraordinary collection of creations by Tang goldsmiths, even though comparable items have recently been discovered at Kalaqin in Liaoning Province (1976) and at Dingmaoqiao in Jiangsu Province (1982).

Indeed, the treasure belonging to the Bin princes is a marvelous example of Chinese gold and silver work at the height of the Tang Period. These items express the goldsmiths' consummate mastery of metalworking techniques, not only for molten metals but for beaten and embossed pieces: chasing, milling, stamping, and filigree work. The same ingenuity is represented by diversity of shapes: bowls with lotus petal decorative motifs, hexagonal or octagonal goblets, flasks which resembled the leather vessels used by horsemen or travelers, urns inlaid with gold, and coffers luxuriously adorned with flowers and birds resembling the decorative motifs used on brocades or on the simple painted wares which served as a substitute in less affluent homes for the gold and silver plates favored by the wealthy. The most impressive piece continues to be a spherical censer (perfume-burner), containing a cup which was ingeniously mounted on two circular pieces attached to a double hub. This clever system allowed the cup of scented fluid to remain horizontal, regardless of the position of the censer.

Apart from these creations whose technical attributes demonstrate the strong influence of Sassanian goldsmiths although their Chinese origin is duly confirmed by the diversity and vigor of floral and animal motifs, there were imported articles revealing the cosmopolitan tastes of the aristocracy during the era. For example, there is an onyx rhyton cup in the shape of a gazelle's head, as well as a glass goblet of Sassanian origin.

Preservation of the Principal Buddhist Shrines

Fascinated by these discoveries whose quasimiraculous existence appears to suggest a feverish treasure hunt, teams of Chinese archeologists have also undertaken diligent efforts to investigate, enhance and safeguard significant monuments whose existence was recognized long ago, such as the vast Buddhist rock shrines. One example is the Binglingsi complex, a jewel of Sino-Indian art from the Tang Period, discovered in 1951. Further excavation and research contributes to historical analysis of techniques,

as well as changes in style, which have been attentively examined by prior specialists and connoisseurs, but *in situ* investigations possess the advantage of offering corroboration for previously developed theories.

Accordingly, the Dunhuang Research Institute, established in 1951, has spent more than thirty years removing sand and providing protection against erosion of a vast complex of decorated caves and stucco statues known as "Mogao" in Gansu Province, where shrines existed from 366 A.D. until the end of the fourteenth century.

154
Urn with two handles. Pottery with bluish glaze and brown ornamentation. Tang Period (618–907). Discovered during 1977–1978 at the Tangcheng kilns in Yangzhou (Jiangsu). Height: 15.4 cm. Neck diameter: 9.4 cm. Nankin Museum.
As one of the few complete pieces discovered at the Tangcheng kilns in Yangzhou, this urn demonstrates the beauty of the decorated pottery being produced at this time in a center which contributed extensively to the transmission of many techniques of Chinese craftsmen to Japan. Yangzhou was also one of the first Chinese cities to be known to Europeans because Marco Polo stayed there during the thirteenth century in order to fulfill his obligations. Thus far, the efforts of Chinese archeologists (in 1975 and subsequently during 1977–1978) have primarily concentrated upon the pottery kilns. Future projects shall likewise permit investigation of the workplaces of goldsmiths and stone-carvers.
Cf. *Wenwu*, 1980, 3, p. 13 and pl. 4, no. 3.

At this site it was first necessary to reinforce the facade with pillars and supporting stone walls, both inside and outside, for a natural cliff made of alluvial deposits containing a mixture of sand and small stones. The fragility of this particular site is attributable to its exposure to intense sandstorms from the Gobi Desert. Extensive erosion has occurred in nearly half of the original caves, or at least within the antechambers. Archeologists in search of salvageable treasures have pursued intensive efforts to restore the wall paintings created upon a base of clay, mud and lime, and have attempted to restore connections among the various caves by rebuilding the external network of corridors and wooden passageways that formerly permitted long processions of worshippers to clamber through the enormous anthill that this place of worship must have originally resembled.

At the same time the government of China established an institute for preserving the Yungang Caves. Its first task was to overcome the desert-like desolation of this site through extensive reforestation. Now there is a semblance of the original natural setting as it once appeared during the period when the Northern Wei ruled northern China from their capital in Datong. At this location too, a certain zest for life appears to have prevailed at the outset. In 1955 the wooden access structures were repaired, and between 1959 and 1961 the eastern and western ends of the caves were restored. Large-scale excavations which took place from 1972 until 1975 permitted the discovery of interesting traces of the past: a Northern Wei sculpture in Cave Number 12, representing a building with a tile roof; traces of a stone floor from the Northern Wei Period within Caves 9 and 10; and portions of a wooden superstructure built in front of the same caves under the Liao rulers. It was also possible to clear new caves filled for centuries with sand, dirt and debris. One of these caves, which was dug between Caves 4 and 5 at a significantly later point, is square-shaped, its center marked by a pentagonal *stupa*. A similar space was created between Caves 13 and 14, although the bare walls suggest that work did not continue. Finally, above Cave

Number 3 there is a niche containing a Maitreya image; according to legends, this is where the monk Tan Yao who established the shrine spent his hours meditating.

Archeologists are currently attempting to reach the caves and the niches still relatively inaccessible. Their efforts are sometimes rewarded by significant discoveries: Northern Wei and Liao paintings in the niches west of Cave Number 11, or in the same vicinity, statues attributed to the year 489. These statues are wearing Chinese-style robes and sashes such as would have been a novelty during that era when Toba garments seem to predominate.

The Longmen caves have also benefited from these extensive efforts to restore and investigate national historical treasures. Bas-reliefs honoring donors, inscriptions, and decorative elements are constantly being discovered, thereby permitting exhaustive sociological and stylistic research. The same situation exists at Dazu in Sichuan Province where Buddhas and bodhisattvas typically representing tenth century art or the beginning of the Song Period, are surrounded by fascinating human and animal figures originating from the Taoist afterlife.

Although these discoveries are quantitatively important, the qualitative aspect appears less striking because the fundamental result is corroboration for previously identified tendencies. Apart from the fact that such discoveries allow more thorough evaluation of phenomena because they provide more accurate statistics, they also allow more effective appraisal of the scope of a phenomenon which was attributed solely to northern China for far too many years. Today, it is possible to examine reality in a more vivid light. On one hand, there is indeed as Chinese archeologists say, a "belt of cliffside shrines" in Northern China, extending from Dunhuang to Longmen by way of Majishan, Tianlongshan, Gonxian and Yungang. During the past thirty years, however, discoveries and exploration throughout China have attested to the breadth of a phenomenon which was mistakenly believed to be closely associated with the caravan routes. Today, the provinces of Guangdong, Hunan and Guizhou are the only regions where rupestrian shrines have not been discovered. One may wonder whether similar shrines may soon be unearthed in those provinces. In other words, the great temples and the pilgrimages that they inspired covered every accessible portion of China: beginning in Central Asia or Southeastern Asia by land, or even along the coasts where ships arrived.

155
Guanyin (Avalokitesvara). White marble. Tang Period (618–907). Discovered in the ruins of the Xingqinggong at Changan (Xi'an, Shaanxi) in 1952. Height: 73 cm.
This Guanyin seated upon a lotus-shaped pedestal strongly reflects the zenith of Tang art. The full face, the folds of her neck, and the abundance of jewelry are aspects which indicate the influence of Indian art, which was already significant by the time of the Northern Qi Dynasty (550–577) and had become obvious by the second half of the seventh century. The result was the creation of works constituting a dramatic departure from the principles of elongation and almost calligraphic stylization which were typical of art from the Northern Wei Period.
Cf. *Kaogu*, 1959, 10.

Illuminating Relationships with Japan

Lastly, there are many situations where archeology lends support to historical texts, including texts that were carefully preserved in Japan even though they became relatively unknown in China. For example, a Japanese source indicated that in 843 (the second year of the reign of Tianbao), a Chinese monk departed from Yangzhou (Jiangsu Province) to bring Buddhism to the archipelago. Instead of undertaking a solitary journey, he was accompanied by a sizable retinue whose members, in addition to religious masters, included a jade carver, painters, sculptors who could create Buddhist statues, calligraphers and craftsmen who engraved stelae. During subsequent centuries, it appears that the relocation of Yangzhou's artistic splendor only survived in Japan. The demise and the eventual disappearance of talents that were exceptional enough to win recognition across the sea is undoubtedly attributable to an Imperial edict banning foreign religions and the ensuing decline of the Tang dynasty.

Recent archeological discoveries have contributed to renewed appreciation for the creations of these forgotten craftsmen, as well as corroborating Japanese texts. A stone elephant was discovered in 1964, and eight Buddhist statues were found in 1976. The most impressive find during the same year was a ceramic bust (14 centimeters high). Such likenesses were an extremely rare genre in Chinese art, at least if one accepts the image that scholars sought to perpetuate after the Ming dynasty.

As a result of archeological discoveries, Chinese and Japanese scholars are attempting to redefine historical characteristics which were shared by both nations at certain times. Some foreign observers still prefer to stress the difficulties between the civilizations of China and Japan. They would truly be shocked by the birth of a new perspective that is steadily gaining strength in China, namely a tendency to emphasize the ancient and recognizable bonds that have joined the archipelago to the mainland in spite of the observable individuality of both nations. Of course, political concerns are present, but this form of research can contribute to improved understanding of the subtle mechanisms that govern exchange and development of ideas among different peoples and nations; in fact, being a "foreigner" is often useful in promoting such understanding.

It is appropriate to adopt this same outlook in approaching the many brief articles which Chinese archeological journals now provide in regard to the Buddhist temples of Xi'an, whose vestiges are now being avidly hunted by archeologists. During the period of their greatest influence, these places of worship which fell into disuse or disappeared after the tenth century contributed in various ways to the education of the most eminent masters of Japanese Buddhism during the Tang Period.

One example is Qinglongsi in southern Xi'an. This is where Kukai (774–835), who introduced the Zhenyan (Shingon) sect in Japan, came to study the secrets of esoteric Buddhism in 805 or 806.

The temple, established at the site of a former residence of the Qin princes, had been founded in 582 by the Sui emperor Wendi, who devoted considerable energy to restoring Chang An, which had essentially been in ruins since the end of the Han Period. The monastic community's activities received approval from the Tang emperor in 621 and were later consecrated to Guanyin in 662 after a monk from Suzhou had brought a Guanyin *sutra* (*Guanyinjing*) to the temple. Nevertheless, the name Qinglongsi was not adopted until 711. The temple was destroyed a century and a half later in 845 when foreign religions were proscribed; the destruction was so widespread that knowledge of the temple's precise location ultimately disappeared.

In 1963 archeologists undertook exploratory excavations but they did not resume their work until ten years later, in 1973, and then in 1979 and 1980. It appears that they successfully determined the location of the temple in spite of the limited archeological discoveries: tiles, a small gilded bronze Buddha, another Buddha created from a silver alloy, and the remains of a third Buddha fashioned from "three colored" ceramic materials as well as fragments of a red terra cotta shrine-pagoda and fragments from several murals. These finds confirm that the site contained a Buddhist place of worship consisting of several buildings, maybe Qinglongsi.

All of the elements contributing to the vitality of Tang Buddhism appear to have been entirely eradicated for more than a thousand years and, in this particular case archeologists' efforts closely resemble a meditation on the theme of impermanence. In the interim, however, certain interesting and possibly controversial ideas are coming to light. For example, there is the theory concerning the origins of *hiragana,* the Japanese cursive script which is traditionally believed to have been developed by Kukai from a simplified version of the Chinese alphabet. Today, it appears that Japanese who were studying in China created this instrument so that they could rapidly transcribe in their own language the enormous quantities of knowledge that they were obliged to absorb within a relatively short period of time. At least, this is the viewpoint upheld by scholars in China.

VIII.   THE SONG DYNASTY

Traces of Shipyards

With respect to the Song Period, contemporary archeology is primarily bringing to light certain elements of exceptional importance in the history of technology, especially in the field of navigation.

For nearly ten years excavations at the Quanzhou (Fujian) shipyards have uncovered the remains of magnificent sea-going vessels which subsequently permitted Zheng He (1375–1435) to complete seven voyages to the "Western Ocean," even as far as Mozambique. Balanced by heavy keels with watertight compartments in the holds, a stern rudder, and after 1119, a compass, (the mode of operation of which was described by Shen Gua (1031–1095), these vessels were capable of carrying several thousand people. Henhouses and small vegetable gardens on the deck made it possible to meet the food requirements of these "floating cities."

These impressive relics from the coasts of southeastern China may confirm one of the theories currently advanced by Chinese historians. It is their belief that the Djurchets' invasion of northern China in 1125, as well as relocation of the Imperial government to the mouth of the Yangtze, was merely a political counterpart and a culmination for a phenomenon which had already existed since the rise of the Song dynasty at the end of the tenth century; namely, the intellectual and technical superiority of southern China.

Ceramics

Ceramic creations are also perceived differently than they were fifteen years ago. Now it is less appropriate to speak of astonishing discoveries than of significant clarifications concerning previously identified categories whose dates or provenance had been defined in an imprecise manner. There have been interesting technical clarifications, such as those provided by continued investigation of the Yaozhou kilns mentioned previously.

The tenth century was distinguished by significant progress in regulating kiln fires. These advances were attributable to several changes, beginning with elementary improvements in the internal layout of kilns. During the Tang Period, for example, wares were fired on triangular supports, leaving traces that appear as recesses on all of the bowls and plates of that era. In the tenth century, potters began to use small studs which left only slight imprints on the base and permitted hot air to flow more freely around their products. Finally, there was the fundamental achievement of learning how to regulate intense flames. In 1973, three kilns from the Song Period were discovered at Yaozhou. Approximately 3 meters long and 1.2 meters wide, these kilns contained a duct of 2.5 meters in order to convey air from a rectangular hearth at one end of the kiln. On the other side, two large chimneys, the lower portions of which were covered by a wall containing holes permitted combustion gases to escape. By opening or closing these holes, a potter could freely reduce or increase the air flow inside his kiln. Thus, it was possible from then on to adjust baking temperatures downward. During the Five Dynasties Period, therefore Yaozhou began to produce the blue-green wares which later became the famous celadons of the Northern Song. These were monochromatic wares, because all of the Song ceramic wares, or at least the majority of luxury items, can be identified by rejection of polychromy or the efforts to obtain color contrasts that so deeply fascinated artisans of the Tang Period.

Recent excavations have also uncovered another important object: a grinding wheel with a diameter of 5.5 meters. This contrivance was essentially comparable to a cider press: heavy stone wheels turned within a circular channel to crush the clay,

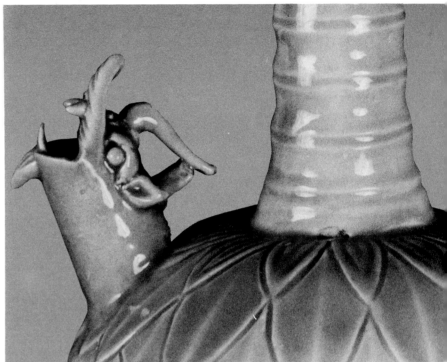

156-157
Kundika pouring pot. White Ding pottery with ornamentation engraved beneath the glaze. Northern Song Period (second half of tenth century). Discovered in the Qingzhongyuan pagoda (995) at Dingxian (Hebei) in 1969. Height: 60.5 cm.
The pouring spout is enhanced by a mask representing a unicorn or a playfully fashioned chimera. This piece had been concealed inside a stone vault with painted walls along with gold and silver coins, and fifty-five other ceramic objects.
Cf. *Wenwu,* 1972, 8, p. 44 and pl. 6, no. 1.

158
Jug in the form of a parrot. Pottery with brownish-orange glaze. Northern Song Period (960–1125). Discovered in 1969 in the Qinglingsi pagoda (977) at Dingxian (Hebei). Height: 15.6 cm. Waist diameter: 11 cm.
This charming piece from the beginning of the Song period evokes qualities which master craftsmen in northern China would attempt to perpetuate under the Liao rulers (916–1125).
Cf. *Wenwu,* 1972, 8.

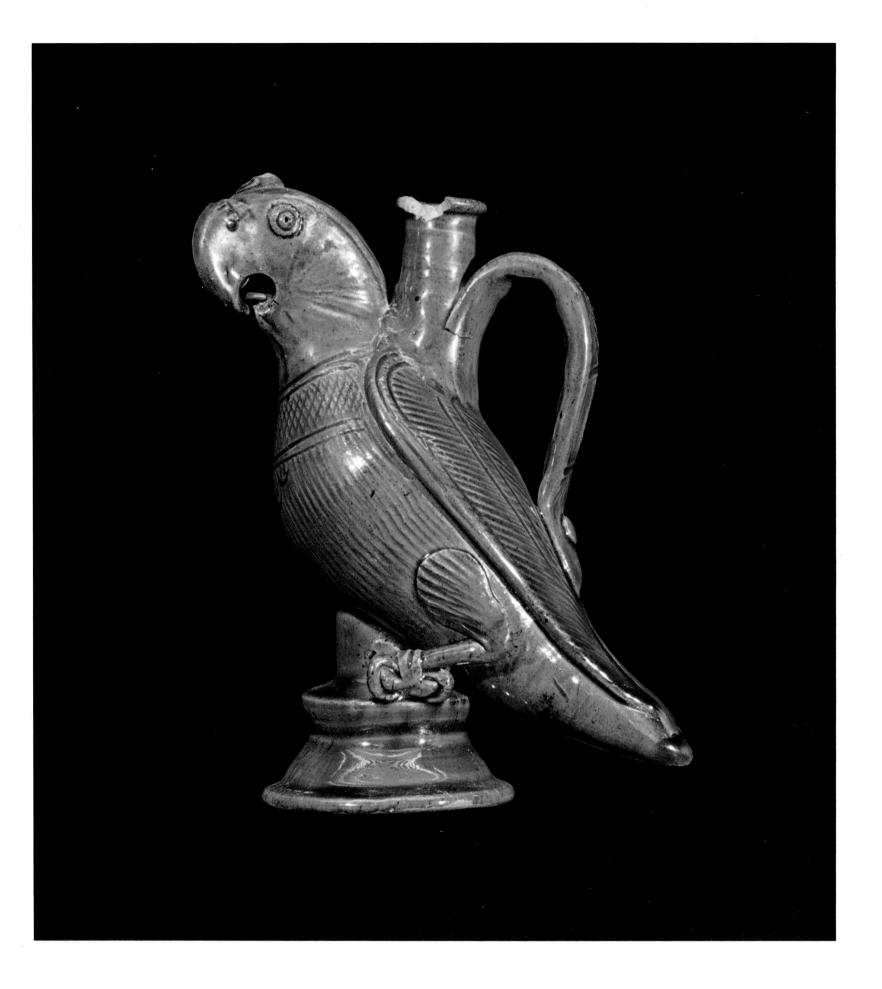

159

Kundika pouring pot. White Ding pottery with incised ornamentation beneath the glaze. Northern Song Period (second half of tenth century). Discovered in the Qingzhisi pagoda at Dingxian (Hebei) in 1969. Height: 15.4 cm. Waist diameter: 11 cm.

The term *kendi* or *kundi,* derived from the Sanskrit word *kundika,* refers to a water pitcher, or, in its original form, a drinking jug containing a spout. Examples exist throughout Asia from Persia to Japan. This particular *kundika* possesses a slender shape, like that of pitchers which Buddhist iconography placed in the hands of the Avalokitesvara (Guanyin) bodhisattva. Pilgrims usually carried pitchers of this type on their jouneys. In addition to this charming piece of white pottery, the treasure buried within the foundation of the Qinglingsi pagoda consisted of an exceptionally abundant horde. In addition to 700 gold, bronze, or ceramic creations, there were more than 27,000 bronze coins, which were used in China from the Warring States Period (475 B.C.–221 B.C.) until the beginning of the Northern Song Period (end of tenth century).
Cf. *Wenwu,* 1972, 8.

160

Vase with a "lotus" foot. Pottery with bluish glaze. Incised decoration beneath the glaze. Song Period (eleventh century–thirteenth century). Discovered at Jingdezhen in 1977. Height: 22.6 cm. Neck diameter: 3.3 cm. Foot diameter: 7.5 cm.

Until recently this type of vase was considered relatively rare, although recent excavations have yielded several specimens.
Cf. *Wenwu,* 1980, 2, p. 73 and pl 8, no. 1.

in order to prepare the potter's materials more adequately. Although this same method was described at the end of the Ming Period in a treatise known as the *Tiangong kaiwu* (1638), comparably ancient examples intended for producing potter's clay had not been discovered heretofore.

Greater knowledge of Song ceramic production was also obtained from finds at Linan (Zhejiang) in 1969. This site contained an abundance of *bisiyao,* "secret wares" that were actually celadons from Yuyao with a muted green glaze applied to a porcelain like sandstone body. The foundation pit of a pagoda at Dingxian (Hebei Province), which was likewise discovered in 1969, contained comparable treasures. A lavish collection of 700 gold, silver and jade items was accompanied by elegant white wares, including a conch shell decorated with carved waves beneath the glaze.

Lastly, we should also mention the finds unearthed during the past thirty years at Longquan (Zhejiang) and items discovered at Nanchang and Jingdezhen in Jiangxi. In those locations, an entire repertoire of charming subjects evoking the subsequent ceramic sculpture of the Yuan Period emerged, alongside a high-quality production of ordinary items. The world of the theater is extensively represented, both at Jingdezhen and at certain sites in Jiangxi where several operatic characters were discovered in 1975 in the form of mortuary pieces (*mingqi*) of an unprecedented type. Aside from their artistic or anecdotal qualities, these figurines provide evidence of the rise of the opera in China long before the Yuan dynasty, which certainly played a decisive role, but solely by encouraging a dramatic genre which had existed since an earlier period. Today, an extremely scientific survey of the clays and other materials used in Longquan products, including those intended for ordinary purposes, is being completed with the aim of establishing more precise knowledge about wares that have previously been described in overly subjective terms.

In every region of China, discovery of the remnants of kilns tends to demonstrate the extensiveness of methods that are largely comparable from one province to another: examples have been unearthed at Zhaozhou in Guangdong (discovered in 1954–1956), at Putian in Fujian (excavations in 1968 and 1976), at Cicun in Shandong (excavations in 1976) and also in Shaanxi, where two ancient porcelain kilns were identified in 1975.

Furthermore, fifty years of research and discoveries have partially reconstructed the history of the famous "blue and white" *qinghua* creations. For a considerable time it had been believed that production was limited or circumscribed to the Jingdezhen

161
Pouring vessel in the form of a mermaid. White pottery. Liao Period (916–1125). Discovered at Shicao (Liaoning) in 1976. Height: 15.3 cm. Length: 19.3 cm. Foot diameter: 7.7 cm.
This pouring vessel represents a relatively rare category: baroque pottery constituting not only utensils but sculptures. The young maiden's head, which is adorned with two heavy side plaits, possesses a doll-like, almost babyish face. Her hands are supporting a pouring spout in the form of a dragon's head. The waist of the vessel is in the form of a fish whose tail evokes movement through the water. An opening for filling this vessel is located on the back of the fish, along with fins which are undoubtedly those of a mermaid or of a siren whose feet are suggested by the claws appearing on the foot. This specimen constitutes an excellent example of the artistic originality of the Liao. Although they had been sinicized, they never forgot that they were Khitans, who had originally inhabited the steppes as animal-breeders and hunters. The Liao were always fascinated by observation of the world and transposition of images into simple forms which were combined so as to provide audacious associations.
Cf. *Wenwu,* 1981, 8, p. 68 and pl. 8, fig. 5.

kilns in Jiangxi or to this general vicinity. Some scholars attributed the origins of *qinghua* to the Song Period, whereas others proposed the Yuan Period or even later eras.

Reconsideration of these perspectives actually began independently of field archeology when John A. Pope in the United States demonstrated in 1952 and 1956 the high quality of "blue and white wares" from the Yuan Period while also confirming the relative diversity of the most ancient specimens. These findings persuaded some scholars to consider earlier origins as well as multiple provenances. On the basis of items found in an early fourteenth century tomb that was discovered at Hangzhou in

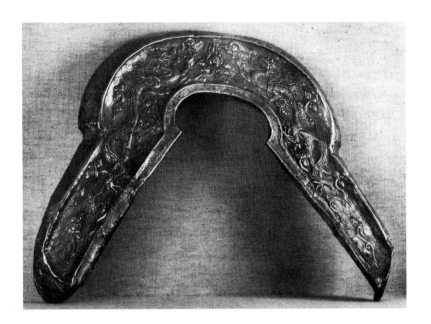

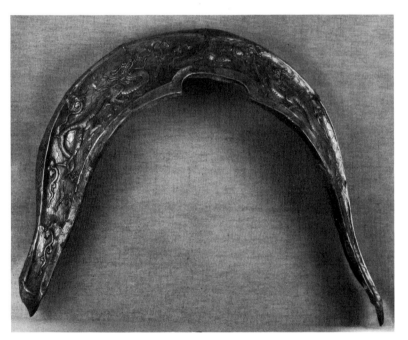

162-163

Saddle bow ornament. Gilded silver, with *repoussé* work. Liao Period (916–1125). Discovered at Chefong (Liaoning) in 1953. Height: 27.7 cm.

The pommel ornament (Illustration 162) was attached to the cantle ornament (Illustration 163). These items were found in the tomb of Xiao Julie, the son-in-law of Taizu, the first Liao emperor (reign: 907–927). Mortuary furnishings within the tomb also included white pottery and harness trappings. In this instance, it is possible to observe the two dragons placed on either side of the Buddhist pearl against a background composed of waves. Cf. *Kaogu xuebao,* 1956, 3, p. 13 and pl. 5, nos. 1–3.

164

Actor figurine. Jingdezhen pottery with traces of polychromy. Southern Song Period (1127–1279). Discovered at Poyang (Jiangxi) in 1975. Height: 20 cm. Jiangxi Provincial Museum.

A Southern Song tomb which was discovered at Poyang at the end of 1975, contained twenty-one statuettes intended as companions who would accompany the decedent and his spouse. Four other statuettes are comparable to this one. According to the epitaph, the tomb was occupied by Hong Zicheng (1186–1264), a prominent official who was a member of a famous family of scholars during the Song Period, although his rank did not permit an unduly large tomb. Thus, the originality of its furnishings compensated for quantity and lavishness. The statuettes depict theatrical performers whom the deceased official must have admired greatly. It is known that since the Han Period, it was customary for tombs to contain large retinues of entertainers, musicians and dancers. Hence, it is hardly surprising that the rise of the theatre would have led to the creation of suitable figurines. The unusual aspect is that these statuettes provide evidence of the development of the theatre in northern and southern China *(zaju* and *xiju)* as early as the Song and Jin Periods (1115–1234), and prior to the Yuan Period (1271–1368). Cf. *Wenwu,* 1979, 4, pp. 6–8.

1978, recent excavations offer support for the latter hypothesis.

Today, there is nothing to contradict the conclusion that production of *qinghua* wares originated in the Changsha region, where painted ceramic objects had been produced during extremely ancient eras. In turn, bluish adornment was introduced at the end of the Song Period, when full mastery of intense heat was achieved. Whereas importing of "Moslem blue" wares was traditionally attributed to the Yuan Period, it is highly probable that this category had already been introduced under the Tang rulers, in conjunction with multiple Sino-Persian encounters. Because of the quality of its pastes, the Jingdezhen pottery works must have played a leading role, but one should also recognize the importance of Jizhou, also in Jiangxi Province. During the Song Period, Jizhou produced items comparable to the famous *cizhou* of northern China: Song and Yuan tombs discovered within this region since 1949 have yielded many specimens. Among the pieces with a brownish or black floral decor on a white background, it has been possible to discover other ceramic products with bluish decoration. Today, these specimens have been recognized as the earliest "blue and white wares," which are attributable to an already ancient technique reinvigorated by the introduction of different pigments. Lastly, if any doubts persist, it should be recalled that "blue and white" wares have been discovered among the treasures buried in the foundations of certain Northern Song pagodas at Longquan in Zhejiang, notably the "Jinshata" pagoda.

To archeologists, the society of the Song Period, therefore, emerges as a favorable milieu, distinguished by the presence of a vast group of craftsmen seeking to achieve perfect creations with a variety of materials: ceramics, of course, but also precious metals or even lacquer. In terms of Chinese lacquer, connoisseurs are especially familiar with Yuan or Ming items produced by spectacular techniques, but there is an entire aspect of this material and of lacquer craftsmanship that has barely existed in China for an extended period of time, namely, the subtle techniques for creating gold and silver inlays. In Japan, perfect specimens of this type of work are still produced under the name *makkinru* or *maki-e*. Beautiful lacquer-work of this kind, which had been extremely rare in China for centuries, reappeared in 1977 and in 1978 during excavation of a Song tomb at Wujin in Jiangsu Province where there was an abundance of samples attributed to the year 1042.

Lastly, the expansion of this fascinating civilization is observable in an especially obvious form in the creations of ethnic groups who appear to have politically overcome the Song in northern China. For example, there are the painted walls of a Liao tomb (916 – 1125) discovered in 1972 at Qianwulibuge in Jilin Province, or in certain Jin tombs: Jiaozuo (Henan, 1973) and Jishan (Shanxi, 1979). One frequent characteristic of these tombs is the presence of an octagonal burial vault, in addition to a square antechamber, in accordance with a design that is typical of the peoples of northern China. When a tomb's walls were of stone, they were decorated with compositions whose style resembles the traditional style of scrolls containing historical paintings. The persons who are identified by inscriptions are depicted by carved lines or relief work. In tombs with brick walls, human figures and architectural components were recreated in still-life simulations in order to provide the illusion of an actual dwelling, with columns, capitals, doorways, windows, furniture and even family servants.

In keeping with the customs of these regions, the deceased were accompanied by *mingqi* in both compartments of the tomb. Picturesque figures were also included among the *mingqi* of Jiazuo (Laowanya): musicians, comedians, and dancers with pointed hats or caps, some of whom were exhibited in Europe (1973) and subsequently in the United States. It is undoubtedly necessary to regard these figurines as evidence of the extent to which inhabitants of the steppe were fascinated by forms of entertainment and dramatic art that had developed in China since the Tang Period but were carefully kept outside the confines of official art. One of the singular merits of archeology is to contribute artifacts when historical texts are deficient: at times, the written word is untrue, but an artifact never is.

IX. THE YUAN DYNASTY

For many centuries, the Sino-Mongolian society of the Yuan Dynasty was the target of direct and indirect censures from scholars who never fundamentally accepted the complete subjugation of the empire by foreign rulers. One of the contributions of modern archeology is that it has indeed directed our eyes toward the creations of a period which, for better and for worse, profoundly shaped China's history.

Discoveries in Dadu (Beijing)

One of the most interesting aspects has been the unfortunately short-lived rediscovery of Dadu, the capital which the Yuan emperors began to erect in 1267 in the same location as modern Beijing. The Yuan enclave was significantly changed by the Ming dynasty, who enlarged it in a southerly direction in order to establish their "Northern Capital." Beijing has been the capital of China there.

One exceptional discovery (1969) owes its origin to ambitious projects, which are always beginning anew in China, and paradoxically, to the devastating strength of the Cultural Revolution. This discovery consisted of a barbican which protected the Gate of Harmony and Equity (*Heyimen*), which was located within the western wall in the vicinity of the present-day Xizhimen district. *Heyimen* was actually one of Dadu's eleven gates, and safeguarded an enclosed area with a perimeter of 28,600 meters. *The History of the Yuan* (*Yuan Shi*) described the circumstances that led to erection of this defensive structure. In 1358, rebellious peasants had gained control of the outskirts of Dadu. Fearing the worst, Emperor Shun ordered immediate construction of means of defense at each of the eleven gates leading into the Imperial city, as well as the installation of

165
Qinghua vase "with the three friends." Pottery with blue decoration under the glaze. Yuan Period (1271–1368). Discovered at Poyang (Jiangxi) in 1976. Height: 17 cm. Neck diameter: 5.7 cm. Foot diameter: 5.9 cm.
This vase which was discovered at the same time as another *qinghua* ("blue and white" ware) specimen contains the famous "three friends" decorative arrangement: a pine, a plum tree, and a bamboo tree. The pine suggests longevity while the plum tree suggests the return of spring and eternal youth. The bamboo tree symbolizes intelligent flexibility and the scholar's indomitable spirit. The "three friends" theme which Song scholars had popularized, was often reproduced by the potters who created the first "blue and white" wares during the Yuan Period.
Cf. *Wenwu*, 1980, 2, p. 73 and pl. 8, no. 4.

drawbridges to prevent attackers from crossing the moat. This hastily begun project was completed in less than one year. In 1969 the inhabitants of Beijing discovered one of the redoubtable barbicans. Supported by an earthen wall (24 meters thick at the bottom) that was coated with bricks, this structure was 22 meters high. Heavy blocks of stone and a brick arch enclosed a passageway which was 4.6 meters wide, 6.68 meters high, and 10 meters thick. Three rooms for sentinels were situated directly above the entrance, and special ducts made it possible to douse the wooden door-panels that sealed the gateway to reduce the risk of destruction by fire. On the basis of current knowledge, it does not appear that a comparable form of military architecture was developed any earlier in China. Unfortunately, as soon as the barbican had been photographed and measured, demolition of Beijing's walls — not to be confused with the walls of the Forbidden City — implacably continued. Thus, the Heyimen barbican has ceased to exist.

Ceramics and the Origin of "Blue and White" Wares

Certain traces of the Yuan capital Dadu continue to be unearthed at the various construction sites that are a ubiquitous feature of Beijing's landscape. In 1970 a large copper urn containing two celadons and nine "blue and white" pieces from the Yuan Period were discovered near the Drum Gate (*Jingulou dajie*). Similarly, a black and white vase and a superb specimen of lacquer inlaid with mother of pearl were found within the brick terrace of a dwelling from the Yuan Period. The fine fragments of mother of pearl had been arranged so as to evoke the legendary palace of Guanghan, which the Chinese think of when they gaze at the moon.

It is tempting to attribute a symbolic meaning to a discovery which was widely acclaimed in 1976, when the remains of a large Chinese vessel from the much-maligned Yuan Period were found near the Korean coast at Sinan. The cargo consisted of 7,168 items, including 6,457 ceramic pieces. Within the latter category, there were 3,466 celadons, 2,281 specimens of white wares from Longquan and Jingdezhen, and 117 black-and-rainbow-colored pieces known as *jian,* which are referred to as *temmoku,* or "heaven's eyes," in Japanese. In addition, there were 700 *jun* objects adorned with splashes of violet as well as more than 500 ceramic pieces produced in other regions, particularly

Korea. The sunken ship's cargo also included 130 bronzes, lamps, censers, coins made of copper and bronze, lacquer, gems, animal hides, and wooden objects. Because the ship had rested at a depth of twenty meters for several centuries, two-thirds of the cargo had been fossilized.

When did this ship sink? Archeologists have been able to determine the date by considering several factors. Chapter 70 of the *True History of Hongwu* (*Hongwu Shili*) states that at the end of 1371, Hong Wu the first Ming emperor, forbade his subjects to travel on the high seas or engage in private trade. This edict was one of several measures intended to curtail and eliminate the activities of pirates who were raiding the Chinese coast. Although the edict was not promulgated until 1371, Zhu Yuanzhang (Hong Wu) had already been enforcing it for several years in conquered regions. In fact, he had seized Zhijiang in 1367. Thus, the ship could only have departed from China at an earlier point.

We do not know which port it sailed from. There are multiple possibilities. Mingzhou? Quanzhou? Another port? Similarly, the destination has not been clearly determined. Was it Japan or Korea? Both the Koreans and the Japanese deeply admired the types of wares that this ship was carrying. It is not inconceivable that the vessel sank while departing from Korea for the archipelago, for it still contained a substantial cargo of such items as *temmoku* or Korean wares that were especially popular in Japan.

This particular discovery furnishes unimpeachable evidence of the renown that China's principal kilns had gained in other nations during this period. In fact, significant expansion of the Longquan kilns had begun during the earliest years of the Yuan Period, when smaller kilns were erected in the vicinity of the main facility known as the *Dayao*. More than 150 new kilns were established, and it is possible to trace the increasing prosperity of this region by the enlargement of the circle of new kilns around the center, especially in an easterly direction. Furthermore, the

166
Octagonal ping vase. Pottery with blue and white decoration. Yuan Period (1271–1368). Discovered at Baoding (Hebei) in 1964. Height: 51.5 cm. Beijing, Palace Museum.
This vase and another similar vase, which constitute a pair, marvelously represent the technique of the first "blue and white" wares (*qinghua*) produced during the Yuan Period. A sumptuous decorative motif which presents a glimpse of dragons playing amid the waves has been traced with "Mohammedan" blue (imported cobalt pigment) upon a porcelain-like sandstone underlayer (visible at the base) which had been coated with a white slip. On the shoulder-piece, it is possible to observe four medallions containing flowers or phoenixes and unicorns (*qilin*). The foot contains four medallions with flowers.
Cf. *Wenwu,* 1965, 2, p. 17 and pl. 11, nos. 1–2.

167-170

Four zaju actors. Terra cotta. Yuan Period (1271–1368). Discovered at Jiaozuo (Henan) in 1963. Height: 33 to 38 cm.

These actors and the dancer remind us that, under the Yuan emperors and with the support of these Mongol rulers of China, drama achieved success and continued to thrive during subsequent centuries.
Cf. *Wenwu,* 1979, 8, pp. 8, 9, 14.

171

Large guan vessel with a lid. Pottery. Red decoration under the glaze. Yuan Period (1271-1368). Discovered at Haidian, Beijing in 1961. Height: 66 cm. Neck diameter: 25.3 cm. Waist diameter: 47 cm.

The virtuosity of potters during this period is demonstrated by the elegant motif of flowering stems and valances appearing on this vessel with twelve lobes (nine on the lid). It also reflects an interesting quest which, although it began under the Yuan Dynasty, did not truly end until the Ming Period: this was the quest for a red underglaze *(liulihong).* Copper oxide pigments, because of their instability, often tend to produce a bluish gray during the initial stages. The results were similar to those achieved with *qinghua* ("blue and white" wares) because the first specimens tinted with copper oxide pigments are often difficult to distinguish from *qinghua* wares.
Cf. *Wenwu,* 1972, 8, pp. 52–53 and pl. 8, no. 5.

luxurious items discovered in tombs or in Dadu confirm that China's Mongol rulers were infatuated with Longquan wares. At least for the fourteenth century, it has been possible to classify these wares according to a relatively precise chronological framework as a result of recent finds.

Under the Yuan emperors there was also additional expansion of the activities of the Jingdezhen pottery works, which had already existed during the Tang Period and had prospered during the Song Period. In this region there were more than 300 public and private kilns producing green and white wares, as well as bowls and dishes known as *shufu,* still produced at the Hutian kilns. This transformation was truly the beginning of a process of expansion that during the Ming Period converted Jingdezhen into an industrial production center.

Still, this evidence does not permit reliable interpretation of the mysterious history of the *qinghua.* The cargo of the wrecked ship did not include any "blue and white" pieces, a fact that would seem to demonstrate that even though production of *qinghua* items expanded under the Yuan emperors, these wares were not intended for ordinary use. It is also possible that they had not yet contributed to the growth of a thriving export trade that did emerge subsequently. At least this circumstance may have been true with respect to Korea and Japan, whose inhabitants preferred less ornate wares. It was different in regions west of China: fragments of "blue and white" wares from the Yuan Period have been discovered as far away as Sudan even though they are of ordinary quality. In China itself "blue and white" porcelain seems to have been extremely rare during this period: specimens have only been discovered at a few sites, as in the case of the Jintan collection found in Jiangsu Province in 1966.

These treasures included an unusually beautiful urn with "blue and white" decoration (height, 26 centimeters; neck diameter, 22.2 centimeters; waist diameter, 35.5 centimeters), where dragons encircle the waist. The dragons' four disproportionately long and twisted claws ultimately merge with clouds, which are prolonged as arrows resembling flashes of lightning. The base of the urn and the bottom portion of the neck are adorned with mantling. The blue decoration is relatively transparent although it does contain small black specks, while the deep and dense white of the glaze has a milky appearance.

An indication of the great value of the urn is the fact that it was buried at the same time as a superb assortment of silver items, including a deep platter whose sides contained an embossed motif resembling the dragons on the urn, although this particular motif continues in the form of a somewhat grotesquely

172

Jun vase on its base. Lavender and violet pottery with blue glaze. Yuan Period (1271–1368). Discovered at the base of the northern wall of Beijing in 1972. Height: 63.8 cm. Waist (vase) diameter: 17.5 cm. Neck diameter: 15 cm. Diameter of base: 19.2 cm.

This beautiful lavender-blue vase which is tinged with violet has a brown trim. Its profile, with two zoomorphic handles, is reminiscent of the Sassanid amphoras which were so highly esteemed during the Tang Period. The vase is a *jun,* representing production techniques which were perfected during the Song Period.

Cf. *Kaogu,* 1972, 6 (comparable specimen: page 31).

173

Lion. Stone. Yuan Period (1271–1368). Discovered in 1964 at the base of the northern wall of Beijing. Height: 27 cm. Length: 24 cm. Width: 24 cm.

This stone lion is one of the few traces of Dadu, the Yuan capital. Although the lion was a typical protective symbol for Buddhist temples this energetic beast is reclining, in a pose typical of domesticated animals.

Cf. *Kaogu,* 1972, 6, pl. 11, no. 1.

174

"Blue and white" (qinghua) urn. Pottery with blue ornamentation beneath the glaze. Yuan Period (1271–1368). Discovered at Jintan (Jiangsu) in 1966. Height: 26 cm. Neck diameter: 22.2 cm. Waist diameter: 35.5 cm. Zhenjiang Museum.

In addition to interesting specimens of silversmiths' work, the Jintan treasure contained this beautiful "blue and white" urn. It attests the level of quality which potters during the Mongol Period had achieved with these wares. It is probable that the Jintan treasure was hidden shortly after 1350 in order to protect it from the destructive turmoil which, after the mid-thirteenth century, accompanied the rapid decline of Mongol authority in southern China and the seizure of power by a new native-born dynasty, the Ming. The principal decorative motif is a rampant dragon with four claws. Beneath the neck of the urn, there is a set of escutcheons where motifs representing good fortune alternate with floral decoration.

Cf. *Wenwu,* 1980, 1, p. 59 and pl. 6, no. 1.

175

Pitcher with lid. Pottery with blue and red decoration beneath the glaze. Yuan Period (1271–1368). Discovered at Baoding (Hebei). Height: 42.3 cm. Neck diameter: 15.2 cm.

This extremely beautiful pitcher whose lid is adorned with a lion is characterized by extremely complex decoration. The body, which is visible at the foot, is distinguished by an ochre hue, and it was coated with a white slip. Blue decorative motifs, as well as motifs in red, were painted upon the slip in accordance with the delicate "red beneath the glaze" *(liulihong)* technique which had been developed during the Yuan Period. As a result a surface which is demarcated by double scalloping in barbotine is adorned with a blue and red floral pattern. In turn, the blue portions are represented by a multiplicity of shapes: valances on the foot and the lid; friezes around the neck and on the edge of the lid; and medallions containing lotus motifs with a background of waves upon the shoulder.

176

Vase with horseman. Pottery with "blue and white" ornamentation beneath the glaze. Yuan Period (1271–1368). Discovered at Nankin (Jiangsu) around 1955. Height: 44.1 cm. Nankin Museum.

This "blue and white" vase, which is fully typical of the prevalent technique during the Yuan Period (the motif beneath the glaze was applied upon a white slip which conceals the ochre of the underlayer), is a *meiping,* a vase intended for plum blossoms. The specimen is noteworthy on account of the variety and vivacity of its floral decoration where a human figure also appears. This combination is directly inspired by traditional Chinese paintings of horses and riders, which were admired by the Mongol rulers.

shaped handle; nine small cups with craftmen's inscriptions or signatures; as well as three urns and six platters, one of which has a lotus petal and *vajra* motifs associated with esoteric Buddhism. The treasure also included silver jewelry and coins. The inscriptions appearing on the silver wares have permitted establishment of a *terminus a quo,* or an earliest possible date. Furthermore, the unpretentious outward appearance of this hoard suggests that it may have been concealed in haste under the pressure of dramatic events. Accordingly, Chinese archeologists have regarded this circumstance as a reflection of the turbulence that marked the collapse of the Yuan dynasty.

At the opposite end of China, at Huochengxian in Mongolia, a somewhat smaller treasure-urn (diameter, 50 centimeters; depth, 60 centimeters) was discovered during the winter of 1975. Its contents included bowls, platters of various sizes and a bronze stem cup. This hoard was attributed to the Yuan Period, and two series of excavations took place during 1976 and 1977. The most outstanding pieces were a platter and a large dish with "blue and white" decoration. Amid a floral motif, the edges of the platter contain the *fulu* characters invoking good fortune, while two phoenixes adorn the inner surfaces of the dish.

Coins discovered together with these ceramics confirmed the Yuan origins of the collection. Some small coins contained the inscription "*Alimoli,*" which was undoubtedly the name of the town that was there during the Yuan Period. These coins provide the first concrete evidence of a town whose location had never been precisely determined despite fifteen years of investigations by archeologists, even though this town is cited in historical texts. Thus, entire civilizations have been rediscovered as a result of the actions of misers or merely through the actions of men who were frightened and wanted to protect their belongings. It is also interesting that this find primarily contained "blue and white" wares. In other words, they were still regarded as prized possessions during this period when they were a novelty. For these reasons, it is possible that Huochengxian may soon acquire considerable importance.

X. THE MING DYNASTY

After the Yuan dynasty ended China appears to have entered a period that contemporary archeologists have been rather slow to approach for various reasons.

One such reason applies to most countries. Private collections and museums still contain abundant quantities of items from a more recent past. We are familiar with them and may encounter them frequently, without feeling any need to seek similar examples elsewhere. When there is an insufficient number of interested persons, or when funds are inadequate — an extremely widespread situation — human and financial resources tend to be allocated to indispensable excavations that may yield unknown artifacts to the detriment of research which would provide less immediately impressive results.

However, Western observers are somewhat astounded to find that such a detached attitude is maintained toward the early Ming Period. In Europe the fifteenth and sixteenth centuries are regarded as fascinating eras whose creations are rare treasures, whereas an entirely different situation exists in China. Despite its grandeur, the Ming dynasty is accurately perceived as an immediate prelude to the Qing dynasty, which is associated with the political, moral and economic collapse of the empire and the difficult beginnings of a renewal still laden with uncertainties. Whereas it is possible for historians to pursue a coherent perspective, it is more difficult for patriotic people examining these less remote periods to encounter the same image of a majestically thriving society that, within its own context, had already reached its apogee during the twelfth century. Scholars from every nation, including China itself, have attempted to delineate the many factors that had rapidly led to a shocking ossification of Chinese culture by the nineteenth century. These circumstances may explain why only a limited number of studies concerning the Ming and Qing Periods are being published at this time. It is possible that the "interval" along the vast and prolific river of Chinese history is still too brief for historians to consider themselves sufficiently capable of impartiality.

Another reason is primarily of a theoretical nature. What, indeed, are proper boundaries for archeology? In the West there appears to be a simple answer. Louis Réau has observed that "if archeology constitutes a means of explaining the past by studying its monuments there is no reason to refrain from speaking of an archeology for the seventeenth or even the nineteenth century." Although this same principle would be applicable to China, a somewhat different accent emerges. There the true domain of archeology tends solely to encompass evidence that can compensate for the lack of historical texts. Instead of adopting a theoretical perspective, historical research in China is carried out and primarily based on practical principles. The special domain of archeology consists of eras that preceded the origins of writing, although a relative lack of written documents allows the boundaries of archeology to be extended as far as the beginnings of Imperial rule. Since official archives as an administrative instrument were established during the Han Period, archeology is often perceived in China today as being confined to development of information that permits dating of unfamiliar relics or of relics whose existence is only indicated by written descriptions. Thus, archeology is frequently regarded as a source of confirmation for occasionally obscure accounts of eras from the Han to the Song Period, or as a means of enriching overly simplified interpretations of the artistic and technical feats of the past. For eras subsequent to the Song Period, archeology only appears useful as a means of clarifying minor points or of providing firm supporting evidence for monographs. Studies pertaining to the pottery kilns are an example of this tendency. Furthermore, when Chinese archeologists approach the Ming

Period, they have a sense of entering a contemporary realm that is represented by an overabundance of artifacts and texts. Indeed, they feel that they have little to contribute.

Nevertheless, archeological evidence from the Ming Period undeniably exists. For example, in 1970 while the Cultural Revolution was still taking place, archeologists investigated the tomb of Zhu Dan, tenth son of Zhu Yuanzhang who founded the Ming dynasty. The young prince who had died when he was

nineteen years old was buried at Zhangzhai (Zhouxian) in Shandong Province. His tomb was a vast underground structure covered with heavy bricks and extending nearly 100 meters into the side of a mountain. Inside the tomb the deceased prince was accompanied by a thousand terra cotta statues and by traditional funerary objects. Whereas none of these items truly provided new knowledge with respect to the arts or techniques of this period, the paintings and calligraphy found within the tomb have significantly enriched China's heritage. The prince's treasures included calligraphy in the "fine gold" style of the Southern Song emperor Gaozong (1127–1162), as well as two paintings. One painting depicted butterflies and hibiscus blossoms, while the other showed sunflowers. In addition, the tomb contained more than 300 printed texts from the Yuan Period. Recently, excavations have taken place at tombs in the Nanjing region (1977, tombs of Xu Pu and his spouse), near Nanchang in Jiangxi Province (1979, tomb of Zhu Yiyin), and at Sinan in Guizhou Province (1980, tomb of Zhang Shenzong

177
The Dingling: the tomb of the Ming emperor Shenzong (Wanli) (1573–1619).
The thirteen Ming tombs, which are a favorite attraction for Beijing's inhabitants and have been one of the few excursion sites open to foreigners, are situated within an extremely beautiful mountainous setting forty kilometers northwest of Beijing. The most recent (Ming Period) sections of the Great Wall are located nearby. Triumphal arches, the Sacred Way *(shendao),* steles, and outer and inner walls demarcate the visitor's path toward the center of the tomb, which is open to the public.

178
Tomb of Emperor Wanli: sacrificial chamber. The three white marble thrones are ready to be used by the spirits of the emperor and his two wives, who are also buried within this tomb. All of the urns are suitably arranged for ceremonial use. At the center, the largest urns, which are adorned with the five-clawed Imperial dragon, served as "10,000 year lamps" which were intended to burn "forever."

and his spouse). All of these tombs contained the customary allotments of artifacts and documents, such as "bills of sale" (*maidiquan*) granting property titles to the deceased in imitation of earthly life, or in a purely imaginary form.

When Ding Ling, the burial site of the Ming emperor Wanli (who ruled from 1573 to 1619), was opened, the public had an opportunity to visit one of the most spectacular funerary monuments from this era — an immense underground palace built of stone. The sepulchre included an antechamber, a vast corridor, two side vaults and the actual burial vault. Throngs of visitors have come to this site to admire the three reconstructed sarcophagi — the emperor's sarcophagus had been placed between those of his two wives — or the coffers which had formerly contained their belongings. All of the funerary objects are displayed in small ground-level exhibition halls adjacent to the tomb, or more frequently, in museums in Beijing. Extensive construction has been completed at the tomb entrance, with the result that its appearance and more specifically its "atmosphere" have been significantly altered. A concrete road and steps have been built for the many Chinese and foreign visitors who are eager to observe the ostentation of another era or, as the explanatory placards indicate, the quality of the tomb's materials and workmanship as well as the grandeur of a structure whose completion required the efforts of several thousand men per day for many months. This is the contemporary face of archeology as a means of promoting tourism and as a source of foreign exchange. This type of burden has been imposed upon every period, from modern times to prehistory. Thus, prestigious publications exalt the historical attractions of Xi'an, from the Neolithic village at Banpo to the monument that commemorates the arrival of the Eighth Route Army.

179
Tomb of Emperor Wanli: passageway leading to burial vaults.

Archeological research of recent periods also displays other more scholarly aspects. Many belong to the domain of epigraphy which is, of course, a pertinent science in relation to antiquity, although the artistic richness of other materials renders its contributions less prominent for eras prior to the end of the Tang Period. In contrast, epigraphic research pertaining to pre-modern or modern periods has awakened considerable interest among archeologists who are attracted by pure research or by its contemporary relevance. Hence, we can readily recognize the extent to which archeology, the science of the past, can also contribute to the present. At one time or another everyone has encountered references to the complex issue of China's borders with the Soviet Union. This is a problem that Father Gerbillon and the envoys who negotiated the Treaty of Nertchinsk were already attempting to solve at the end of the seventeenth century! Accordingly, it would not be possible to regard as merely coincidental the fact that commentaries accompanied by archeological observations were published in 1974 with respect to the Ashihata cliffside inscriptions which had been discovered in 1891, or inscriptions appearing on stelae (discovered in 1885) at the Yongning monastery (Yongningsi) at Liaoyang in Liaoning Province.

The cliffside inscriptions lauded the virtues of Song Guozong who, after receiving the title "General Ming Wei," journeyed to these remote northeastern regions during the reign of Yong Le (1403-1424) and again during the reign of Xuan De (1426-1435). In turn, the stelae contain inscriptions citing the arrival of a thousand soldiers and twenty-five large ships in 1411 in order to consolidate Chinese military authority within this region.

At the other end of China a similar purpose was associated with excavations along the southeastern coast in the Xisha Islands during 1974. The objective was to demonstrate, on the basis of an abundant harvest of ceramic creations from the Tang up to the Qing Period that this archipelago has a cultural identity that unites it with the Chinese mainland. Hence, for eras closer to our own it is indeed possible to consider the benefits of archeology in these terms.

Certain other discoveries, however, will always belong to the domain of pure scholarship. One example is the recovery of two forgotten works by the scholar Song Yinxing (1615-1645), who was the author of the famous *Tiangong kaiwu* (1637). His treatises, *"Concerning the Heavens" (Tan tian)* and *"Concerning the Weather" (Lun qi)*, which were popularized scientific works, reappeared in Jiangxi Province. Similarly, in 1965, archeologists digging at Guangshan in Henan Province unearthed a bronze shield that belonged to the movement known as the Red Turban Army (*Hongjinjun*), whose rebellion led to the collapse of the Yuan Dynasty and allowed Zhu Yuanzhang to take power. Priceless physical landmarks of this kind ultimately shed light upon the paths that historians must pursue.

CONCLUSION

Chinese archeology is not confined solely to "*Han*" regions whose boundaries and characteristics have sometimes been a source of intense debates. Indeed, we have briefly referred to this topic. Today, the broad question of identity emerges in relation to every important center of civilization: where do regions end and nations begin?

China's current government, which officially maintains a respectful stance toward the identities of local cultures, is attentively promoting the development of archeology in regions inhabited by "minorities." Political concerns likewise seem to explain this approach but how would it be possible to adopt a different policy in relation to peoples who sometimes played a decisive role in China's own history, having been not only adversaries but admirers of the attainments of the Central Plain? The problem of peripheral cultures is extremely complex because many ethnic groups and influences have come into play, creating cultural composites significantly different from those of Imperial China. Their creations were often fragile, traveling through time in a brief instant, whereas other creations became integral components within vast cultural chains that linked these cultures through Central Asia or the Middle East to the West by means of complicated and sometimes debatable pathways.

This phenomenon is not a new element. For example, the art of the Ordos region (or Sino-Siberian art) was admired by collectors at the turn of the century, and numerous specimens can be found in Western collections. Salmony's 1933 study of this topic continues to be relevant. Nevertheless, there are many properly identified and properly dated items today which represent a solid foundation for more comprehensive investigation of artifacts and of the societies that they represent.

For example, the marvelous creations of the Kingdom of Dian, which existed in Yunnan Province two thousand years ago, have been accessible since 1955. Similarly, the recent development of archeological research pertaining to the Kingdom of Chu, which existed during the Warring States Period, has revealed previously unsuspected affinities between the art of the southwestern mountain-dwellers and the creations of central China's inhabitants.

The Xiongnu, the fearsome northwestern neighbors whom the Great Wall ultimately failed to deter, had been remotely perceived through Si Ma Qian's descriptions. Indeed, recent discoveries have tended to confirm or to enrich the historian's masterful portrayal of the Xiongnu. Today, their civilization, which differed so significantly from China's agrarian society, is gradually coming to light at sites in Inner Mongolia. But it is still difficult to establish dates for relics from the end of the era of China's kings. In general, efforts to determine chronological limits are aided by the presence of Chinese artifacts buried at a given site or in close proximity. For example, certain artifacts from the Warring States Period, which were unearthed 500 meters from the site, provided reference points for attributing the Xiongnu tombs at Aluchaideng to a period several centuries before Christ. Hence, these are some of the oldest Xiongnu tombs to have ever been discovered.

The two tombs, where serious deterioration had been caused by the extremely sandy soil at this heavily wooded site that was highly suitable for human habitation, were discovered in 1972, and excavations began in 1973.

The burial accoutrements included 218 gold artifacts as well as certain silver items. Splendid jewelry, rectangular plaques adorned with images of animals in combat, and even a head-dress with a decorative bird placed at the top were created by highly diversified techniques such as casting, hammering and embossing. The tomb appeared to belong to a ruler. The assortment of jewelry, typical of items found in Xiongnu tombs from the seventh century to the third century B.C., confirms Si Ma Qian's descriptions of the fascination for ornaments among the rulers of this group that was so deeply feared by the Han. It is not surprising that these breeders of horses, sheep and deer would have created exceptional specimens of zoomorphic art, but Chinese archeologists have emphasized that images of tigers, horses, and goats may also represent the totems of clans within a society that was essentially dependent upon hunting.

Recent discoveries appear to indicate that there were four phases in the development of the zoomorphic objects that were ordinarily found along China's northern borders and in the provinces of Hebei, Shanxi, Shaanxi and Ningxia, or at least among ethnic minorities. From the end of the Shang Period until the beginning of the Zhou Period (thirteenth to ninth century B.C.), the predominant form of ornamentation at first consisted of animal heads that were extensions of the handles or hilts of bronze swords, knives and daggers. Subsequently, from the end of the Western Zhou dynasty to the beginning of the Spring and Autumn Period (ninth to sixth century B.C.), metal-workers discovered open-work, such as the famous round plates with coiled animal motifs. Typical of this metal work is the Xiajiadian category. Then, during a third phase extending from the end of the Spring and Autumn Period to the Warring States Period (sixth to second century B.C.), rectangular plates appeared alongside the round ones, which remained popular. The most elegant theme, namely that of combat among real or mythical beasts, originated at this time. The art of the Xiongnu who inhabited the Ordos steppes emerged during this phase. Finally, under the Western and Eastern Han Dynasties (second century B.C.–second century A.D.), there was extensive development of rectangular plates with open-work, which were worn as waist ornaments.

Hence, archeological research pertaining to China's peripheral regions is gradually developing: relics from the Yangshao culture at Suibin in Heilongjiang (discovered in 1973); ceramic adaptations of Shang and Zhou bronze motifs at Baijinbao in Helongjiang (discovered in 1974); numerous Han relics along the entire periphery of China; lavish tombs with paintings illustrating the life of a local dignitary during the Eastern Han Period (25–200 A.D.), at Holingol in Inner Mongolia (discovered in 1972); and Tang tombs filled with brocades, paintings, and mortuary figurines discovered in Turfan in 1972–1973. At the other end of China the originality of Yunnan appears to be consistently represented by various discoveries such as the twenty-seven tombs at Lijiashan (1972), which contained more than a thousand items, including elegant bronzes with the well-known motif of a tiger attacking the peaceful water buffalo.

Such lengthy enumerations only offer an approximate concept of the tasks facing Chinese archeologists at the present time, notwithstanding frequent official expressions of a desire to proceed deliberately and cautiously instead of digging hastily in the excitement of a "treasure hunt." Constantly confronted by the urgent need for excavations intended to preserve

180
Plaque in the form of a lion. Gold leaf worked by *repoussé* technique. Han Period (fourth century B.C.–third century A.D.). Discovered during 1976–1978 at Alagou (Xinjiang) in the Autonomous Uighur Region (Tomb M 30). Height: 11 cm. Length: 20.5 cm.
This ornamental plaque, which had shattered into several fragments, was found in one of the eighty-five tombs attributed to ethnic minorities in the vicinity of Alagou. Excavations at these tombs took place between 1976 and 1978. Insofar as it is possible to reconstruct the tomb today, Tomb M 30 appears to have been the tomb of a young woman who was buried with an entourage of slaves. The mortuary furnishings permit attribution of the tomb to the Western Han Period (206 B.C.–24 A.D.). The stylistic affinities between this plaque and the art of the steppes, from the Ordos to the Black Sea, are undeniable.
Cf. *Wenwu,* 1981, 1, pp. 18–22 and pl. 8, no. 4.

monuments and relics, which arises from the public works projects incessantly being promoted in China, they also face a need to publicize, study and interpret their discoveries. Otherwise, their many finds will merely accumulate as a vast assortment of uninvestigated objects. Under the dynamic guidance of Professor Xia Nai, the Archeological Institute publishes two significant periodicals: *Archeology* (*Kaogu*), that was originally intended primarily to provide reports concerning excavations, and the *Journal of Archeology* (*Kaogu*), that is an inexhaustible source of studies and first-hand information. The latter publication (since 1981) is accompanied by an exceptionally useful selective bibliography of Chinese publications pertaining to archeology.

Furthermore, nearly every prefecture or provincial university during recent years has begun to publish its own series of scientific periodicals where archeology receives well-deserved attention. *Archeology and Cultural Relics* (*Kaogu yu wenwu*), which is published by the University of Shaanxi in Xi'an, continues to be one of the most interesting new journals, whereas the quality of its counterparts often varies greatly. Similarly, museums, such as the Palace Museum (*Gugong Bowuguan*) in Beijing, or the Shanghai Museum (*Shanghai Bowuguan*), have begun to publish scholarly journals containing studies of items in their respective collections. This represents a far-reaching venture when one remembers that all of the principal discoveries from excavations tend to be entrusted to the principal regional museums.

Recently, archeological congresses have taken place in a different city each year: Xi'an in 1979, Wuhan in 1980, and Hangzhou in 1981. The first of these congresses pursued the objective of assessing archeological research during the past thirty years and defining current perspectives. The second congress, which was held in the true center of the Chinese mainland, devoted its efforts to studying the civilization of the Kingdom of Chu, whose prolific creations and multiple ramifications have been frequently cited throughout the present text. In turn, the third congress which took place in the former capital of the Southern Song Dynasty, returned to a broader, more classification-oriented perspective of present-day arche-

ology. The most recent report, which is now being prepared for publication, is intended to provide methodical descriptions of archeological research in each province. In this way, the report will renew and broaden the vision expressed by a compilation that was published in 1979, within the context of the first archeological congress, namely *Thirty Years of Archeology* (*Zhongguo kaoguxue sanshi nian*). An extremely beautiful Japanese edition of this publication was released in 1981 by the Heibonsha publishing company.

It is also important not to overlook the excellent journal *Cultural Relics* (*Wenwu*), which is published by the Cultural Relics Publishing House (*Wenwu chubanshe*). As the title indicates, its orientation is not solely archeological. Thus, important discoveries are often described within articles that, even though they provide less physical detail than reports appearing in *Archeology* (*Kaogu*) or in the *Journal of Archeology* (*Kaogu xuebao*), offer informative summaries and carefully situate these discoveries within the context of knowledge concerning China's history. The verifications and differing points of view emerging from consultation of these publications contribute to the growth of a living science that, among specialists, tends to transcend the political framework, so often emphasized in museums, and therefore comes to occupy an especially prominent position in the eyes of the populace.

Lastly, collections of studies, works whose length would not permit publication in periodicals without sacrificing brevity, or the indispensable reproductions of newly-discovered treasures are included among miscellaneous publications by the *Wenwu chubanshe,* such as monographs printed on ordinary paper or luxurious albums containing multiple color plates.

In general, one could get the impression that archeology is at this time one of the most active areas of research in China. It incontestably seems to be one of the most effective ways of acquainting other nations with Chinese culture. Indeed, archeology miraculously conveys a bountiful dream that influences every cultivated person, since it permits the world to discover creations that, above and beyond uniquely Chinese esthetic canons, evoke a response from everyone who encounters them?

APPENDIX

NOTES

1 H. Maspéro, *La Chine antique,* p. 1.

2 An Zhimin, "The neolithic archaeology of China. A brief survey of the last thirty years," *Kaogu,* 1979, 5, p. 393–403; English translation by Chang Kuang-chih, *Early China,* 5, 1979 –1980, p. 35–45.

3 "Excavation of a neolithic site in Dahe village near Zhengzhou," *Kaogu xuebao,* 1979, 3, p. 301–374.

4 "Excavation at San-li-ho in Chao-hsien, Shantung province," *Kaogu,* 1977, 4, p. 262–267.

5 "A report on the excavation of the Chengzi site in Zhucheng county, Shandong province," *Kaogu xuebao,* 1980, 3, p. 387–402.

6 Han Kangxin, Pan Qifeng, "On the racial type of the Dawenkou population," *Kaogu xuebao,* 1980, 3, p. 387-402.

7 H. Maspéro, *La Chine antique,* p. 22, 25–26.

8 "Excavation of the place remains of the early Shang at Erlitou in Yen-shih county, Henan province," *Kaogu,* 1974, 4, p. 234–248 and "Reconnaissances and trial diggings of the Erlitou sites in South Shanxi," *Kaogu,* 1980, 3, p. 203–210, 278.

9 "Excavations conducted to the South of Hsiao-t'-un village in Anyang," *Kaogu,* 1975, 1, p. 27–46 and "Excavation of the Yin tombs in the western section of Yin-hsü, 1969–1977," *Kaogu xuebao,* 1979, 1, p. 27–146.

10 "New finds of significance in the excavation of Yin-hsü. A well preserved royal tomb at Hsiao-t'un," *Kaogu,* 1977, 3, p. 151–153.

11 "Excavation of tomb no. 5 at Yin-hsü in Anyang," *Kaogu xuebao,* 1977, 2, p. 57–98.

12 H. Maspéro, *La Chine antique,* p. 40.

13 Bagley, Robert W., "P'an-lung ch'eng: a Shang city in Hupei," *Artibus Asiae,* XXXIX, 3/4, 1977, p. 165–219.

14 Kane, Virginia C., "A reexamination of An-yang archaeology," *Ars orientalis,* vol, 10, 1975, p. 93–110.

15 Vandermeersch, Léon, *Wangdao ou la Voie royale,* Paris, EFEO, 1977, vol. I, p. 32–33.

16 "Excavation of the western Zhou dynasty bronze pit at Fengchu village in Qishan county, Shaanxi province," *Wenwu,* 1979, 11, p. 12–15 and Fu Xinian, "First discoveries of western Zhou architecture at Fengchu (Qishan) in Shaanxi," *Wenwu,* 1981, 1, p. 65–74, and Fu Xinian, "A primary inquiry into the remains of the western Zhou buildings at Shaochen village in Fufeng county, Shaanxi province," Wenwu, 1981, 3, p. 34–45.

17 Vandermeersch, Léon, op. cit., vol. II, p. 484.

18 H. Maspéro, *La Chine antique,* p. 124.

19 H. Maspéro, *La Chine antique,* p. 263.

20 "The remains of the city of Chu at Jijiahu in Danyang county, Hubei province," *Wenwu,* 1980, 10, p. 31–41 and Goa Zhixi, Xiong Chuanxin, "Remains of things done by Chu man in Hunan," *Wenwu,* 1980, 10, p. 50–60.

21 "The Chu tombs of the Spring and Autumn Period at Xiasi in Xichuan county, Henan province," *Wenwu,* 1980, 10, p. 13–20 and "Excavation of the tomb no. 1 at Xiasi, Xichuan, Henan," *Kaogu,* 1981, 2, p. 119–127.

22 "Excavation of the ancient tomb of Hougudui at Gushi county, Henan province," *Wenwu,* 1981, 1, 1–8.

23 H. Maspéro, *La Chine antique,* p. 263.

24 H. Maspéro, *La Chine antique,* p. 339–340.

25 "The occupant and the chronology of tomb no. 1 at Wangshan," in *Acts of the First Archeological Congress,* 1979, p. 229–236.

26 "Excavation of the tomb of Zeng Houyi at Suixian county in Hubei province," *Wenwu,* 1979, 7, p. 1–24 and 32–39.

27 "Excavation of the tombs of the state of Chung Shan in the War-ring States Period at Pingshanxian, Hebei province," *Wenwu,* 1979, 1, p. 1–31.

28 Yang Hongxun, "A study of the king's mausoleum of Warring States Zhongshan kingdom and "Zhao Yu Tu"," *Kaogu xuebao,* 1980, 1, p. 119-138 and Fu Xinian, "A study of "Zhao yu tu" and its mausoleum planning unearthed from Zhongshan kingdom royal tombs of the Warring States Period at Pingshan county," *Kaogu xuebao,* 1980, 1, p. 97–118, and Huang Shengzhang, "Further notes on the royal tombs of the Zhongshan kingdom at Pingshan," *Kaogu,* 1980, 5, p. 444–447.

29 H. Maspéro, *La Chine antique,* p. 175.

30 L. Vandermeersch, *Wangdao,* vol. II, p. 383.

31 "Gold and silver coins of the state of Chu found at Gucheng village, Fugou county, Henan province," *Wenwu,* 1980, 10, p. 61–66.

32 "Excavation of the Spring and Autumn Period copper smelting remains at Tonglushan, Hubei province," *Wenwu,* 1981, 8, p. 30–39 and "Restauration of copper smelting shaft furnace at Tonglushan, Hubei province," *Wenwu,* 1981, 8, p. 40–45.

33 Lei Congyun, "Iron tools of the Warring States Period: discoveries and first conclusions," *Kaogu,* 1980, 3, p. 259–265.

34 H. Maspéro, *La Chine antique,* p. 351.

35 Hulsewé, A.F.P., "The Ch'in documents discovered in Hupei in 1975," *T'oung Pao,* LXIV, 4–5, 1978, p. 175–217.

36 Translated by Ed. Chavannes, vol. II, p. 193–195.

37 "Technique of making terra–cotta soldiers and horses at the time of the First Emperor," *Kaogu yu wenwu,* 1980, 3, p. 108–119.

38 "Clearing up some Qin tombs at Shangjiao village in Lintong," *Kaogu yu wenwu,* 1980, 2, p. 42–50.

39 Translated by Ed. Chavannes, vol. II, p. 195.

40 Translated by Ed. Chavannes, vol. II, p. 58.

41 Yuan Zhongyi, "Inscriptions on the pottery made in the workshop run by the central government of the Qin dynasty," *Kaogu yu wenwu,* 1980, 3, p.83–92 and Yuan Zhongyi, "Studies on the inscriptions of the pottery made in private owned workshops of the Qin dynasty," *Kaogu yu wenwu,* 1981, 1, p. 95–100.

42 "Excavations of the site of palace no. 3 in Xianyang, capital of the Qin dynasty," *Kaogu yu wenwu,* 1980, 2, p. 34–41.

43 Translated by Ed. Chavannes, vol. II, p. 174–176 and 283.

44 Cheng Te-k'un, "Chi'in-Han mortuary architecture," *The Journal of the Institute of Chinese Studies of the Chinese University of Hong Kong,* XI, 1980, p. 193–269.

45 Lu Zhaoyin, "A preliminary study on the jade funerary clothes of the Han dynasty," *Kaogu,* 1981, 1, p. 51–58.

46 "Excavation of the Western Han dynasty wooden-chambered top at Daishu in Laixi county, Shandong province," *Wenwu,* 1980, 12, p. 7–16.

47 Yao Shengmin, "Survey of the site of the Ganquan palace of the Han dynasty," *Kaogu yu wenwu,* 1980, 2, p. 51–60.

48 "Excavation of the Han dynasty tomb no. 40 at Dingxian, Hebei," *Wenwu,* 1981, 8, p. 1–10.

49 "Han dynasty bamboo slips from Han tomb no. 40 at Dingxian," *Wenwu,* 1981, 8, p. 11–12.

50 Henricks, Robert G., "Examining the Ma-wang-tui silk texts of Lao-tzu, with special note of their differences from the Wang Pi text," *T'oung Pao,* LXV, 4–5, 1979, p. 166–199.

51 Fu Xingyu, "Some questions on the map of the military regions," *Kaogu,* 1981, 2, p. 171–173.

52 "Excavation of Liu Ci's tomb dating from the West Han dynasty at Linyi in Shandong," *Kaogu,* 1980, 6, p. 493–495.

53 Yu Weichao, "Notes on the Eastern Han dynasty images of Buddha," *Wenwu,* 1980, 5, p. 68–77.

54 "Excavations of four granaries in the imperial city of Luoyang, eastern capital of the Sui and Tang dynasties," *Kaogu,* 1981, 4, p. 309–314.

55 Li Zhiyan, "A preliminary study on the pottery from tombs of the Sui and Tang dynasties in Xi'an area," *Kaogu yu wenwu,* 1981, 1.

56 Zhuo Zhenxi, "New discoveries from the reconnaissance and excavation of the Yaozhou kilns," *Kaogu yu wenwu,* 1980, 3, p. 54–62.

57 "An investigation of Tongguan kiln-sites of the Tang dynasty at Changsha," *Kaogu xuebao,* 1980, 1, p. 67–96.

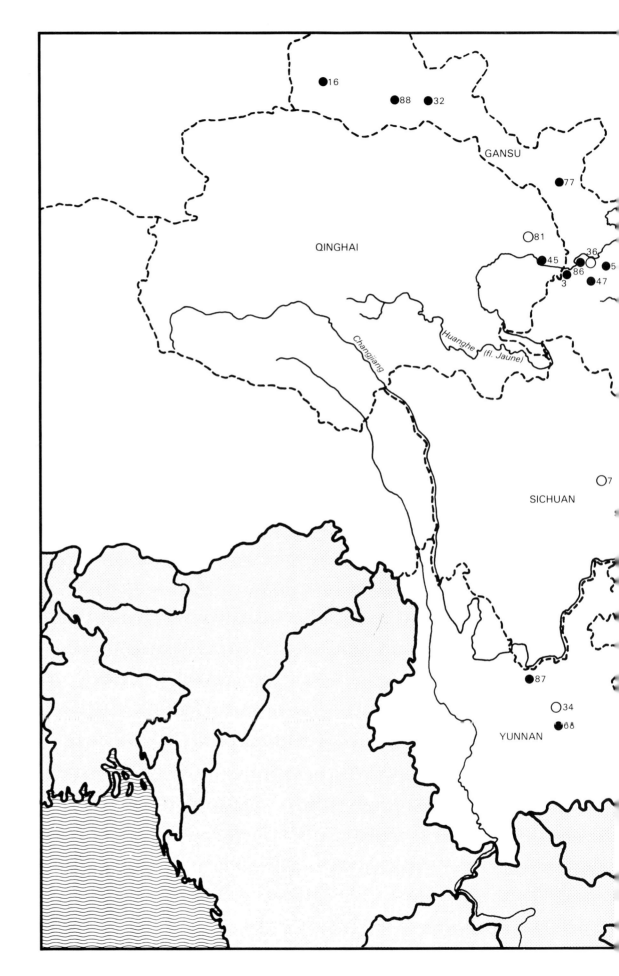

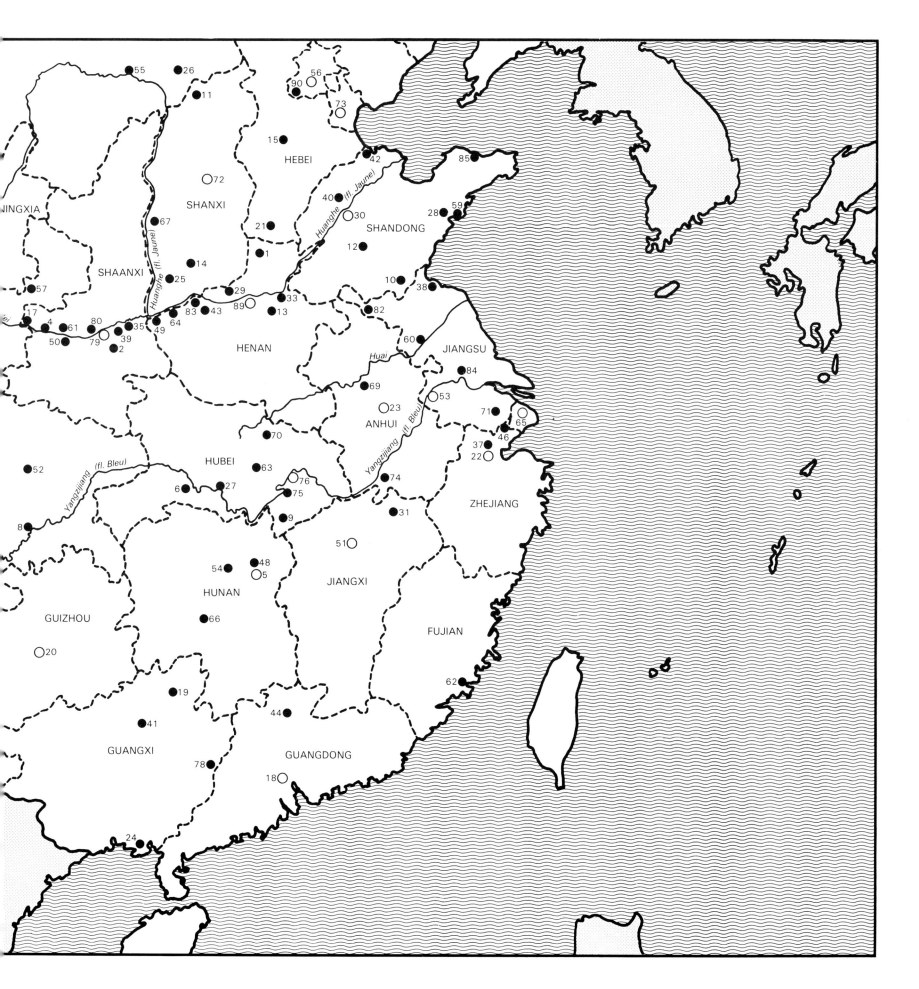

NINGXIA

●55 ●26

●11

●56
90○ ○56

○73

15●

HEBEI

○72

SHANXI

40 *(fl. Jaune)*

85●
42●

SHAANXI
●67
Huanghe (fl. Jaune)

21●

○30

SHANDONG

28●
59●

●1

12●

14●

●25

10●

29●
33●

38●

●57

89○

82●

17●

83● 43●

13●

4● ●61 ●80

60●

●35

49● 64●

●84

50● 79○ 39●

HENAN

Huai

JIANGSU

●2

○23

53○

ANHUI

69●

71●

○65

Yangzijiang (fl. Bleu)

46●

●52

70●

37●

Yangzijiang (fl. Bleu)

HUBEI

63●

22○

6● 27●

76○

74●

75○

9●

31●

ZHEJIANG

51○

54● ●48

○5

JIANGXI

HUNAN

●66

FUJIAN

GUIZHOU

○20

62●

●19

41●

44●

GUANGXI

GUANGDONG

78●

18○

24●

227

PRINCIPAL ARCHEOLOGICAL SITES IN CHINA

Preparing a list of the principal archeological sites in China is a difficult task because the relative importance of established data is constantly being modified by archeologists' endeavors. Thus, we shall only provide a selection (200 entries) covering the periods cited within this book, at the point when it was entrusted to the printers. We have not included sites which are already listed in specialized archeological indexes of the type provided in our colleague Cheng Te-k'un's studies on archeology of the Shang and Zhou Periods which first appeared during the 1960s.

ANYANG   (Henan)
Discovered during the Song Period (960-1279) although scientific excavations only began after 1928. Anyang continues to be the most important Shang site to have been discovered thus far.
Also see: DASIGONGCUN, HOUGANG, HOUJIA-ZHUANG, WUGUANCUN, XIAOTUN, XIBEIGANG, YINXU.

BAIJI   (Jiangsu)
Discovered in 1965. Tombs with engraved slabs from the Eastern Han Period (25-220 A.D.).

BAIJINBAO   (Heilongjiang)
Discovered in 1974. Relics from a culture that predated establishment of the empire.

BALING   (Shaanxi)
Mausoleum of an Early Han emperor, Wen (179-157 B.C.).

BANPO   (Shaanxi)
Discovered in 1954. This is the most important Neolithic site (4500-2500 B.C.) of the Yangshao culture to have been thus far discovered.

BAOJI   (Shaanxi)
Since 1925-1926 bronzes from the Zhou Period were found in the vicinity of this site, where relics from the Neolithic Yangshao culture were discovered in 1959. In 1974, tombs from the Zhou Period (tenth century B.C.) were discovered in the locality known as Rujiazhuang.

BEISHOULING   (Shanxi)
Discovered in 1959. Neolithic Yangshao site.

CHANG'AN   (Shaanxi)
The ancient capital of the Han and Tang rulers occupied the same location as modern Xi'an. The first extensive report on excavations, published in 1959, pertained to Damingong, the principal palace of the Tang capital (618-907).

CHANGPING   (Beijing)
Discovered in 1981. This site contained two tons of Shang bronzes, including 56 exceptionally valuable specimens. No studies describing this discovery thus far have been published.

CHANGYANG   (Hubei)
Discovered in 1956. The site contained the remains of a Neanderthal man who lived from 200,000 to 300,000 years ago.

CHENG RENTAI, Tomb of   (Shaanxi, near Xi'an)
This tomb (seventh century A.D.), excavated in 1972, contained "three-colored" wares (*sancai*) with yellow or green glazes that had been colored after baking.

CHENGZI   (Shandong)
Neolithic Longshan site (about 2500-2400 B.C.).

CICUN   (Shandong)
Excavated in 1976. Pottery kiln from the Tang (618-907) and Song Period (960-1279).

CISHAN (Hebei)
Early Neolithic site from 5000 to 6000 B.C.

DABOTAI (Beijing)
Discovered in 1974–1975. Tomb with wooden compartments (referred to as "Chu" tomb) from the Western Han Period (206 B.C.–220 A.D.).

DADU (Beijing)
Extensive excavations in 1969 uncovered traces of the former capital of the Yuan Dynasty (1279–1368) in the same location as modern Beijing.

DAHE (Henan)
Discovered in 1972. Neolithic site with Yangshao and Longshan items (5000–2100 B.C.).

DAISHU (Shandong)
Discovered in 1978. A tomb from the Han Period (end of first century B.C.) contained a jointed wooden effigy (height: 193 centimeters).

DASIGONGCUN (Henan)
One of the sites at Anyang, capital of the Shang Dynasty (1350–1100 B.C.).

DASONGYUAN (Jiangsu)
Discovered in 1975. Pottery kiln from the Six Dynasties Period (fourth to sixth century A.D.).

DAWENKOU (Shandong)
Discovered in 1959. Eponymous site for a Yangshao and Longshan Neolithic culture (about 5000–2100 B.C.).

DAXI (Sichuan)
Discovered in 1959. Inhabited by a Neolithic culture around 2500 B.C.

DEHUA (Fujian)
Discovered in 1953. New discoveries in 1961. Excavations took place in 1976 and pottery kilns from the Song Period (960–1279) were found here.

DENGFENG (Henan)
Excavated in 1977. Foundry from the Warring States Period (473–221 B.C.).

DINGCUN (Shanxi)
Discovered in 1954. Late Paleolithic Clacthonian site.

DINGLING (Beijing)
Mausoleum of the Ming emperor Wanli (ruled from 1573 to 1619).

DINGMAOQIAO (Jiangsu)
Discovered in 1982. A sizeable hoard of silver (nearly 1,000 items) was discovered in the foundations of a residence from the Tang Period (618–907). In size and quality this treasure can be compared with the Hejiacun treasure (discovered in 1970), but these items often appear to have deteriorated significantly.

DINGXIAN (Hebei)
Discovered in 1973. Ruins of a walled town and tombs from the Western Han Period (206 B.C.–24 A.D.). Tomb Number 40 contained a jade shroud with gold threads and a large collection of manuscripts. This significant discovery overshadowed the prior one (1969) of a treasure from the Song Period (960–1279), consisting of gold, silver and jade items as well as ceramic products.

DONGXIAFENG (Shanxi)
Bronze Age site comparable to Erlitou in Henan Province (about 2100–1600 B.C.).

DUJIANGYAN (Sichuan)
Discovered in 1974. Extensive irrigation structures were accompanied by a stone statue (Eastern Han Period, 25–220 A.D.) of Li Bing who had been prefect of the Shu region (Sichuan) during the reign of the First Emperor.

EGOUBEIGANG (Henan)
Discovered in 1977. This Yangshao site from the Neolithic Age contained a terra cotta bust of a man (about 5300 B.C.).

ERLIGANG (Henan)
Discovered in 1952. This site belonged to Zhengzhou, capital at the beginning of the Shang Dynasty (sixteenth century B.C.).

ERLITOU (Henan)
Discovered in 1954. This site, inhabited by the Longshan culture at the end of the Neolithic Age, was also inhabited at the beginning of the Shang Dynasty. (A palace from around 1600 B.C. was discovered in 1960.) Perhaps traces of the Xia Dynasty will be found between these two strata.

FANCUI (Henan)
Tomb from the Bei Qi period (550–577), that contained proto-*sancai*.

FENGHUANGSHAN (Hubei)
Tombs from the Han Period (second century B.C.–second century A.D.). The remains of a mummy were found here.

FUFENG (Shaanxi)
Discovered in 1962. This significant site from the Warring States Period also yielded other relics, including tombs from the Early Shang Period (sixteenth century B.C.–fourteenth century B.C.), at Famen in 1973, and Zhou bronzes (around 1100–771 B.C.) in 1976.

FUZHOU (Fujian)
Discovered in 1975. Southern Song (1127–1279) fabrics in an excellent state of preservation were found here.

GANQUANGONG (Shaanxi)
Discovered in 1978–1979. Ruins of a palace complex from the Han Period (end of first century B.C.–beginning of first century A.D.).

GONGXIAN
Discovered in 1958–1959. Foundry from the Han Period (206 B.C.–220 A.D.).

GOURONG (Jiangsu)
Primitive tumulus from the Shang Period (around 1600 B.C.–1100 B.C.).

GUANGSHAN (Henan)
Discovered in 1965. A shield belonging to the Red Turban movement that revolted against the Yuan Dynasty was discovered within this district. Yuan power ended in 1368.

GUANGZHOU (Guangdong)
Among various discoveries in the Guangdong region, two of the most important in the history of science are: in 1958 the discovery of a tomb from the Eastern Han Period (24–220 A.D.) that contained a funerary replica (*mingqi*) of a ship with a stern rudder and, during 1974–1976, discovery of the remains of a shipyard from the Qin and Han Periods.

GUANYINDONG (Yunnan)
Late Paleolithic site discovered in 1964.

GUCHENG (Henan)
Discovered in 1974. Gold and silver coins from the Warring States Period (475–221 B.C.) had been hidden here.

GUWEI (Henan)
Tumulus from the Warring States Period (475–221 B.C.), containing the remains of a ceremonial pavilion.

HEJIACUN (Shaanxi, south of Xi'an)
Discovered in 1970. This site yielded a treasure that included many gold items from the Tang Period (eighth century A.D.).

HEMUDU (Zhejiang)
Neolithic site on the Lower Yangtze River.

HETAO (Inner Mongolia)
Late Paleolithic site.

HEZHANG (Guizhou)
Discovered in 1976. Tombs from the Qin Period (221–207 B.C.).

HEZHONGYUAN (Jiangsu)
Complex of towns or walled villages from the Eastern Han Period (25-220 A.D.).

HOLINGOL (Inner Mongolia)
Group of tombs with paintings from the Eastern Han Period (25-220 A.D.).

HOUGANG (Henan)
Site within Anyang, capital of the Shang Dynasty (around 1350-1100 B.C.). Hougang contained many remnants of dwellings.

HOUGUDUI (Henan)
One of the tombs (Number 1) in the necropolis discovered at this site contained the remains of the wife of Duke Jing (515-451 B.C.) of the Kingdom of Song.

HOUJIAZHUANG (Henan)
Site within Anyang, capital of the Shang Dynasty, discovered in 1934. Some of the burial grounds (Xibeigang) at Houjiazhuang contained royal tombs.

HOUMA (Shanxi)
Discovered in 1957. Important site from the Warring States Period (475-221 B.C.). Texts on strips of bamboo were discovered in 1965.

HUOCHENGXIAN (Inner Mongolia)
Discovered in 1975. A treasure from the Yuan Period (1271-1368) included coins, gold items, and "blue and white" ceramic creations (*qinghua*).

JIAOZUO (Henan)
Discovered in 1973. Tombs from the Jin Period (1115-1234) and Yuan Period (1271-1368).

JIAYUGAN (Gansu)
Discovered 1972-1973. Tombs with paintings from the Eastern Han Period (25-220 A.D.) and Six Dynasties Period (fifth-sixth centuries).

JINAN (Hubei, Jiangling)
Excavations in 1975-1980 unearthed a walled city which had been the capital of the Kingdom of Chu (Warring States Period, 475-221 B.C.).

JINAN (Shandong)
Discovered in 1969. Several tombs from the Western Han Period. One tomb contained a terra cotta composition portraying acrobats and musicians on a platform performing for dignitaries sitting on both sides of the stage.

JINCUN (Henan, near Luoyang)
Glass objects which had been imported during the Warring States Period (475-221 B.C.) were discovered at this site.

JINGDEZHEN (Jiangxi)
Extensive research and discoveries have taken place since 1966 at this famous center for production of ceramic wares and porcelain, that began to thrive during the Tang Period (618-907).

JINTAN (Jiangsu)
Discovered in 1966. A treasure (silver items and "blue and white" wares) from the Yuan Period (1271-1368) was found here.

JIUQUWAN (Hunan)
Copper mines in operation during the ninth and eighth centuries B.C.

JIZHOU (Jiangxi)
During the Song Period (960-1279), this kiln produced wares comparable to the *cizhou* from Northern China, as well as ceramic items with bluish decoration.

KEZUO (Liaoning)
Discovered in 1973. Shang and Zhou bronzes (around thirteenth to eighth centuries B.C.) had been stored in the kilns at this site.

KONGWANGSHAN (Jiangsu)
Buddhist bas-reliefs (Han Period).

LAIWU (Shandong)
Discovered in 1972. Foundry for iron agricultural tools during the Western Han Period (206 B.C.-24 A.D.).

LANGJIAZHUANG (Shandong)
Discovered in 1971. A large tomb from the Warring States Period (475-221 B.C.) contained luxurious items that demonstrated the prosperity of the Kingdom of Qi during this period.

LANTIAN (Shaanxi)
Discovered in 1963. Remains of a slightly older hominid than *Sinanthropus*. This creature lived from 600,000 to 700,000 years ago.

LEIGUDUN
See SUIXIAN.

LEITAI
See WUWEI

LIANGZHU (Zhejiang)
Neolithic site on the Lower Yangtze River.

LIANHUABAO (Liaoning)
Iron smelting site that was active during the Warring States Period (475-221 B.C.).

LI FENG, Tomb of (Shaanxi, near Xi'an)
Excavations in 1973. The tomb contained many *sancai* from the second half of the seventh century.

LIJIASHAN (Yunnan)
Discovered in 1972. This site, with many tombs from the Western Han Period (206 B.C.-24 A.D.), exemplified the art of the Kingdom of Dian.

LIJIAZUI (Hubei)
Excavated in 1974. This site is located east of Panlongcheng, a walled town from the Shang Period (c. 1600-1100 B.C.).

LI JINGXUN, Tomb of (Shaanxi)
A nine year old child was buried in this tomb, discovered in 1957 at Xi'an. Li Jingxun was the granddaughter of the wife of Xuandi of the Bei Zhou (557-581 A.D.). Customary objects as well as ceramic figurines and toys were arranged around the stone sarcophagus.

LINAN (Zhejiang)
During excavations between 1958 and 1965, tombs from the Five Dynasties Period (tenth century) were found at this site. The tombs contained astronomical maps, where specific colors or motifs had been used to identify various regions. A pottery kiln was discovered in 1969. In 1978, the tomb of Qian Kuan, which contained an astronomical map as well as white pottery from the late Tang Period (ninth century), was discovered here.

LINGBAO (Henan)
Discovered in 1972. Eastern Han tombs (second century A.D.) contained interesting architectural models, as well as terra cotta *liubo* (backgammon?) players and parts from an arbalest.

LINTONG (Shaanxi)
The mausoleum of the First Emperor (221-207 B.C.) was erected within this locality and there have been constant discoveries since 1974.

LINYI (Shandong)
Discovered in 1972. The site contained tombs from the Western Han Period (206 B.C.-24 A.D.) with lavish funerary furnishings, including important manuscripts as well as items that later evolved into the jade shroud: headdresses, gloves, leggings.

LIUJANG (Guizhou)
Discovered in 1958. The site contained the remains of a *homo sapiens* who lived 30,000 to 40,000 years ago and possessed Mongolian features.

LIULIHE (Beijing)
Discovered in 1972. Cemetery from the Western Zhou Period (ninth century-770 B.C.).

LONGQUAN (Zhejiang)
Many discoveries during the past thirty years have contributed to an understanding of the activities of this famous center of ceramic production that was already thriving during the Song Period (960-1279).

LONGSHAN (Shandong)
Eponymous site for the final phase of the Neolithic Age in China (about 2500-2100 B.C.), characterized by the production of delicate and lustrous pottery that was completed or retouched on lathes. This type of pottery was usually black.

MABA (Guangdong)
Discovered in 1958. Remains of a Neanderthal man who lived approximately 100,000 years ago.

MAJIABANG (Zhejiang)
Discovered in 1959. Inhabited by a Lower Yangtze Neolithic culture.

MAJIAYAO (Gansu)
Discovered in 1958. Neolithic Yangshao site, that was inhabited around 3000 B.C.

MANCHENG (Hebei)
Discovered in 1968. Western Han tombs, containing the jade shrouds of Liu Sheng and Touwan (second century B.C.).

MAOLING (Shaanxi, Xi'an)
Tomb of the Western Han emperor Wu (140-87 B.C.). In May 1981, an unknown tomb was discovered along the outer boundary of the sacred enclosure. Its mortuary furnishings included an unprecedented find: a bronze horse entirely covered with gold (height—62 centimeters; length—76 centimeters). (Currently on display at the Xi'an Museum. See Figure 23.)

MAPIGU (Jiangsu)
Discovered in 1975. Pottery kiln from the Six Dynasties Period (fifth-sixth centuries).

MAPUTOU (Shanxi)
Bronze Age site, comparable to Erlitou in Henan.

MAWANGDUI (Henan)
Discovered during 1972-1974. Three tombs from the Western Han Period (end of third century A.D.) contained the remains of Li Cang, Marquis of Tai, who was the Prince of Changsha's chancellor, and the remains of his wife and his son. Tomb Number 1 (the wife's tomb) contained a painted silk banner, Tomb Number 3 another banner, as well as exceptionally important texts and three maps.

MEISHAN (Henan)
Discovered in 1958. Site inhabited by the Longshan culture. New discoveries in 1970 uncovered a stratum of the Erlitou type (Phases I and II). Excavations during 1975 led to discovery of a "Meishan culture," representing the beginnings of the Bronze Age in the Central Plain region.

MEIXIAN (Shaanxi)
Site from the Zhou Period (around 1100-771 B.C.).

MENGXI (Hunan)
Discovered in 1966. This site was inhabited by a Neolithic culture that existed around 2400 B.C.

MENGZHUANG (Henan)
Excavations during 1976-1977. Village from the beginning of the Shang Period (same level as the Erligang culture at Zhengzhou, around 1600 B.C.).

MIAODIGOU (Henan, Sanmenxia)
Discovered in 1966. This site contained two cultural strata: one represented the Yangshao culture (4500-2500 B.C.), and the other contained gray pottery (2700 B.C.).

MIXIAN (Henan)
Tombs with paintings from the Western Han Period (206 B.C.-24 A.D.).

MIZHI (Shaanxi)
Discovered in 1971. Eastern Han tomb (107 A.D.) was adorned with carved slabs containing mythological scenes.

NANCHANG (Jiangxi)
Excavated in 1973. Pottery kilns from the Han Period and Six Dynasties Period (fifth–sixth centuries).

NANSHANGENG (Liaoning)
Discovered in 1963. A tomb from the ninth to eighth centuries B.C. contained interesting bronzes of provincial origin.

NANZHAO (Henan)
Discovered in 1979. Remains of a *Sinanthropus*.

NINGBO (Zhejiang)
Discovered in 1974. Pottery from the Tang Period (618–907) and Five Dynasties Period (907–960), intended for export markets.

NINGXIANG (Hunan)
Discovered in 1960. A cooking vessel (*fangding*) with four legs and a rectangular body, whose four sides were adorned with human faces (Shang Period, around 1600–1100 B.C.) was found here.

OUMAKOU (Shanxi)
Excavations in 1963. One of the principal stone-cutting quarries in Northern China at the beginning of the Neolithic Age.

PANLONGCHENG (Hubei)
Excavations in 1974. Walled town from the Shang Period (around 1600–1100 B.C.).
See LIJIAZUI.

PEILIGANG (Henan)
Early Neolithic site. Inhabited approximately 5000 to 6000 years B.C.

PINGLU (Shanxi)
Tombs with paintings from the Han Period (first century A.D.).

PINGSHAN (Hebei)
Excavations from 1974 to 1979. Five royal tombs from the Warring States Period (475–221 B.C.). Tomb Number 1 contained a bronze plaque that provided a map of the mausoleum area.

PU QIANQIU, Tomb of (Henan, near Luoyang)
Discovered in 1976. This site contained the oldest funerary paintings to have ever been discovered. These paintings are from the Han Period (second to first century B.C.).

PUTIAN (Fujian)
Discovered in 1958. New discoveries in 1976. This site contained a pottery kiln that was active during the Tang Period (618–907).

PUYANG (Henan)
Tomb from the Bei Qi Period (550–577) containing proto-*sancai*.

QIANWULIBUGE (Jilin)
Discovered in 1972. Tomb from the Liao Period (916–1125).

QIJIA (Gansu)
Discovered in 1959. Important Neolithic settlement.

QILIHE (Henan)
Discovered in 1972. Eastern Han (25–220 A.D.) tomb near Luoyang. In addition to other accoutrements, this tomb contained two especially interesting items: a large lamp with multiple arms and a well-shaped urn adorned with two figures of acrobats balancing upon the edge, as a superstructure.

QINGLIANGGANG (Jiangsu)
Discovered in 1951. Neolithic Yangshao culture.

QINGZHOU (Shandong)
Site where gold and silver coins from the Warring States Period (475–221 B.C.) were discovered.

QISHAN, FENGCHU (Shaanxi)
Discovered in 1977. Palace complex from the Zhou Period (around 1100–771 B.C.).

QUANZHOU (Fujian)
The remains of sea-going vessels with watertight holds, built during the Song Period (960–1279), were discovered at this site during 1973–1974.

QUJIALING (Hubei)
Discovered in 1954. Neolithic village, around 2500 B.C.

RENJIAPO (Shaanxi)
Possible identification of the Baling, the mausoleum of the Han emperor Wen (180–157 B.C.).

RUJIAZHUNG
See BAOJI.

SANLIHE (Shandong)
Neolithic Longshan and Bronze Age site.

SANMENXIA
See MIAODIGOU and SHANGCUNLING.

SHANBAOYINGZI (Jilin)
Discovered during 1973–1974. Relics from the Warring States Period (475–221 B.C.). Devices for weighing grain were accompanied by an edict issued by Qin Shi Huangdi (221 B.C.) in order to standardize weights and measures.

SHANGCUNLING (Henan, Sanmenxia)
First discoveries in 1956. New discoveries in 1975. Tombs from the Warring States Period (475–221 B.C.) contained valuable bronzes: a *fangli* urn with scroll-like ornamentation and a lamp decorated with human figures were found in Tomb Number 5.

SHANGYUANJIA (Gansu)
Discovered in 1967. Seventeen bronzes from the Qin Period (221–207 B.C.). One of these bronzes contained an edict concerning standardization of weights and measures. A portable rotary lamp made of bronze was also found here.

SHIJIAYUAN (Shaanxi, Chunhuaxian)
Discovered in 1979. This site from the Western Zhou Period (1120–771 B.C.) contained the largest *ding* tripod to have been found thus far: it was 140 centimeters high, with a diameter of 120 centimeters and weighed 226 kilograms.

SHIJIAZHUANG (Hebei)
Discovered in 1978. Tombs from the Eastern Han Period (25–220 A.D.).

SHINING (Guangdong)
Discovered in 1976. Six small boats from the Eastern Han Period (25–220 B.C.) were found here.

SHIZHAISHAN (Yunnan)
Discovered in 1955. Relics from this site provided knowledge about the impressive civilization of the Kingdom of Dian during the Han Period (200 B.C.–200 A.D.).

SHOUXIAN (Anhui)
Discovered in 1955. Tomb of the Marquis of Cai, from the Warring States Period (475–221 B.C.). In 1979, gold and silver coins from the same period were discovered here.

SHUINI (Henan)
Site from the Spring and Autumn Period (770–476 B.C.), close to Luoyang. Iron tools which are among the oldest iron tools discovered thus far were found at this site.

SIMAJINLONG (Shanxi)
Discovered in 1972. A Northern Wei tomb (386–534) contained the oldest glazed *mingqi* to have been identified thus far.

SINAN (Korea)
Discovered in 1976. Wreckage of a Chinese ship that carried ceramic products. This vessel, sunk during the fourteenth century, lay 20 meters below the surface of the sea.

SONGCUN (Shaanxi)
Discovered during 1965–1966. Tombs from the Kingdom of Qin (300 B.C.) contained the skeletons of five horses.

SONGSHAN (Shandong)
Discovered in 1978. Carved work on stone from the Han Period (200 B.C.–200 A.D.).

SUIBIN (Heilongjiang)
Discovered in 1973. Relics from a Neolithic culture of the Yangshao type.

SUIXIAN (Hubei)
Excavations during 1977–1978. The tomb of Zeng Houyi from the Warring States Period (475–221 B.C.) contained more than 7,000 items, including a set of more than 64 bells and important manuscripts on bamboo sheets.

SUJIALONG (Hubei)
Tomb from the Warring States Period (475–221 B.C.) containing bronzes and large chariots.

TIANXINGGUAN (Hubei)
Excavations in 1978. Tombs from the Kingdom of Chu (300–200 B.C.). Tomb Number 1 contained 2,500 mortuary items.

TONGGUAN (Hunan)
Discovered in 1957. This site was the source of the oldest Chinese pottery (ninth century) with a painted underglaze.

TONGLUSHAN (Hebei)
Discoveries in 1965 and in 1973, with excavations after 1974. Two mine shafts from the Spring and Autumn Period (770–475 B.C.) and the Warring States Period (475–221 B.C.).

WANGDU (Hebei)
Tombs containing paintings from the Eastern Han Period (25–220 A.D.).

WANGHUI (Sichuan)
Tombs with stone sarcophagi from the Han Period (200 B.C.–200 A.D.).

WANGSHAN (Hubei)
Discovered in 1965. The site contained a large tomb (Number 1) from the Warring States Period (475–221 B.C.).

WANJIABA (Yunnan)
Discovered in 1975. This site was the source of the oldest bronze drums to have been discovered thus far. It is possible that these drums were from the Western Zhou Period (1100–771 B.C.).

WEININGXIAN (Guizhou)
Discovered in 1976. Tombs from the Qin Period (221–207 B.C.).

WENDENG (Shandong)
Discovered in 1973. Cast iron weights (32 kilograms) from the Qin Period (221–207 B.C.).

WUCHENG (Jiangxi)
Site from the Shang Period (around 1600–1000 B.C.).

WUGUANCUN (Henan)
Discovered in 1950. Site of Anyang, the capital of the Shang Dynasty (around 1550–1100 B.C.).

WUJIN (Jiangsu)
Excavations during 1977–1978. Beautiful lacquer items from the Song Period (960–1279).

WUWEI (Gansu)
Discovered in 1969. Two hundred and twenty relics crafted from lacquer, gold, other metals, bone, and stone were found here but the most famous find consisted of a collection of bronzes, including fourteen chariots and seventeen horses accompanied by forty-five grooms or mounted guardsmen (average height: 40 centimeters). This vast retinue was accompanied by a unique bronze statue, referred to as "the flying horse" (height: 34.5 centimeters).

WUYANGTAI (Hebei)
Discovered in 1973. Weapons from the Han Period (200 B.C.–200 A.D.). Some of these weapons were made of steel.

WUZUOFEN (Hubei)
Discovered in 1973. Tombs from the Western Han Period (206 B.C.-24 A.D.) contained beautiful bronzes and lacquer work.

XIADU
See YAN XIADU.

XIANGSHAN (Zhejiang)
Discovered in 1978. Kilns for proto-celadons from the Tang Period (618-907).

XIANGYUN (Yunnan)
Tombs from the Han Period (200 B.C.-200 A.D.), with bronze sarcophagi.

XIANYANG (Shaanxi)
Impressive finds since 1962. This was the capital city established by the First Emperor (221-207 B.C.).

XIAOBAIYANGCUN (Shaanxi, Xi'an)
Discovered in 1973. Tomb from the Western Han Period with zoomorphic bronzes.

XIAOTUN (Henan)
This is the most important location within Anyang, the capital of the Shang Dynasty. The earliest excavations took place from 1928 until 1937. Since 1949, more than 200 Shang sites have been discovered here.

XIASI (Henan)
Excavations during 1978-1979. Tombs from the Warring States Period (770-476 B.C.) contained bronzes which had been produced by the *cire perdue* method.

XIBEIGANG (Henan)
One of the burial sites within Houjiazhuang, at Anyang, the Shang capital. The earliest excavations of royal tombs began during 1934.

XINDU (Sichuan)
Discovered in 1978. Extremely beautiful bas-reliefs (on brick) from the Han Period (200 B.C.-200 A.D.).

XINGLONG (Hebei)
Discovered in 1953. Foundry from the Warring States Period (475-221 B.C.).

XINYANG (Henan)
Discovered in 1957. A tomb from the Warring States Period (475-221 B.C.) contained a carillon.

XUANHUA (Hebei)
Discovered in 1971. A tomb from the Liao Period (916-1125) was decorated with murals that portrayed scenes from daily life, as well as an astronomical map.

XUJIAYAO (Shanxi)
Discovered in 1975. This site contained the earliest microliths to have been identified in China thus far (dating from the beginning of the last glacial period).

XUZHOU (Jiangsu)
Discovered in 1952. Numerous Han tombs (200 B.C.-200 A.D.) with carved decorative work.

XUYI (Jiangsu)
Discovered in 1982. A treasure from the Warring States Period (475-221 B.C.), including a gilded bronze urn with a golden lid (9 kilograms), was found here.

YANGJIAWAN (Shaanxi, Xianyang)
Discovered during 1965-1970. One tomb contained a retinue of mortuary miniatures, consisting of 3,000 horses and soldiers (approximately 70 centimeters high) from the period of the First Emperor (221-207 B.C.).

YANGSHAO (Henan)
Eponymous site for the first phase of the Neolithic Age in China, characterized by the use of painted lead-based pottery, usually red.

YANG SIXU, Tomb of (Near Xi'an)
This tomb (around 740), discovered in 1958, contained not only lavish mortuary furnishings, but also two marble statues (height of approximately 40 centimeters) representing hunters.

YANGZHOU   (Jiangsu)
Numerous discoveries, including Tang pottery decorated with floral motifs (1975) and, in 1977, a tomb from the Han Period that contained pieces of glass. Painted sculptures from the Tang Period (618–907) were also discovered in 1977.

YAN XIADU   (Hebei)
Discovered in 1958. Capital of the Kingdom of Yan during the Warring States Period (475–221 B.C.). Armor and weapons were found here.

YAOZHOU   (Shaanxi)
Excavations during 1973–1974. There was a prolific kiln during the Tang Period, that became exceptionally well-known during the Song Period (960–1279).

YI DE, Tomb of   (Shaanxi, near Xi'an)
Discovered in 1971. Tomb of a member of the Imperial family. Built in 706.

YINGZHEN   (Henan, near Zhengzhou)
Excavations in 1975. Foundry from the Han Period (200 B.C.–200 A.D.).

YINQUESHAN   (Shandong)
Discovered in 1972. Tomb from the Han Period (134 B.C.) containing a mortuary banner and important texts on bamboo sheets.

YINXU   (Henan)
The "ruins of Yin" in Anyang. This is the most important Shang Dynasty site and was discovered as early as the Song Period. See ANYANG.

YONG TAI, Tomb of   (Shaanxi, near Xi'an)
Discovered in 1960. This tomb of a member of the Imperial family was built in 706.

YUANMOU   (Yunnan)
Discovered in 1965. This site contained the remains of a hominid believed to have lived 1,700,000 years ago.

YULONGTAI   (Inner Mongolia)
Discovered in 1974. Xiongnu tomb (400 B.C.–200 A.D.).

YUNMENG   (Hubei)
Discovered in 1975 (at Xiaogan). There was an important tomb from the Qin Period (221–207 B.C.) containing many texts on bamboo sheets.

ZHAOLING   (Shaanxi, near Xi'an)
Excavations in 1972. Certain tombs adjacent to the mausoleum of the Tang emperor Taizong (626–649) contained interesting statues of chimeras and of human beings.

ZHAOWUDA   (Liaoning)
Discovered in 1963. Cast iron weights from the Qin Period (221–207 B.C.).

ZHAOZHOU   (Guangdong)
Discovered in 1954. Pottery kilns from the Tang Period (618–907) and from the Song Period (960–1279).

ZHENGZHOU   (Henan)
Discovered in 1952. Ancient Shang Dynasty (sixteenth century B.C.) capital.
Also see: ERLIGANG, BAIJIAZHUANG.

ZHIZILING   (Hunan, near Changsha)
Tomb Number 34 contained iron tools from the Spring and Autumn Period (770–446 B.C.) that are among the oldest iron tools to have been discovered thus far.

ZHONGSHAN   (Hebei)
Kingdom represented by the Pingshan site. See PINGSHAN.

ZHONGZHOULU   (Henan)
Discovered during 1954–1955. Objects at this site included jade fragments that could be fitted together to cover a face, when they were sewn onto a shroud. End of Spring and Autumn Period (770–476 B.C.).

ZHOUKOUDIAN (Hebei)
Discovered in 1921. Remains of a hominid, the *Sinanthropus,* or "Peking Man," who lived 500,000 or 600,000 years ago.

ZHOUYUAN (Shaanxi)
Discovered in 1977. This site contained 10,500 oracle bones (Shang Period, about 1600–1100 B.C.).

ZHUDAN, Tomb of (Shandong)
Excavations in 1970. Tomb of the tenth son of the founder of the Ming Dynasty (end of fourteenth century–early fifteenth century).

ZHUMAZUI (Shaanxi)
Discovered in 1977. Tombs from the Shang Period (fourteenth century B.C.), northwest of Xi'an.

ZIDANKU (Henan)
Discovered in 1973. A tomb at this site contained two paintings on silk from the Han Period (200 B.C.–200 A.D.).

ZIYANG (Sichuan)
Discovered in 1951. Paleolithic site.

ZUOJIAGONGSHAN (Hunan)
Discovered in 1954. Tomb from the Warring States Period (475–221 B.C.) containing the oldest paint brush to have been discovered thus far.

Fig. 23 *Horse.* Gilded bronze at the time of the Western Han Dynasty. Discovered in 1981 in an unknown tomb that was found near Maoling in the mausoleum of Emperor Wu (140–87 B.C.). Height 62 cm. Length 76 cm. Based on *Wenwu,* 1982, 9, pl. 1.

CHRONOLOGY OF PRINCIPAL ARCHEOLOGICAL DISCOVERIES IN CHINA SINCE 1950

1950   *Wuguancun* (Anyang): royal tombs

1951   *Ziyang* (Sichuan): human remains discovered at a late Paleolithic site.

Resumption of excavations at *Zhoukoudian*.

Discovery of 145 tombs of the early and late Han dynasties in the vicinity of Changsha (Hunan).

Discovery of the *Qingliangang* Neolithic culture in Jiangsu.

Binglingsi (Gansu): Buddhist cave temples.

1952   Discovery of the Shang *Erligang* culture (*Zhengzhou*).

1952   *Xinglong* (Hebei): more than 70 iron implements from the Warring States Period.

1954   The oldest known paintbrush discovered at *Zuojiagongshan,* near Changsha (Hunan), in a tomb from the Warring States Period.

Banpo (Xi'an, Shaanxi): discovery and initial excavations of an important complex of Neolithic sites.

Dingcun (Shanxi): Paleolithic artifacts.

Qujialing (Hubei): discovery of a Neolithic culture.

1955   *Shizhaishan* (Yunnan): discovery of the civilization of the Kingdom of Dian (Western Han Period).

Lijiacun (Shaanxi): several inscribed bronzes from the Western Zhou Period.

Discovery of the mural at Luoyang (Henan) from the Eastern Zhou Period.

Shouxian (Anhui): Tomb of the Marquis of Cai (Warring States Period).

Excavations in the region of *Sanmenxia* (Henan) in search of Xia relics.

Discovery of the walls of the Shang city at *Zhengzhou* (Henan).

1956   *Banpo:* excavations carried out on a grand scale and construction of museum over main site.

Tombs of the Xiongnu people (400 B.C.-200 A.D.) in Liaoning.

Discovery of Changyang man (Hubei), who lived some 200,000 to 300,000 years ago.

Miaodigou (Sanmenxia, Henan): discovery of Yangshao Neolithic culture.

Beginning of excavations of the Han city of Changan.

Shangcunling (Henan): more than 200 tombs from the Western Zhou and also from the Spring and Autumn Period.

1957   *Houma* (Shanxi): a city of the Spring and Autumn Period and of the Warring States Period.

Beginning of excavations of the Tang city of Chang'an.

Xinyang (Henan): a Chu tomb.

Zuinan (Anhui): 30 zoomorphic bronzes from the Shang Period.

1958   Beginning of excavations at Yan *Xiadu* (period of the Warring States 475-221 B.C.), Hebei.

Opening of the Banpo Museum.

Discovery of *Maba* man (Guangdong), who lived approximately 100,000 B.C.

Discovery of Liujiang Man (Guangxi), who lived approximately 30,000-40,000 years ago.

Gongxian (Henan): discovery of foundries from the Han Period (200 B.C.-200 A.D.).

1959   *Majiabang* (Zhejiang): discovery of a Neolithic culture.

Dawenkou (Shandong): discovery of an important Neolithic settlement, represented by over 100 burials.

Zhoukoudian (Hebei): new discovery of a fragment of a human fossil.

Daxi (Sichuan): discovery of a Neolithic culture.

1960   *Erlitou* (Henan): remains of palace complex of the Shang (1600-1100 B.C.).

1962   Work on the Sui and Tang cities of Changan.

1963   Discovery of Lantian man (Shaanxi), who lived 600,000-700,000 years ago.

1964 *Guanyindong* (Guizhou): discovery of a Lower Paleolithic site.

1965 Discovery of Yuanmou man (Yunnan), who lived 1,700,000 years ago.

Yangjiawan (Shaanxi): a funerary military procession of more than 3,000 people and horses (Western Han Period).

Wangshan (Hubei): three large Chu tombs.

Houma (Shanxi): important texts, written on bamboo slips from Kingdom of Jin (Warring States Period).

1966 *Zhoukoudian:* cranium of Sinanthropus discovered.

1968 *Mancheng* (Hebei): two tombs from the Western Han Period contained jade burial shrouds (second cent. B.C.).

1969 Bronze funerary army discovered at *Leitai* (Gansu).

1970 *Heijiacun* (Xi'an): more than 1,000 pieces of Tang gold and silverwork.

1971 Tombs of *Zhang Huai* and *Yi De* near Xi'an, Shaanxi (beginning eighth century).

1972 *Linyi* (Shandong): two tombs with a wealth of important texts of the Western Han Period provided important manuscripts (second–first centuries B.C.).

Mawangdui (Hunan): Tomb no. 1 (that of the woman), end third cent.–beginning first cent. B.C.

Liulihe (Beijing): site of the Shang-Zhou Period (about 1100 B.C.).

1973 *Tonglushan* (Hubei): first discovery of copper mines active since the end of the Zhou (eighth cent. B.C.).

Mawangdui (Hunan): discovery of Tombs no. 2 and 3.

Excavations at *Anyang:* Yinxu, Xiaotun; discovery of more than 1,800 oracle bone inscriptions.

1974 *Lintong:* terra-cotta army of Qin Shi Huang, First Emperor of China (221–207 B.C.).

Quanzhou (Fujian): sailing ship from the end of the Southern Song Period (1127–1279).

Pingshan (Hebei): important tombs of the Kingdom of Zhongshan (Warring States Period).

Guangzhou (Guangdong): discovery of a naval boatyard of the Qin and Han.

1975 *Xujiayao* (Shanxi): Paleolithic remains.

Yunmeng (Hubei): important tombs of the Qin and Han Periods (200 B.C.–200 A.D.) containing important texts written on bamboo slips, useful for interpreting other texts.

1976 *Anyang:* tomb of Fu Hao (about twelfth century B.C.).

Fufeng (Shaanxi): important bronzes from the Western Han (about 1100–771 B.C.).

1977 *Zhouyuan* (Shaanxi): 10,500 oracle bones of which 170 were inscribed (Shang Period).

Excavation of a site in *Dengfeng,* Henan, which also contained what seemed to be the remains of a city of the Xia dynasty.

1978 *Suixian* (Hubei): Tomb of Zeng Houyi (about fourth cent. B.C.).

First archeological works undertaken in Tibet; excavation of a Neolithic site.

1979 *Pingshan* (Hebei): tomb of one of the kings of Zhongshan dating to the period of the Warring States (475–221 B.C.).

1980 Continuation of excavations at Jinan (Jiangling, Hubei) ancient capital of the Kingdom of Chu (400–200 B.C.).

1981 *Changping* (Beijing): discovery of an important collection (weighing more than 2 tons) of Shang bronzes, among which 56 pieces were of particular interest.

1982 *Xuyi* (Jiangsu): discovery of some 38 valuable gold objects, placed inside a wine jar, dating to the Warring States Period (200 B.C.). The latter, made of gilt bronze, was adorned with a gold lid in the form of a tiger, weighing nine kilograms.

BIBLIOGRAPHY

All the documents of articles, reviews, excavation reports have come from China. These works have been published in special journals (*Kaogu, Kaogu xuebao, Wenwu, Kaogu yu wenwu*) and in such books as in the Acts of the First Chinese Archeological Congress of 1979. Apart from a certain number of important references, the list has not been expanded. The *Kaogu Journal*, since 1981 (no. 5, p. 475 and no. 6, p. 569), publishes an annual bibliography and methodically lists the principal archeological excavations in China of that year. Professionals and amateurs alike refer to this journal.

References to works in French, English and German are offered to a more educated public. Also, the articles in each of these works comprise important documentation.

AKIYAMA, Terukazu, *Arts of China. Neolithic cultures to the Tang dynasty: Recent discoveries,* Tokyo, 1968.

AN, Zhimin, "The neolithic archeology of China. A brief survey of the last thirty years," *Kaogu,* 1979, 5, p. 393–403; English translation by Chang Kwang-chih, *Early China,* 5, 1979–1980, p. 35–45.
Archeological treasures excavated in the People's Republic of China, Cat. of exhibition held in Japan in 1973 (in Japanese).

BAGLEY, Robert W., "P'an-lung-ch'eng: a Shang city in Hubei," *Artibus Asiae, 39,* 3/4, 1977, p. 165–219.
____, see FONG, Wen, *The great Bronze Age of China.*

BARNARD, Noel, *Bronze casting and bronze alloys in ancient China,* Monumenta Serica Monograph, XIV, Tokyo, The Australian National University and Monumenta Serica, 1961, XXIV.
____, "The incidence of forgery among archaic Chinese bronzes: Some preliminary notes," *Monumenta Serica,* 1968, 27, p. 61–168.

BARNARD, Noel and SATO, Tamotsu, *Metallurgical remains of ancient China,* Tokyo, 1975.

BOBOT, Marie-Thérèse, *Chinese art,* Paris, 2nd ed., 1980.

BODDE, Derk, *China's first unifier: A study of the Ch'in dynasty as seen in the life of Li Ssu* (280?–208 BC), Hong Kong, 1967.

BRINKER, Helmut and GOEPPER, Roger, *Kunstschätze aus China, 5000 v. Chr. bis 900 n. Ch. Neuere archäologische Funde aus der Volksrepublik China,* Zurich, 1980.

CHANG, Kwang-chih, "Chinese archeology since 1949," *Journal of Asian Studies,* vol. XXXVI, no. 54, Aug. 1977, p. 623–646.
____, *The archeology of ancient China,* New Haven and London, 3rd ed., 1977 and 1979.
____, *Shang civilization,* New Haven and London, 1980. *Changsha Mawangdui yihao Han mu (Han Tomb No. I at Mawangdui, Changsha),* 2 vol., Beijing (in Chinese).

CHENG, Te-k'un, *Archeology in China.* Vol. I: *Prehistoric China,* Cambridge, 1959 (1966); sup. to Vol. I: *New lights on prehistoric China,* Cambridge, 1966; Vol. 2: *Shang China,* Cambridge, 1960; Vol. 3: *Chou China,* Cambridge, 1963.
____, *An introduction to Chinese art and archeology: The Cambridge outline and reading lists,* Cambridge, 1973.
____, "Ch'in-Han architectural remains," *Journal of the Institute of Chinese Studies of the Chinese University of Hong Kong,* 9, 2, 1978, p. 1–81.
____, "Ch'in Han mortuary architecture," *Journal of the Institute of Chinese Studies of the Chinese University of Hong Kong,* vol. XI, 1980 p.193–269.

COTTERELL, Arthur, *Le Premier Empereur, la plus grande découverte archéologique du siècle,* Paris, 1981.
____, *Des profondeurs de la terre chinoise,* Paris, 1982.

DEWALL, Magdalena von, "Der Gräberverband von Wu-kuan-ts'un/Anyang," *Oriens Extremus,* VII, 1960, p. 129–151.
____, "New data on early Chou finds. Their relative chronology in historical perspective," in *Symposium in honor of Dr. Li Chi,* II, Taipei, 1966.

EGAMI, Namio, "Migration of the cowrie shell culture in East Asia," *Acta Asiatica,* 26, Tokyo, 1974, p. 1–52.

ELISSEEFF, Danielle and Vadime, *La civilisation de la Chine classique,* Paris, 1979.

ELISSEEFF, Vadime, "La préhistoire de l'Asie Nordorientale," in *L'homme avant l'écriture* (dir.: A. Varagnac), Paris, 2nd ed., 1967.

____, *Trésors d'art chinois, récentes découvertes archéologiques de la République populaire de Chine,* Cat. from the Paris exhibition in 1973.

FINSTERBUSCH, Käte, *Zur Archäologie des Pei-Ch'i (550–577) und Sui-Zeit (581–618), mit einem Fundkatalog,* Munich Asiatic Studies, Wiesbaden, 1976.

FONG, Mary H., "Four Chinese royal tombs of the early eighth century," *Artibus Asiae,* 35, 4, 1973, p. 307–334.

FONG, Wen, *et al., The great Bronze Age of China. An exhibition from the People's Republic of China,* London and New York, 1980.

FONTEIN, Jan and WU, Tung, *Unearthing China's past,* Boston, 1973.

FRANKE, Otto, *Geschichte des chinesischen Reiches,* Berlin, New York, 1948–1965.

FRIEND, Robert, "New archeological work in China," *East and West,* ISMEO, XXII, 3–4, Sept.–Dec. 1972, p. 233–247.

FU, Xinian, "First finds on the traces of Western Zhou architecture at Fengchu (Xishan, Shaanxi)," *Wenwu,* 1981, I, p. 65–74 (in Chinese).

____, "A primary inquiry into the remains of the Western Zhou buildings at Shaochen village in Fufeng county, Shaanxi province," *Wenwu,* 1981, 3, p. 34–45 (in Chinese).

GAO, Zhixi, "A chronology of Chu Tombs (Hunan)," in *Acts of the First Archeological Congress,* 1979, p. 237–248 (in Chinese).

GERNET, Jacques, *Le monde chinois,* Paris, 1972.

GOEPPER, Roger, *Kunst und Kunsthandwerk Ostasiens,* Munich, 1968.

HANSFORD, S., Howard, *A glossary of Chinese art and archeology,* London, 1954, 2nd ed., 1972.

HERVOUET, Yves, "Découvertes récentes de manuscrits anciens en Chine," in *Summaries of proceedings for April–June, 1977 at the Académie des Inscriptions et Belles-Lettres,* Paris, 1977, p. 379–393.

HO, Ping-ti, *The cradle of the East, an inquiry into the indigenous origins of techniques and ideas of neolithic and early historic China, 5000–1000 B.C.,* Hong Kong, 1975.

HOU, Ching-lang, "Ts'in Sculpture," *Arts asiatiques,* XXXIII, 1977, p. 133–181.

HENRICKS, Robert G., "Examining the Ma-wang-tui silk texts of Lao-tzu, with special note of their differences from the Wang Pi text," *T'oung Pao,* vol. LXV, 4–5, 1979, p. 166–199.

HULSEWE, A.F.P., "The Qin documents discovered in Hubei in 1975," *T'oung Pao,* vol. LXIV, 4–5, 1978, p. 175–217.

JIA, Lampo, *Nos ancêtres les Chinois, la préhistoire de l'homme en Chine,* Paris, 1982.

Jianming Zhongguo lishi tuben (Illustrated edition of a concise history of China), Tianjin, 1978–1981, 6 vol. (in Chinese).

KANE, Virginia, C., "The independent bronze industries in the south of China contemporary with the Shang and Western Chou dynasties," *Archives of Asian Art,* 28, 1974–1975, p. 77–107.

____, "A reexamination of Anyang archeology," *Ars orientalis,* 10, 1975, p. 93–110.

KEIGHTLEY, David N., "The Bamboo Annals and Shang-Chou chronology," *Harvard Journal of Asiatic Studies,* 38, 1978, p. 423–438.

____, *Sources of Shang history. The oracle bone inscriptions of Bronze Age China,* Berkeley, Los Angeles, London, 1978.

LEE, Shermann E., *Chinese art under the Mongols: The Yuan dynasty (1279–1368),* The Cleveland Museum of Art, 1968.

LEI, Congyun, "Iron tools from the Warring States Period: Discoveries and first conclusions," *Kaogu,* 1980, 3, p. 259–265 (in Chinese).

LI, Chi, *Anyang,* Seattle, 1977.

LI, Xuequin, *The Wonder of Chinese Bronzes,* Beijing, 1980.

LI, Zhiyan, "A preliminary study on the pottery from tombs of the Sui and Tang dynasties in Xi'an area," *Kaogu yu wenwu,* 1981, I (in Chinese).

LIU, Dunzhen, *La maison chinoise* (translation from *Zhongguo zhuzhai gaishuo,* Beijing, 1957), Paris, 1980.

LIU, Yubei and XIONG, Lin, "Hoard of Yuan's blue and white and underglazed red wares found in Gao-an county, Jiangsu province," *Wenwu,* 1982, 4, p. 58–69 (in Chinese).

LOEHR, Max, *Ritual vessels of Bronze Age China,* New York, 1968.

LOEWE, Michael, "The manuscripts from tomb number three Ma-wang-tui," *China: Continuity and change, Papers of the XXVIIth Congress of Chinese Studies, 31.8.–5.9. 1980,* Zurich University, Zurich, 1982, p. 29–57.

LU, Zhaoyin, "A preliminary study on the jade funerary clothes of the Han dynasty," *Kaogu,* 1981, I, p. 51–58 (in Chinese).

MEDLEY, Margaret, *The Chinese potter. A practical history of Chinese ceramics,* Oxford, London, 1976, 1977.

_____, *Yuan porcelain and stoneware,* London, 1974.

NEEDHAM, Joseph, *Science and civilization in China,* Cambridge, 7 vol., 1954–1971.

Newsletter. East Asian Art and Archeology, Ann Arbor, University of Michigan, Biannual publication since 1977. *New Archeological Discoveries in China: Antiquities since the Cultural Revolution,* Beijing, 1973. *New Archeological Discoveries in China,* Beijing, 1980.

PIRAZZOLI-T'SERSTEVENS, Michèle, *Chine,* coll. "Architecture universelle," Friburg, 1970.

_____, *La civilisation du royaume de Dian à l'époque Han, d'après le matériel exhumé à Shizhaishan (Yunnan),* Paris, Ecole Française d'Extrême-Orient, vol. XCIV, 1974.

_____, "Extrême-Orient, préhistoire et archéologie. Chine: paléolithique, néolithique et âge du Bronze", Supplement I to the *Encyclopedia Universalis,* Paris, 1980, p. 582–590.

_____, "Le mobilier en Chine à l'époque Han," *Journal des Savants,* January–March 1977, p. 17–42.

QIAN, Hao, CHEN, Heyi and RU, Suichu, *Out of China's earth. Archeological discoveries in the People's Republic of China,* Beijing, New York, 1981

RAWSON, Jessica, *Ancient China, art and archeology,* London, 1980.

SEKINO, Takeshi, *Chugoku kokogaku sanjunen (Thirty years of Chinese archeology).* Translated and adapted from *Wenwu kaogu gongzuo sanshi nian* (Beijing, 1979), Tokyo, 1981 (in Japanese).

_____ ,*Shang Zhou kaogu (Archeology of the Shang and Zhou dynasties),* Beijing, 1979 (in Chinese).

SULLIVAN, Michael, *Chinese art, recent discoveries,* London, 1973.

_____, *The arts of China,* Los Angeles, London, 1977.

_____, *Chinese landscape painting.* Vol. II: *The Sui and Tang dynasties,* University of California Press, 1980.

Tang Li Xian Li Zhongjun mu bihua (Murals in the tombs of Li Xian and Li Zhongjun of the Tang dynasty), Beijing, 1974 (in Chinese). *Tang Li Xian mu bihua (Murals in the tomb of Li Xian),* Beijing, 1974 (in Chinese).

THILO, Thomas, *Klassische chinesische Baukunst, Strukturprinzipien und soziale Funktion,* Leipzig, 1977.

Treasures from the tombs of Zhongshanguo kings: An exhibition from the People's Republic of China, Tokyo, 1981 (in Japanese).

TWITCHETT, Denis C., *The Cambridge history of China.* Vol. 3: *Sui and Tang China, 589–906, Part I,* Cambridge, 1979.

VANDERMEERSCH, Léon, *Wangdao ou la voie royale. Recherches sur l'esprit des institutions de la Chine archaïque,* Paris, Ecole Française d'Extrême-Orient, 1977–1980, 2 vol.

WATSON, William, *Archeology in China,* London, 1960.

_____, *Ancient China: The discoveries of post-liberation Chinese archeology,* London, 1974.

_____, *L'art de l'ancienne Chine,* Paris, 1979.

Wenwu kaogu gongzuo sanshi nian (Trente ans de travail archéologique), 1949–1979, Beijing, 1979 (in Chinese).

WU, Zhenfeng, *Shaanxi chutu Shang Zhou qingtongqi,* 6 vol. (in Chinese).

XIA, Nai (HSIA Nai), *Essays on archeology of science and technology in China* (with summaries in English), The Institute of Archeology, Chinese Academy of Social Sciences, Beijing, 1979.

_____, "Chinese archeology in the last thirty years," *Kaogu,* 1979, 5, p. 385–392 (in Chinese).

XU, Xitai, "An archeological record of Chou-Yuan," *The Journal of the Institute of Chinese Studies,* 1981, vol. XII, p. 153–183 (in Chinese).

Zhongguo mingsheng cidian (Dictionary of Chinese archeological sites), Shanghai, 1981 (in Chinese).

Zhongguo taoci shi (History of Chinese ceramics), Beijing, 1982 (in Chinese).

ZHUANG, Wei, *Four Great Discoveries of Old China,* Beijing, 1981.

INDEX

PHOTOGRAPHIC CREDITS

The authors submitted all of the photographic documentation to Ingrid de Kalbermatten.

We thank the institutions which are responsible for providing us with the reproductions that are in this work. The numbers refer to the illustrations.

Cultural Relics Publishing House, Beijing 9, 11–22, 24, 31–33, 36, 37, 40, 42, 50–64, 69, 70, 85, 89–97, 110 115, 116, 118, 124, 125, 134, 138, 142, 145, 154, 160 161, 164–169, 174–176, 180

Philippe De Gobert, Brussels 106, 149, 159, 172

Leo Hilber, Friburg 34, 35, 68, 71–78, 139, 150

J. L. Klinger, Heidelberg 1–8, 10, 23, 25, 28–30, 38, 41, 43 65–67, 79, 81–83, 99, 102, 109, 113, 114, 117, 122, 123, 126, 127, 130, 132, 133, 143, 144, 148, 156, 157, 162, 163, 170, 171

Propyläen Verlag, Berlin 178, 179

Rijkmuseum, Amsterdam 44–49, 84, 86–88, 98, 100, 101, 103–105, 107, 108, 111, 112, 119, 128, 129, 135–137, 140, 141, 146, 151, 155, 158, 173

Author's archives 26, 27, 80, 120, 121, 131, 152, 153, 177

The authors express their gratitude to the editors of Office du Livre and to their collaborators for their efforts in improving the quality of the reproductive material. The also wish to thank the editors of Wenwu chubanshe for their cooperation in supplying a number of extremely useful documents.